This book examines the English rural community, past and present, in its variety and dynamism. The distinguished team of contributors brings a variety of disciplinary perspectives to bear upon the central issues of movement and migration; the farm family and rural labour force; the development of contrasting rural communities; the portrayal of rural labour in both 'high' and popular culture; the changing nature of religious practice in the English countryside; the rural/urban fringe, and the spread of notions of a rural English arcadia within a predominantly urban society.

Fully illustrated with accompanying maps, paintings and photographs, *The English rural community* provides an important and innovative overview of a subject where history, myth and present debate are inseparably entwined. A full bibliography will assist a broad range of general readers and students of social history, historical geography and development studies approaching the subject for the first time, and the whole should establish itself as the central analytical account in an area where image and reality are notoriously hard to unravel.

The ENGLISH RURAL COMMUNITY

COMMUNITY

Image and analysis

Edited by

BRIAN SHORT

*School of cultural and
community studies,
University of Sussex*

CAMBRIDGE
UNIVERSITY PRESS

Published by the Press Syndicate of the University of Cambridge
The Pitt Building, Trumpington Street, Cambridge CB2 1RP
40 West 20th Street, New York, NY 10011–4211, USA
10 Stamford Road, Oakleigh, Victoria 3166, Australia

© Cambridge University Press 1992

First published 1992

Printed in Great Britain at the University Press, Cambridge

A catalogue record for this book is available from the British Library

Library of Congress cataloguing in publication data

The English rural community: image and analysis/edited by Brian Short
   p.   cm.
Includes bibliographical references and index.
1. England – Social conditions.   2. England – Rural conditions.
3. Peasantry – England – History.   I. Short, Brian, 1944– .
HN398.E5E53   1992
307.72′0942–dc20   91–22153   CIP

ISBN 0 521 40537 9 hardback
ISBN 0 521 40567 X paperback

CE

Contents

Contributors

Dr PETER AMBROSE has taught at the University of Sussex since 1965. Originally a geographer, he has been associated with the university's Urban Studies degree since its inception in the School of Cultural and Community Studies in 1974. Current interests include comparative housing research in Western Europe, continual monitoring of the London Docklands redevelopment, and advisory work concerning transformations in housing policy in several central and east European countries. His publications include *The Property Machine* (1975) and *Whatever Happened to Planning?* (1986).

Professor JOHN BARRELL is Professor of English in the School of English and American Studies at the University of Sussex and has published widely on the history of literature and art. His most recent books are *The Birth of Pandora and Other Essays* (1991) and *The Infection of Thomas De Quincey* (1991).

Dr ALUN HOWKINS is Senior Lecturer in History in the School of Cultural and Community Studies at the University of Sussex. He left school at 15 and worked at a variety of jobs in rural areas before going to Ruskin College in 1968. He graduated in History from Oxford and completed his Doctorate at Essex. He has published widely on rural social history and other areas. He is the author of *Poor Labouring Men: Rural Radicalism in Norfolk 1870–1923* (1985) and *Reshaping Rural England 1850–1925* (1991).

MALCOLM KITCH is Reader in History in the School of English and American Studies at the University of Sussex. He has written on sixteenth-century religious history and migration to London in the later Stuart period. He is currently researching into rural migration in eighteenth-century England.

Dr STUART LAING is Assistant Director at Brighton Polytechnic and was previously Senior Lecturer in Media Studies in the School of Cultural and Community Studies at the University of Sussex. His previous publications include *Representations of Working-Class Life 1957–64* (Macmillan 1986) and the jointly authored *Disorder and Discipline: Popular Culture 1550–present* (Temple Smith 1988).

vi

JOHN LOWERSON is Reader in History, Centre for Continuing Education, University of Sussex, and an Anglican priest working in a country parish. He is the author of *Victorian Sussex* (1972), *A Short History of Sussex* (1980), co-author of *Time to Spare in Victorian England* (Hassocks 1977) and *Trends in Leisure, 1919–39* (1979), and has written numerous papers on local and regional studies and the recent history of sport and leisure.

Dr BRIAN SHORT is a lecturer in Human Geography in the School of Cultural and Community Studies at the University of Sussex. His research has centred on the historical and contemporary aspects of the geography of South East England, and more recently on the landownership structure of Edwardian England and Wales. Publications include the jointly authored *South East England from 1000 AD* (Longmans 1990). He is currently editor of the *Sussex Archaeological Collections* and a member of the executive committee of the Sussex Rural Community Council.

Dr JOAN THIRSK was formerly Reader in Economic History in the University of Oxford, and Professorial Fellow of St Hilda's College. She is general editor of the eight-volume series, *The Agrarian History of England and Wales* (Cambridge University Press 1967–) and was a contributor to volumes IV and V. Much of her work has centred on agriculture and rural society in the sixteenth and seventeenth centuries, as her volume of collected essays, *The Rural Economy of England* (Hambledon Press 1984) shows.

Dr SUSAN WRIGHT is Lecturer in Social Anthropology in the School of Cultural and Community Studies at Sussex University. Her current research on community development in North East England follows employment as a rural community worker and research on decision-making processes in rural Britain. Her continuing interests in processes of interaction between people and state organisations, empowerment, and locally generated development stem from doctoral research on the impact of state policies on tribal organisation in Iran. She is co-editor (with H. Buller) of *Rural Development: Problems and Practices* (Aldershot 1990).

Acknowledgements

This book springs from a lecture course at the University of Sussex, and in a sense all those people who have helped to make those lectures possible have thereby contributed to the production of this book. The continuing support of Dr Stuart Laing, Dean of the School of Cultural and Community Studies until 1991, has been invaluable. The editor also wishes to thank all the contributors, who responded so warmly and quickly in an increasingly hectic academic environment.

Over the years during which the course has run, many other colleagues and very many students have also contributed in ways valuable yet incalculable. Specifically however, we would wish to acknowledge the help of the Media Services Unit at the University of Sussex; of Susan Rowland, cartographer in the Geography subject group, who prepared the maps and diagrams with her usual skill and speed; of Valerie Short who transcribed much of the original material from which these chapters have come; and of the staff in the University of Sussex library for their efficiency. Help with illustrations was also generously provided by James Barlow, Judy Gielgud, Denis Hutchinson, Nigel Llewellyn, Marcia Pointon and John Stubbings. The index was prepared by Ann Hudson.

The editor and publisher would like to thank the following for permission to reproduce illustrative material: Aerofilms (fig. 10.4); the Barber Institute of Fine Arts, the University of Birmingham (fig. 6.9); the Beamish North of England Open Air Museum (figs 5.2 and 5.3); the Bridgeman Art Library (fig. 4.3); Bobby Mitchell, BBC London, and Joy Tonkin, production assistant, *The Archers*, BBC Pebble Mill (figs 7.3 and 7.4); Cheltenham Art Gallery and Museums (figs 6.6–6.8); Colour Library Books Ltd (fig. 1.3); the Marquess of Tavistock and the Trustees of the Bedford Estates, Woburn Abbey (figs 6.4 and 6.5); the Ministry of Defence and The Welsh Office (fig. 10.1); the National Railway Museum (fig. 1.2); the Art Gallery of Ontario, Toronto (fig. 6.10); the Royal Photographic Society (fig. 1.1); the Tate Gallery, London (fig. 6.2); and the Yale Center for British Art (figs 6.1, 6.3, and 6.11–6.14). Every effort has been made to reach copyright holders: the publishers would be pleased to hear from anyone whose rights they have unwittingly infringed.

Thanks are also due to Richard Fisher of the Publishing Division of Cambridge University Press for his continuing interest in the project, and his many helpful suggestions.

BRIAN SHORT

Falmer, Sussex

January 1991

Images and realities in the English rural community: an introduction *1*

BRIAN SHORT

Less than 20 per cent of the population of England and Wales lives in the countryside, a space covering about 80 per cent of the land area. So why produce another book dealing with this minority and their histories, their cultural and economic impacts, past and present? Indeed, as one member of a recent conference on rural issues asked, why not 'do away with rurality' altogether as a conceptual tool?[1] Do we need it? This chapter aims to introduce the themes of the volume and to address the question as to whether we really do need any further studies of the English rural community.

The changes in population distribution between rural and urban England since the first census in 1801 have been enormous, threatening to marginalise the culture and society as well as the economic contribution of the countryside. But has this culture been marginalised? Certainly the economic importance of the countryside, measured in terms of its agricultural output compared with total Gross Domestic Product has dwindled over the last 100 years, but threading through all the contributions in this volume is the belief expressed by Raymond Williams that:

Rural Britain was subsidiary, and knew that it was subsidiary, from the late nineteenth century. But so much of the past of the country, its feelings and its literature, was involved with rural experience and so many of its ideas on how to live well, from the style of the country-house to the simplicity of the cottage, persisted and even were strengthened, that there is almost an inverse proportion, in the twentieth century, between the relative importance of the working rural economy and the cultural importance of rural ideas.[2]

Therefore agriculture, for example, now accounts for just 2 per cent of our GDP, and the wellbeing of the farming fraternity (it is still male-dominated) no longer determines the significance of the countryside to the nation to any real extent. Once what was good for the farmer was thought good for the countryside, but today, when the restructuring of the post-Fordist economy is bringing demands for rural locations for new constellations of industries and new forms of social and economic relations in our villages, there is now almost a presumption against that. When farmers marched through Whitehall in October 1990 in protest against threatened reductions in European Community subsidies, they gained few friends and found little support. New power blocs have arisen to challenge the older landed hegemonies, and certainly many village residents are ideo-logically or pragmatically opposed to further intensification and industrialisation of farm and countryside.

Much of this opposition springs from a rightful concern with ecological and aesthetic damage. But the damage to the rural community goes unheeded too often. As Louis Simond (French-born but resident in America) remarked of the Norfolk countryside in June 1810:

> The scale of agriculture is such, that I saw five pair of fine horses with five harrows at work in one field ... Large farm-houses are seen with all their out-houses substantial and complete – very few cottages. I do not know how and where the common labourers live.[3]

The 'invisibility' of the poor in rural England, engendered by a series of state legislative moves from the beginning of the nineteenth century which displaced the poor from view, and by a series of mechanical innovations which removed them from the harvest fields and even the threshing floors, helped perpetuate and uphold a myth of arcadian beauty which could be seized upon and utilised in selective imagery for a great variety of purposes. The English countryside was contrasted with the English town (especially the industrial town) and found not only to be aesthetically superior, but somehow sounder in social character and moral purpose, strength of physique, and English virtue. Attitudes ranged from the nostalgic to the apocalyptic, eugenic and Utopian.[4] But from whatever standpoint it was viewed – from the performing arts to creative literature, from high to popular culture, and from historical description to social scientific analysis – the countryside appeared desirable and also capable of satisfying the need for conspicuous consumption from a wide spectrum of society. To live in the countryside, at least in middle-class eyes, was to possess a 'positional good' which was worth defending stoutly.

Thus to be truly English by the beginning of the twentieth century was to be rural. Urban stereotypes could easily be conjured up, but it was not the town that was fought for in Flanders but the English countryside; not even London, but rather the 'South Country' (which of course included Shropshire in its curiously elastic geography but excluded, for example, Cornwall) that was the package of ideas carried across the Channel and reinforced by the Georgian poets.[5] Asked more specifically what he was fighting for, one lieutenant replied: 'English fields, lanes, trees, English atmospheres, and good days in England – and all that is synonymous for liberty.'[6] The sense of identity, the personality, of England was firmly associated with its rural past.

But as with the lieutenant cited above, 'rural' did not really mean rural *people*, and especially not *poor* rural people, who might not even fit stereotypes of poverty by living in picturesque cottages. The countryside was made by working people, but the rural idyll of pastoral from the eighteenth to the twentieth century, itself

Fig. 1.1 'Bringing Home the May' by Henry Peach Robinson, 1862 (Royal Photographic Society, Bath). The picture was said to illustrate Spenser's 'May' in *The Shepheard's Calendar*:

> / ... when all is ycladde
> With pleasaunce, the ground with grasse, the woods
> With greene leaves, the bushes with blossoming buds
> Youngthes folke now flocken in everywhere
> To gather May-buskets and smelling brere;
> And home they hasten the postes to dight
> And all the kirke pillours eare day light
> With hawthorne buds, and sweet eglantine,
> And girlands of roses, and soppes in wine.

The photograph, a composite of nine separate negatives for the figures, was produced from his Leamington studio, with May gathered in the Warwickshire Lanes, and his daughter Edith as the smallest child. Other members of his family and friends were called upon to pose as 'peasants', since country girls were often frightened or suspicious. Dressed in costume and with some of Robinson's range of accessories, 'polite' society played at 'being a rustic' or at a 'Tableau Vivant', both popular pastimes in the Victorian period. (Margaret Harker, *Henry Peach Robinson*, 1988, 34–8 *et seq.*).

an urban product, has largely banished them from the scene. The image was that of an outsider, often looking with 'tourist gaze' and seeing the landscape from a distance, not in detail, and not encompassing all its occupants. And those who did investigate the 'South Country' image beyond the landscape itself were unlikely to delve much deeper than into an assumed organic society based on mutuality, obligations and tradition, influenced by writers and artists such as the skilful Victorian landscape photographer, Henry Peach Robinson, working within a pastoral (almost pantheistic) tradition in the 1890s to produce an image of villages wherein people were in harmony with nature – indeed naturalised. But in what Kit Wright, in referring to some of A. E. Housman's poetry, has called 'bogus peasantism', Robinson found it more effective to have the daughters of landowners pose as 'peasant girls' than to use the real working families, and his support came primarily from the urban-dominated Royal Photographic Society or the lavish *Country Life*[7] (fig. 1.1).

There may be an anti-urban bias in English culture but the bias is itself biassed against the rural community in its totality. When Colin Buchanan declared that its 'spirit of place' had saved Stansted from becoming a huge airport for London, 'place' meant 'landscape' which was devoid of tangible, breathing humans with their own aspirations and problems – including unemployment.[8] And this sense of a missing element, that of the working country person, is only reinforced by the quick resort of many in the Arts to the archetypal. Lob the countryman, with *all* the virtues of countrymen in general, is nothing more after all than a caricature. Little of the reality of real workmen can be gained, nor any of the infinitely shaded degrees of skill and status constituting, for example, levels of country working. So in the absence of real knowledge of country people, abstracts are sought, whether from the arts or the social sciences. And failing that, it seems, the landscape itself becomes the focus of attention.

However, the rural landscape is a notoriously elusive concept to grasp, and its very intangibility, coupled with its enveloping beneficent notions, makes it a powerful weapon in any armoury. But the contributors to this volume set out to remind us that landscapes don't just happen, that they are (and have been) created by and for people, and according to notions sometimes hegemonic, sometimes contested, but always involving people, and usually people living in communities of some kind or another. And if the word 'rural' has its own aura, so too of course does 'community'. Put the two together and the effect is to multiply the mythology to something more than the sum of its constituent parts. Add 'English' and the effect is like a chemical chain reaction which grows and glows, subfusing everything in a good, green light – but an ideological light which can obscure as well as ornament the object of analysis. The mixture is given still greater mystique by the addition of a historical dimension, such that 'rural' is also equated with a reverent antiquity, itself a cocktail of history and legend quite irresistible to the middle-class English (and others). Samuel and Nathaniel Buck's views, Turner's watercolours, or the Gothic novels, for example, convey the 'rural ruin' motif wherein the romantic English ruins naturalise but displace culture from its true historical context, and help create 'Englishness' and national identity.[9] By contrast, as Vaughan reminds us:

Painters of the rural scene in the 20th century have been notorious for their inability to see pylons and silage towers. 'Discussing the Milk Quota' and 'Artificial Insemination Day' are still, I believe, subjects awaiting their debut at the Royal Academy.[10]

Thus those who use the phrase 'English rural community' must be aware of the inherent danger of projecting onto it multiple individual or interpersonal evaluations which cocoon its original shape of meaning. It implies, for example, a 'moral affluence' quite different to the poverty associated with much of past and present urban life. The social relations and social processes within the countryside are envisaged as parts of a residual culture, remnants of a traditional moral economy which in some ways also stands in contrast to the capitalist relations within the town. Perhaps however, enough has been written to demonstrate the falsity of the conceptual separation of town and country, and to demonstrate that capitalism was, and is, 'quite at home in both the long and short grass of rural England': that capitalism did not diffuse from town to countryside, and that pastoral images should instead be seen as 'the propaganda of the victors'.[11]

The dangers of such false imagery are frequently those associated with an unbalanced attitude to countryside issues and planning in the present. The ideology of rural arcadia has a hegemonic grip over our consciousness, it seems, so that it is difficult to conceive of any alternative to the preservation, protection and conservation of rural beauty, even at the expense of human suffering, for 'suffering leaves no mark in the countryside'. Wiener has demonstrated how the quest for rural living has resulted in 'the gentrification of the industrialist' and a lack of investment in British industry which has left us vulnerable in a changing technological world, citing Enoch Powell to the effect that 'The life of nations no less than that of men is lived largely in the imagination'. One might add to this that it is also lived largely in the past, as we have been reminded by Patrick Wright, Robert Hewison and others.[12] The actual or potential 'museumisation' of large parts of the English countryside at the present day is therefore a trend which must be monitored closely in this post-industrial and incipient post-agricultural country.

With such a grip on the national consciousness, it is no wonder that planners, developers and local politicians can see little alternative to the dedication of large areas of the countryside to aesthetic beauty, while paradoxically acknowledging that space must be found for rural housing and service provision, appropriate small-scale industries, and improved transport links. Here again is the need for balanced judgement, so crucial to the English style of rural planning, and while a finely tuned sensitivity to environmental issues is certainly required, so too is an awareness of the need for a living countryside, peopled by working families who can share in the fullness of modern standards as enjoyed by all. Decisions on such issues, and they appear with great regularity, are made by professionals and lay politicians alike who are actually themselves heavily imbued with middle-class notions of English rural idyllicism. Indeed, such notions may well be central to decisions made about living and working in the countryside by many of the service and industrial sectors, who by the fact of their presence may in turn attract more service industries, lower-paid manual and clerical workers, development, employment and planning pressures.[13] Much of the present industrial restructuring process, channelled into certain rural areas and pulled sharply away from others, is constituted by decisions taken by certain groups of individuals who may themselves live in rural areas but who may wish to develop other rural areas. Much of the appreciation of change in the countryside could be enhanced by the inclusion of studies which sought to relate representations of rurality by particular social groups to the political and economic planning processes. One person or group's rural idyll can be used to justify promotion or negation of development and change.[14]

This collection of essays therefore sets out to demystify and deconstruct rural images, and to set them against the reality of country living as it was, and as it exists in the years moving towards 2000. In order to do this, it is also necessary to set the past alongside the present, or rather to see them as indivisible, in order to see how each generation has constantly reinterpreted and reconstructed its past, and to appreciate how we are ourselves shaped by it in the present. Culture, politics, economics, society and place are intricately interwoven in a texture embodying the rural past and present. Thus it is surely correct that attempts to undertake this work encompass the arts and humanities and the social sciences.

The origins of the present volume lie in a series of lectures given at the University of Sussex in the course *English Rural Communities*. The course is interdisciplinary (a 'contextual' in Sussex University parlance) and the collection here represents the thoughts of tutors from Anthropology, English, Geography, History, Media Studies and Urban Studies. While their disciplinary groundings may come through, they are all attempting to present issues and concepts which are not only interdisciplinary in their importance, but are of real concern to our understanding of the rural community. No particular disciplinary knowledge is assumed for the purposes of the original lectures, or for these chapters, but this necessarily means that description of sources and materials, such as verse or paintings, is to some extent prioritised over, for example, the analysis of historical and discursive change. There is a sometimes uncomfortable but always productive tension between disciplinary depth and interdisciplinary breadth which Sussex University tutors have championed. Most of the chapters incorporate new material with previously published work, often the author's own. With the exception of Joan Thirsk, who has contributed to the course as a visiting speaker, all are Sussex University tutors. Rather than attempt to introduce and describe the individual contributions, which speak eloquently enough for themselves, the following pages will instead draw out some of the interconnecting themes which thread through them.

Structures

The authors range widely in spatial scales and in temporal modes, but one concern is that of *definitions and classifications of the rural community* through a variety of historical and contemporary approaches. No-one has attempted to define what they mean by 'rural', somewhat in the spirit of Newby's view that 'what constitutes "rural" is wholly a matter of convenience and ... arid and abstract definitional exercises are of little utility'.[15] Nevertheless it behoves us to discuss concepts of rurality and rural community studies, and these issues have traditionally been the concern of the geographer, the historian and the anthropologist. At least four of the contributions touch directly or indirectly on this theme.

Joan Thirsk makes observations on the interlocking parts making up rural communities and on the historical emergence of regularities in linked regimes of farming patterns and social structures. Paying particular heed to the English Midlands, she investigates the changing economic conditions of farming and rural industry between *c.*1400 and 1750, and the impacts that such changes had on social structures. Such an approach, with economic change as a key variable in understanding community structure, exemplifies a longstanding historical tradition. On the theme of contrasting communities, Brian Short also investigates the long-term underpinnings of what emerged in the early Victorian period as 'open' and 'close' parishes. Based on the notion of regionally uneven development and the spatially uneven acquisition of political power, the Victorian 'model' is examined in the context of South East England. The implications and complications of such a conceptualisation of rural differences are examined in terms of demographic change, social interaction, class relations and local economies. Possible refinements to the concept are considered also, together with its relevance to present-day planning and landscape issues in the South East.

The historical reality of such differences is further explored by Alun Howkins, who focusses his chapter on the farm and the family as much as on the community. Indeed, 'community' is a difficult concept to apply to some of his case study material, drawn as it is from the isolated farms of Northumberland. Nevertheless, social relations within the households, based again on differing regional economies and cultures, are a key element of his contribution, which shows the contrasts at the local level between rural North and rural South. Relationships within the farm family, which was the site of work as well as leisure and cultural and workforce reproduction, included variations in the relations between parents and children, informal support networks and roles, betrothal and marriage, working women and children, and the significance of the living-in farm servant.

Differences within and between communities over a long time period are therefore to be found here, in a wide variety of ecological settings drawn from the North, the Midlands and the South. The complexity and dynamics of such communities are demonstrated, surely necessitating a revision of any concept of progression from 'simple' to 'complex' society through time. Of course, much depends on how the notion of community is predicated. The three contributions described so far look to slightly different criteria: Thirsk to the impact of economic activity on social life; Short to the ramifications leading from land-ownership and power structures; Howkins to the complexities inherent within and between farm families. On the other hand, Sue Wright examines the very issue of the conceptualising of rural communities – in her case by anthropologists – to reveal how the assumptions taken into the study by the researcher have inevitably coloured the results gained at the end. The very notion of community at all is a contested one, imbued as it is with ideological and political conno- tations, and it is therefore certainly not something which should be accepted by researchers dealing with historical or contemporary rurality as unproblematic.

Images

The images of the rural community held by academic researchers are but one part of a wider complex of images held by the English as a whole about their countryside. In *Northanger Abbey*, Jane Austen's heroine, Catherine Morland, is taken on a walk by the discerning brother and sister, Henry and Eleanor Tilney. Henry persuades her to see the landscape revealed to them as a painting to be interpreted and gives a lecture on the Picturesque:

> in which his instructions were so clear that she soon began to see beauty in everything admired by him, and her attention was so earnest that he became perfectly satisfied of her having a great deal of natural taste. He talked of foregrounds, distances, and second distances – sidescreens and perspectives – lights and shades; and Catherine was so hopeful a scholar that when they gained the top of Beechen Cliff, she voluntarily rejected the whole city of Bath as unworthy to make part of a landscape.[16]

The irony is heavy and pervades the novel, but the point is made. We see what we are told about and believe to be there, and the structured interpretation, based on historical and hallowed precedent, deflects commonsense and indeed often renders it banal. Interpretations and images of the English countryside, just as with Catherine's view over Bath, are handed to us as sets of interpretations of interpretations: a double hermeneutic of rural imagery. We are left too often with an image of rurality which strikes discord on more mature reflection or greater research, and which tells us more about the interpreter and the interpretation than about the reality of country living.

This theme of the *production and reproduction of rural imagery*, and the approximation of such imagery to any generally agreed reality, is taken up not only for the case of academic anthropologists by Wright, but also by John Barrell in his study of rural labour as portrayed in English poetry and painting in the eighteenth and early nineteenth centuries. Those who attempted to represent the English countryside and its inhabitants at this time had a limited number of genres open to them, and Barrell demonstrates how the use of such genres affected the scene being portrayed and our subsequent interpretation of it. Certainly the characterisation of rural labour was emphatically related to the prevailing perceptions of the political economists and philosophers of the period. And while Barrell deals with the images generally accepted to be part of High Culture (although the subject matter did not always sit easily with polite society in the eighteenth century), Stuart Laing deals with the images of the rural being produced within Popular Culture. He takes a longer time period – from 1750 to the present, and demonstrates how certain images have persisted despite changes in the media of communication. Taking eighteenth-century poetry, nineteenth-century music hall song and the modern BBC radio *Archers* programme, he analyses the importance of the images, their origins and their purposes.

Many of the other contributions also take up the theme of rural image and ideology, not least that by John Lowerson, which examines the religious and quasi-mystical character shadowing many attitudes to the English countryside. In order to examine such perceptions he describes the changing place of the church in rural society, and the overlap between 'folk' religion and Christianity. Drawing freely on literary sources, Lowerson also investigates the changing image and reality of the rural incumbent, the financial and other problems of the modern church, and its future in the countryside.

Certainly in terms of rural iconography, the parish church is a foremost element in society and landscape. But are we correct in assuming, with Raymond Williams that such churches, symbolising much that held the community together, are nowadays elements of a residual culture?[17] And if so, is the countryside itself perhaps better understood as the stage on which a residual culture enacts its death throes, in the face of creeping (or galloping) urbani-sation? Notwithstanding Williams' eloquent plea that we should not separate the country and the city, since their fates are intertwined and their histories united, the clash between Dominant and Residual – or between the urban commercial and industrial world and that of rural retirement and even torpor – generates a third sub-theme of the volume.

Urban culture and rural change

The Dominant culture of the urbanised world is only really considered in this volume to the extent to which it generates change within the rural community, represents alternative images which some rural dwellers strive to emulate, or represents a world from which many seek to escape. The differences are many-layered and complex. Much rural imagery, as found for example in advertising, has been aimed directly at urban consumers in English society

Fig. 1.2 Southern Railway poster, 'The South Downs', by Walter Spradbury (National Railway Museum).

(fig. 1.2); whereas much urban imagery, with its overtones of metropolitan sophistication, is aimed at rural dwellers elsewhere in the World.

Generally, the ability to move between the urban and the rural has increased as our levels of technical ability and income have ensured the accessibility of even remote rural areas to townspeople looking for weekend breaks, second homes or holidays. The theme of *externally induced change* is an important one addressed here. Most obviously, it is the central focus of Peter Ambrose's chapter on modern rural planning issues. Ambrose deals with the political struggles between the various actors on the rural stage: old capital in the shape of landed interests, even in the 1990s a very dominant feature of English society and landscape; farming interests; the housebuilders; the broad-based and increasingly articulate conservation lobby; central government; and local planners.

The conflicts in the past between these groups have established the structures within which all the groups operate at the present time, but in turn the groups themselves, in their ever-shifting alliances and with fluctuating positions of power, re-define the structures of the future. Many English rural or semi-rural landscapes, such as that of Central Berkshire provide examples of these shifting power relations being played out in a pressurised rural scene.

The immediacy of such an issue as Central Berkshire in the 1990s also raises the ever-present surrounding question as to whether change in rural areas is a relatively new phenomenon, or whether it is endemic. Clearly in Berkshire change threatens to run out of control, but what of change in the historical community? Malcolm Kitch addresses this issue squarely in the context of early-modern England. The related myths of continuity and the organic community form a prelude to a discussion of some central issues in rural population studies: the sources of information and their availability; age-sex and social bias in the demography of migrants; the reasons for movement; the spatial and temporal dimensions of movement; and the extent to which there are long-term historical trends discernible. Movement is seen by Kitch (and by most modern historians) as ubiquitous, though not necessarily long-distance. Change in the shape of a continuous groundswell of movement of families and individuals, was a characteristic of village life in the past, as in the present.

This finding makes it all the more difficult to reconcile reality with those studies which have approached the rural community as if it were a 'self-contained arena of power'. Too many of the early post-war community studies carried out in Wales, the West of England and Scotland, neglected change and thereby helped perpetuate the myth of changelessness in the countryside. And if change was seen, it was internalised within the parish boundaries, and resolved by recourse to a functional equilibrium model of local society wherein change is localised and serves only to reinforce the status quo. Wright describes this feature of these studies, so typical of much social scientific thinking in the 1950s and 1960s, in her chapter. By contrast, and in a longer historical context, Joan Thirsk prefers to note the subtle restructuring of rural life, which might take the form of the interlocking of farming communities from adjacent but contrasting environments, which worked to the benefit of both groups. But again, the parish cannot be seen in isolation, a point which is also very germane to the discussions of local landownership and power in Victorian England undertaken by Short. Change and external contact was the norm, not the exception, although sweeping generalisations must be tempered by reference to local situations. Not all communities were equally outward-looking, and some had, and still have to some degree, locked-in power structures which fiercely resisted change.

Scales of analysis

One of the most interesting questions facing students of the rural world is the extent to which studies of one rural locality are generalisable to a wider range of situations. It is a question which Phythian-Adams has addressed in the context of local history[18] and which has been characterised by Finberg as the tension between 'national history localised' on the one hand, and 'local history *per se*' or 'the biography of little places' on the other. The former, the study of national themes and changes as they worked themselves through at a local level, has a long historical tradition. It was the tradition which enabled Finberg and Hoskins to introduce some of the papers in their *Devonshire Studies* (1952) as 'English history localised in Devon', or to introduce a study of Tavistock as a town which: 'has combined, on a small scale indeed, but in a state of high perfection, the most characteristic elements of English feudal, monastic, parliamentary and industrial history'.

In 1962 Finberg asserted that: 'We may picture the family, the local community, the national state and the supra-national society as a series of concentric circles. Each requires to be studied with constant reference to the one outside it.'[19] The relatively new field of local history now came to be conceived of as one in which a locality was studied for its own sake but also for the light it shed on its region and on national history; often though, through a series of sweeping assumptions about the national scene which were barely sustainable. For Hoskins to assume that the farmers of Wigston Magna could be comparable with all other English farmers, and that such a process of comparison could also illuminate our national thinking, certainly gave local history a boost. Most such studies remained however, thematic and economic or topographical, rather than social, and the fundamental problem of relating their localised subject matter to that of the national level remained largely unresolved.

In the last 30 years the gap between local and national has, however, been straddled in a number of ways, of which two in particular are represented in this volume. Studies in the typology of towns and villages have proceeded, the latter owing much to the work on 'open' and 'close' villages by Dennis Mills. This effectively, as discussed herein by Short, presents a multi-dimensional typology of villages which can be applied at all scales from local to national, although its advocates have mostly proceeded on a village-by-village basis, building upwards and outwards rather than from a national model down to the local particular. The other main attempt at explanation is through the agrarian region, as exemplified in the work of Joan Thirsk, and discussed in her contribution here. Such studies have become increasingly sophisticated since their proximate origins in historical studies in the 1950s, although their existence as an analytical tool in geography has a longer pedigree. Recent examples include the two volumes of the *Agrarian*

History of England and Wales V 1640–1750 (1984 and 1985) and Thirsk's own summary of early-modern studies in *English Agricultural Regions and Agrarian History 1500–1750* (1987).[20] The study of the *pays* has grown logically from this, and it has been the concern of Thirsk and Everitt, for example, to represent the totality of landscape and society, responding to the particular historical moment, in a way which was not achieved in the earlier work of Hoskins, Finberg or Beresford.

The question of response and dynamic change within and between regions has received less attention than the more static period pictures of *pays*, or studies using the *pays* as yet another boundary – larger than that of the individual community – but still artificially limiting. As Phythian-Adams has noted, what we still largely lack are studies of 'The interpenetration of contrasting *pays* ... [and] the manner in which the societies of *pays* in later times may have been inter-connected ...'[21] Similar remarks can be made for the study of the region, which extends the historical boundary of study outward still further, and which has become a popular focus for academics in recent years. Still broader regions are hinted at by such journals as *Northern History*, *Midland History*, and *Southern History*. A 'hierarchy of belonging'[22] can be adduced, which ultimately links the severely local to the provincial and the national.

In recent years the question of local/national interconnections and scales of analysis has received much attention also from geographers, sociologists, anthropologists and philosophers. It is certainly not a historical problem only, nor one attached specifically to the study of the English rural community. There has been, for example, much discussion over the concept of 'locality research', with the concept of the locality as an object of study raising both exciting and problematic issues. In the rural sense it has recently been claimed that we might see events in rural localities as expressions of broader (national or international) processes working themselves out.[23] Leaving aside for the moment the argument that by conceptualising rural areas merely as stages on which wider processes unfold, one is actually undermining rural studies in their own right, since what is important in this approach is the process rather than the rural arena, it is important to note that herein lies belated recognition from the social sciences that the integration of local and national places and processes is long overdue.

The dynamics of countryside and community

The focus of this volume is the English rural community. The term implies a particular scale of enquiry, the community level, and a particular type of location or setting. Nevertheless, all contributors are also at pains to set out the particular processes operating on the rural community, past and present, with a sensitivity to both historical periodisation and locality. Some of these processes might be specified as 'local causal processes', arising from local actions and creating local distinctiveness. Others might be seen as derived essentially from urban, or national or international origins. Thus Barrell's concern with depictions of rural scenes in the eighteenth and nineteenth centuries is fuelled by an interest in national aesthetic or social standards; Laing's paper is in part concerned with the nationally networked and urban-dominated modern media and its reproduction of the images of rurality; Ambrose is concerned with national policy in the fields of planning and housing as they impact on particular rural areas. The papers by Thirsk, Howkins and Short however, emerge out of a concern with local distinctiveness first and foremost. It is the particular fashioning of networks of socio-economic structures and power relations *at the local level*, including those within the rural family, which guide them. However, just as Ambrose is concerned to show the impact of national processes and even international restructuring on particular places, so Thirsk, Howkins and Short also acknowledge the importance of country-wide issues in the understanding of places.

In order to promote the study of English rural communities, we surely now need a tolerant but conceptually tight approach to the English countryside. Such an approach should perhaps aim to integrate our various knowledge bases and approaches, such that we can aim for an interleaving of our understanding of social, economic and political processes deriving from, and operating at, different scales (local, regional, national, international) with a respect for the individuality of place (which again can be conceived of as being at different geographical scales) and with a keen awareness of historical momentum: what one social scientist has referred to as 'the becoming of places'.[24]

Such an approach might also derive strength from knowledge of the fact that rural communities were and are constantly changing, that such change results from the actions, decisions and aspirations of individuals and community groups within the villages and hamlets, as well as from the distant and largely faceless bureaucracies of power structures within which we all move. The physical and human institutional structures of the village, upon which such distantly engendered policies come to rest, determine its impact locally. Neither social theory nor socio-economic processes can be abstracted from the context of the village or other rural scene upon which they come to rest, and to wrench that context from its position in space and time would be to repeat the mistakes of abstraction made in the social sciences in the 1960s and to render any such analysis insubstantial.

This is not to prioritise the place over its inhabitants, or to prioritise either at the expense of a study of process. It is surely by integrating and giving equal validity to all three; and by allowing cultural analysis to inform social analysis and vice versa, that we can make progress. Cultures were created and re-created locally by working villagers; rural economy and geography helped form the myriad rural cultures of the villages and hamlets, alongside the social and religious allegiances described by Lowerson. Traditions were formed, described and resurrected by working villagers and wealthy newcomers interacting (peacefully or in a state of class conflict) in the countryside. The peculiar results of these conjunctions for our present ideological stances towards rurality impel us to consider culture history alongside rural economics; an understanding of changing media representations alongside social history, and so on.

One of the underlying strands connecting the contributions to this volume is the belief that by concentrating attention on the past *and* present of the rural community, we can aspire to appreciate what such policies, attitudes and ideologies meant to the lives of working country people. The village and farm is not, nor has it ever been, self-contained or static but many studies present them as if they were. The countryside contained, and still contains, many poor, but many observers still cannot see them. Nor is this the first era to witness 'rural restructuring', and the contemporary socio-economic shockwaves as disinvestment and policy changes hit agriculture and multi-national companies seek to invest in 'greenfield' sites and 'green' labour, do have some interesting historical analogies. Nevertheless, the rural future without a strong farming presence is still inconceivable for most people. Furthermore, the arcadian image of rural living is slowly being destroyed by the very presence of those who have the money to follow their dream. Realities and images still await reconciliation. It is important that we make strides towards this, since strong rural imagery traps our thoughts, guides our decisions and is a major filter through which present and future rural policies emerge.

It is also the contention of this volume that many of our modern (and past) attitudes to the countryside have been based on myth as much as upon direct observation. And myth allows us to live with the problematic, and even to find pleasure in it, even to the extent, as Janowitz reminds us, of finding pleasure in ruins[25] (fig. 1.3). As Barthes has written:

In passing from history to nature myth acts economically: it abolishes the complexity of human acts, it gives them the simplicity of essence, it does away with all dialects . . . Things appear to mean something by themselves.[26]

Thus the material countryside is shorn of its tensions and politics, and one result is that those actually in need of help are deprived. When the early landscape gardeners set about creating countrysides which resembled paintings, thereby changing reality to fit the image, they started a process which still continues, in many various guises, to the present day. We still inspect our countrysides through a 'Claude glass' of mythology which obscures and directs our perceptions. And perhaps even more worrying is the thought that the mythology now feeds off itself, with little reference back to its origins in reality. When the novels of Thomas Hardy or the screenplay of *Emmerdale Farm* are used as

Fig. 1.3 Countryside reality and the ruin. Castle Rising, N. Norfolk, where a newly built housing estate growing out from Kings Lynn nestles side by side with early medieval and older earthworks (Colour Library Books).

substitutes for the reality of country living, or when people's images of rurality become based around *Archers* weekend visits, there is a threatened separation which carries the rural community mythology industry higher onto its own plane. Is it not time that this was stopped?

It is hoped that the essays which make up this volume will go some way towards reducing the shocking ignorance which we still have about such a large and well-loved part of England; stimulate thought as to why such ignorance has prevailed, and raise questions. In whose interests, for example, does it lie that we should still have such naive ideas? Too often the countryside has served as a stage upon which urban interest groups fight for control, as most prominently perhaps on the Southern Pennines grouse moors in the interwar period. Today, in an age concerned with the 'greening' of politics and the 'greening' of industry, it is important to remember that our cognition of the villages and people of rural England conditions our attitudes to its future, just as it influences the questions we ask of its past. Such are the justifications for this volume, written in the belief that although not all aspects of rurality are covered, enough will have been said to raise questions, prompt discussions and, by better understanding the past and present rural community, to hope for an improved future.

NOTES

1 K. Hoggart, 'Let's do away with rurality' unpublished paper presented to the Rural Economy and Society Study Group, University of Bristol, December 1989.

2 R. Williams, *The Country and the City* (1975 edn) 297.

3 Louis Simond, *An American in Regency England: the Journal of a Tour in 1810–1811* edited by Christopher Hibbert (1968) 57.

4 P. Lowe, 'The rural idyll defended: from preservation to conservation' in G. E. Mingay (ed.), *The Rural Idyll* (1989) 113.

5 A. Howkins, 'The discovery of rural England' in R. Colls and P. Dodd (eds.), *Englishness: Politics and Culture 1880–1920* (1986) 62–88; P. Brandon and B. Short, *The South East from AD 1000* (1990) 336–59.

6 P. Parker, 'Forever England': a book review of C. Dakers, *The Countryside at War 1914–1918* (1987) in *The Listener* 10 December 1987.

7 John Taylor, 'The imaginary landscape' in *Ten-8*, 12 (1983) 9. For the separation of 'landscape' and working countryside see J. Urry, *The Tourist Gaze* (1990) 96–100; Kit Taylor, 'Never mind what it means' (*Times Saturday Review* 2 February 1991), 15.

8 C. Buchanan, *No Way to the Airport* (1981).

9 Anne Janowitz, *England's Ruins: Poetic Purpose and the National Landscape* (Cambridge 1990).

10 W. Vaughan, 'Leisure and toil: differing views of rural life *c.* 1750–1850' in D. Spargo (ed.) *This Land is Our Land: Aspects of Agriculture in English Art* (1989) 9.

11 Roger Sales, *English Literature in History 1780–1830: Pastoral and Politics* (1983) 17.

12 M. J. Wiener, *English Culture and the Decline of the Industrial Spirit 1850–1980* (Cambridge 1981); P. Wright, *On Living in an Old Country* (1985); R. Hewison, *The Heritage Industry: Britain in a Climate of Decline* (1987).

13 N. Thrift, 'Manufacturing rural geography' *Journal of Rural Studies* 3(1) (1987) 77–81.

14 T. Marsden and J. Murdoch, *Restructuring Rurality: Key Areas for Development in Assessing Rural Change* ESRC Countryside Change Initiative Working Paper, 4, 1990.

15 H. Newby, 'Locality and rurality: the restructuring of rural social relations' *Regional Studies* 20 (1986) 209.

16 Jane Austen, *Northanger Abbey* (1803) 1968 Minster Classics edn, 150.

17 R. Williams, *The Country and the City* (1975).

18 C. Phythian-Adams, *Re-thinking English Local History* University of Leicester Department of English Local History occasional paper, fourth series, no. 1 (1987) 1–14.
19 *Ibid.*, 2.
20 Joan Thirsk (ed.), *The Agrarian History of England and Wales v, 1640–1750* part 1 (Cambridge, 1984) and part 11 (Cambridge, 1985); *England's Agricultural Regions and Agrarian History 1500–1750* (Cambridge, 1987).
21 Phythian-Adams, *Re-thinking English Local History*, 11.
22 *Ibid.*, 45.
23 P. J. Cloke, 'Rural geography and political economy' in R. Peet and N. J. Thrift (eds.) *New Models in Geography* vol. 1 (1989) 164–97.
24 A. Pred, *Place, Practice and Structure* (Cambridge, 1986).
25 Janowitz, *England's Ruins*.
26 Roland Barthes, *Mythologies* (1972) 143, cited in John Taylor, 'The imaginary landscape' in *Ten-8* 12 (1983) 3–4.

The evolution of contrasting communities within rural England 2

BRIAN SHORT

This essay explores the long-term evolution of differences within the settlements and fields of the English countryside, differences that have long been recognised:

The traveller from the coast, who, after plodding northward for a score of miles, over calcareous downs and corn-lands, suddenly reaches the verge of one of these escarpments, is surprised and delighted to behold, extended like a map beneath him, a country differing absolutely from that which he has passed through. Behind him the hills are open, the sun blazes down upon fields so large as to give an unenclosed character to the landscape, the lanes are white, the hedges low and plashed, the atmosphere colourless. Here, in the valley, the World seems to be constructed upon a smaller and more delicate scale; the fields are mere paddocks, so reduced that from this height their hedgerows appear a network of dark green threads overspreading the paler green of the grass. The atmosphere beneath is languorous, and is so tinged with azure that what artists call the middle distance partakes also of that hue, while the horizon beyond is of a deepest ultramarine. Arable lands are few and limited; with but slight exceptions the prospect is a broad rich mass of grass and trees, mantling minor hills and dales within the major. Such is the Vale of Blackmoor.[1]

Rural community structures will be examined here in three ways: first to account for how and why the social, economic, political and morphological differences between settlements arose; secondly to examine one classificatory device in use by the early nineteenth century; and thirdly to note some of the complications and implications of these differences. These will be illustrated mainly, though not exclusively, from within South East England, a region which, despite its vanguard position within English history and its European significance, has not received its due share of attention from local and regional historians.[2]

Power and community: a framework for study

Rural settlements don't just materialise. Their genesis, growth and flowering reflect human needs and consciousness at some past time. As such they are clearly the outcome of social process, but once in place they become a part of that very process, with their presence guiding and stimulating further developments, and being both the scene and the outcome of social reproduction. The differences between village, hamlet and isolated farm are explored elsewhere in this volume.[3] However, the communities living amongst these settlements are also variable in

19

complex ways. They differ socially, economically, politically, culturally, and here then is the key question – why should these differences occur?

Rural communities do not exist in a vacuum. Nor have they ever, despite the abstractions of social scientists and local historians. They generally came into existence, grew or declined, as part of a wider network of settlements reacting to external as well as to internal stimuli. Historically such networks have taken many different forms, but they have been associated over the last 1,500 years in England and Wales with spatial and political units of varying sizes, such as the manor, the multiple estate, or sub-county units such as the Kentish Lathe or the Sussex Rape. The origins of such features are disputed, but crucially they all exhibited a strong element of centralised control. They were spatial units of socio-economic domination, often by one family or dynasty. This power was normally exercised from a geographical base: a villa regalis, a town, court, or castle, and thus we have the development of a centralised power base (a *core*) and other constituent settlements within the unit at varying geographical and political distance from the core, ultimately through to the *periphery*. It would surely not be too fanciful to suppose that political power declined historically as some function of physical distance, so that some more remote corners might be almost devoid of centralised influence, getting only a modicum of administration, law and order and whatever passed for civilised society in the frontier zone of that period. Thus both society and space were unequal. Some settlements would have been subjected to greater degrees of exploitation than others, receiving little in return for the appropriation of their resources, an action which subsumed the asymmetrical power relations, translated them into daily, repeatable and 'normal' or 'natural' events, and shaped the very landscapes in and around the settlements themselves. Decisions made at the core settlement would be thrust upon all others.

Historically therefore, most rural communities existed somewhere within a core/periphery continuum. Settlements were *inter-dependent* upon one another, not merely isolated and inward-looking, since their economies were linked directly or indirectly to the needs of people in other settlements. Politically they were unfree, although in reality the inaccessibility of some vills might have rendered them relatively immune from lordship exercised through manorial courts and power bases.

Political power and control of land thus shaped the village. Over time some became completely dominated by individual families, perhaps having been located in the core areas of power, and as such they emerged as what ultimately became known as 'close' communities, with their jobs, houses, and social and religious provision at the discretion of that family. Other communities, more peripheral and further from the core, lacked such powerful families, and were composed instead of smaller farmers, tradespeople and rural industrial workers. They were more 'open' in that their village councils were more generally accessible, and their social structures were very different to those in the 'close' communities.

So one moves through time, from early origins of inter-dependency and power relations, to the more recent recognition of contrasts in rural communities. The key theme in this framework is the location and asymmetrical exercise of power. As Giddens has it: 'Resources are media through which power is exercised, as a routine element ... in social reproduction.'[4] Such a system of exploitation and dependency over rural space, developing and becoming manifest in many various ways, is neither self-contained nor functionalist. It is historically variable in its form, and it rests on the exercise of power over resources and other human beings. It now remains to put more flesh on these conceptual bones or 'structures of domination'.[5]

How and why have the rural community differences arisen?

There are certain intrinsic qualities of the physical environment which encourage or discourage settlement and influence its pattern. Altitude, climate, water supply, soil fertility and topography all affect the pattern of villages and village life. Rackham has rightly drawn attention to the fact that the ordinary rural landscapes of Britain are the result of interaction between human activities and such features of the natural world, and that to see the countryside as artefact and the result of design and ambition alone misses much of the rich complexity of the scene.[6] Whatever case study is taken, this much surely remains true.

While acknowledging the influence of such environmental forces, this chapter will pursue a more socio-political and historical analysis of the contrasting rural settlement patterns and their structures of livelihood, and one which stretches over a very long period of time, because as R. D. Blackmore has it in *Lorna Doone*: 'I know not where the beginning was nor where the middle ought to be.'[7] There is no obvious starting date for when settlement contrasts begin. Remembering that all generations inherit environments created by their forebears for their own needs, and that country people therefore must be seen as operating within many constraints, the processes and patterns of such inheritance are of paramount importance. Such constraints are not just those emanating from the physical environment, since there are constraints also which arise from being born into particular cultural and economic systems. This conjunction of environment, culture and economy gives a particularity to individual places and regions and renders it vital that theoretical ideas about the development of village differences should be grounded empirically in a real environment.

In South East England there is a clear differentiation between the coastal lands and the interior country (fig. 2.1). Around most of the coast, from North Kent to the Romney Marsh and western Sussex, is an environment of more accessible,

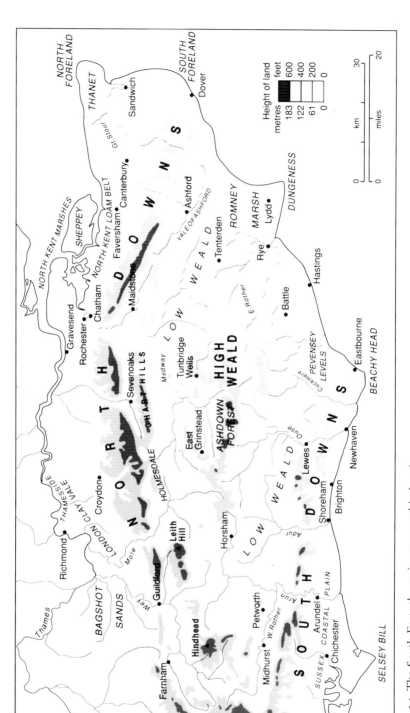

Fig. 2.1 The South East: the main topographical regions.

freer-working soils: the *Coastal Fringe*. It was this area which was the first to be taken up; it was probably the first to be settled during the fourth millenium B.C. It was the area of the first clearances of woodland, and it is therefore an area of enormous investment over long centuries of both human labour and capital. This investment, not surprisingly, was maintained and expanded upon over many generations, with people in each increasingly sophisticated political structure seeking out their own optimum spatial organisation, and both reacting to, and recognising positively, the value of those previous generations of clearance, drainage and reclamation.

So here we have the earliest settled communities, for example along the northern and southern edges of the North and South Downs and on the coasts themselves where feasible, in the fertile brickearth zone of North Kent, and later along the Sussex Coastal Plain around Chichester. We find the quantitative and qualitative importance of such early communities reflected, for example, in the distribution of prehistoric finds from the Neolithic onwards, being predominantly focussed in the Coastal Fringe. Accepting that any prehistoric distribution maps are in part a reflection of chosen areas of archaeological fieldwork, are time-dependent and reflect also the ease of discovery of artefacts, the overwhelming evidence still points to a temporal and spatial dominance of settlement in the Coastal Fringe being held over a very long time. Many such prehistoric communities were probably controlled by or through central place foci of power in the causewayed camps or downland hill forts which acted as nuclei of defence and political power along the chalk downs.[8]

The Interior, by contrast, was far less accessible. This comprised the High and Low Weald (fig. 2.1) and was the area about which Furley wrote in 1871:

a portion of the earth's surface strongly marked for many centuries with the primeval curse of the Almighty ... certain it is that for many a century it was a desert and a waste, neither planted nor peopled, and filled only with wild animals, herds of deer and game.[9]

It was far more populated than was once realised, since the lack of recent arable farming, the overriding presence of woodland which inhibits access and aerial photography, and the heavy clay soils have inhibited fieldwalking and archaeological research. Consequently our knowledge of the prehistoric settlement of the Interior is still rudimentary and biased towards the work of relatively few individuals. It is now thought possible that extensive wealden usage resulted in large clearances by the later Neolithic and Early Bronze Age, but with subsequent soil exhaustion and retreat of settlement.[10] Another resurgence of activity may have occurred with the Late Iron Age building of hill forts and more agricultural clearance.

Certainly the Romans recognised the differences between Coastal Fringe and Interior in the South Eastern territories of the *Regnenses* and *Cantiaci*. Their villas were on soils made productive by earlier investment or through their own system of slave-based production, and their towns and non-villa settlements were also primarily in the 'civilised', already densely cultivated and inhabited part of the region, the Coastal Fringe. During this period therefore, villas spread out along the Sussex Coastal Plain, but there are relatively few known inland at any distance from the foot of the North and South Downs.

Much of the Weald, by contrast, was a specialist area, an Imperial Estate, with certainly the eastern end near present-day Battle producing iron for the Roman fleet, the *Classis Britannica*.[11] Put in a broader context, activities within the interior Weald were strongly subordinated to the wider interests of the Roman empire. Here was a political and military decision: that the Coastal Fringe was to be civilian, 'civilised' and administratively dominant: the Interior an extractive area, not primarily for permanent settlement, and consequently yielding few signs of civilised Roman life.

It would seem that if ever there were periods of settled agricultural activity in the prehistoric and Roman Weald, then soil exhaustion, lack of sustained investment, or political change terminated rather than reinforced that settlement. When the Saxons spread across the South East from their initial land holdings on the Coastal Fringe, they therefore encountered an Interior which had probably reverted to woodland and scrub, and they renewed a cyclical process which has come down to us as a period of woodland clearance, now documented (albeit scantily) and recorded in place-names. Much of the Weald is a heavy clay environment, certainly capable of being farmed but it was also well-suited to woodland, and was used by the Saxon coastal communities initially for seasonal swine pastures (pannage), for timber for building, for fuel and probably for the mining of iron ore. From it came timber and minerals; to it could be sent swine to be fattened. At present the only undisputed evidence for Saxon ironworking in the Weald comes from a site on the Ashdown Forest, dated to A.D. 745 $+90/-65$, but this surely cannot be an isolated industrial find.[12]

That pattern of extraction from the Interior by the elites of the Coastal Fringe which was so early established, came to characterise much of the subsequent history of the region.[13] It is a long-lasting, deep political structure within the South East which sits upon and interacts with the physical structure of the land surface itself. As such it is sensitive to, and recurs within, different historical contexts. Areas of early settlement became dominant in the Coastal Fringe, while areas of the Interior became dependent (fig. 2.2). And that dependence was institutionalised in several ways in the centuries following Roman rule. The mechanisms of dominance included the Coastal Fringe minster church with its wealden dependencies; the Kentish lathe with its royal settlement nuclei always in the Coastal Fringe; the huge multiple estates with their manorial or home farm in the Coastal Fringe and with subordinate interests in the Interior; and the

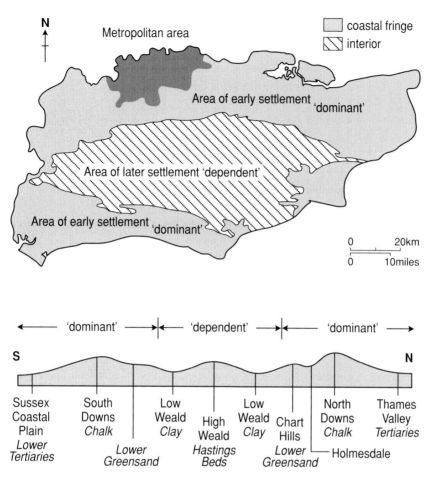

Fig. 2.2 Regions of dominance and dependence in the South East.

Sussex Rapes, the fundamental territorial sub-divisions of that county, with each coming to be controlled from a castle town fortified in the early Anglo-Norman period, and with each town being once again in the Coastal Fringe. Even many parishes, emerging in the Saxo-Norman transition period, could be found with their nucleated villages (of whatever date) within the Coastal Fringe area and dependent parts in the Interior. These long, strip-like parishes are a well-known feature repeated in other early territorial subdivisions in many parts of England.

Thus, the main institutions had power bases in the Coastal Fringe and dependent parts in the Interior long before the advent of feudalism. But with the development of the latter the contrasts between the Coastal Fringe and the Weald mirrored conditions over much of Western Europe. Older manorial and strongly feudal centres emerged under the grip of lordships and baronies, as their advantages of site were institutionalised and as the rights, privileges and dues attached to the person became transferred in time to the land. Within feudalism the dependency of man on man cemented society, and this was also seen in the pattern of their holdings, as units of land acquired prestige and power with their occupiers over other units at a distance from the manorial centre. In the South East these core areas were to be found, of course, in the Coastal Fringe, and here, in common with other older settled areas of Europe, the networks of lordship, dependency and labour-services were most strongly developed.

Although the South East as a whole has been considered to be a part of the feudal core of Western Europe,[14] at a more detailed level of enquiry it becomes clear that there were localised peaks of feudalism in both town and countryside, surrounded by, or adjacent to, more peripheral and less manorialised areas. In the centuries following the Norman Conquest such areas were sought by feudal lords for colonisation, sub-infeudation, assart-tenure and money rents rather than labour-services. This was a preferable way to expand within feudalism, to adjust the system by spatial expansion, rather than to attempt the difficult task of extracting more labour-services from the peasantry within the core areas.

Therefore within the South East the Weald became an important arena in which feudalism attempted to reassert itself, with manorial lords encouraging the assarting of their wealden outliers, and granting lesser manorial status to wealden manors, as a flexible alternative to development in the stultified core areas. Money, not labour-services, could be gained; and the situation became still more obvious after 1350 when strategies of demesne leasing in the Coastal Fringe were also adopted. Even today much of the wealden landscape derives its character from assarting in the years prior to the fourteenth century, and the implications for its later social and economic structures which flowed from its being seen as a feudal pressure-release area were equally significant.

However, by about 1500 the two contrasting environments were sharply diverging as a spatial reaction to the halting transition to a capitalist economy. Much of the Coastal Fringe was by now a highly capitalised, labour-extensive sheep and corn region, with demesnes held by tenant farmers needing relatively few workers for the sheep-corn husbandry of this area. Indeed, surplus labour could be shed, outlying hamlets and small villages might become deserted or shrunken, and innovations came into predominantly large farms held on leasehold or owned by the forerunners of the prosperous yeomen.

The Interior, by contrast was an area of wood-pasture and wood-based industry. Here was a society and economy producing iron (water power had been applied to Chingley Furnace in the Kentish Weald in the early fourteenth century, and the first English blast furnace was established on the slopes of Ashdown Forest at Newbridge in the 1490s); glass; cloth (there were references to fulling mills in the fifteenth century); pottery (by the sixteenth century kilns were located near the centre of the Weald with large market radii) and tiles. Iron ore, limestone, marl and building stones were quarried and timber hewn and worked in a variety of ways. As such, with its profusion of woodlands, roadside wastes and commons, it attracted migrants and the tramping poor; the marginal elements of society who otherwise could find no niche. Ironworks in particular tended to attract vagrants, some of whom might be troublesome. Richard Michelbourne, JP, wrote in 1633:

I sent this sixth of January to the Sessions two woemen and one yonge fellow the one of the woemen is called Nan in the hayre a desperate ruffianly drab shee nameth her selfe to be the wife of one Richard Shinn shee hath used about Freshfield Forge and Sheffield Forge for the space of this two or three yeares and there hath beene of that company eighteene or nineteene at one time and they are such as breede a terror in the Country heereabout she may passe for an incorrigble Rouge . . .[15]

One result of these differential changes was that by the early seventeenth century a demographic reversal had occurred in which the Weald became more heavily populated than the surrounding Coastal Fringe. The latter needed relatively few workers but the Interior needed many and could provide for them. It not only attracted migrants but also retained its own population within the region through patterns of partible inheritance, and through the early marriages and consequent larger families generated by access to rural industrial employment and cottages on wasteland.

However, by about 1640 the Wealden iron, glass and cloth industries had more or less peaked.[16] This wood-pasture region was now set on a de-industrialising process throughout the seventeenth and eighteenth centuries, which gradually stripped out the early-modern employment opportunities, but which had no wealth of agriculture to fall back on, starved as it always had been of capital investment in this extractive robber-economy.

Thus we can perceive regional patterns of dominance and dependence, deference and obligation beginning to emerge from the mists of antiquity; and we have the channelling of surpluses and produce from the Weald to the non-Weald. It is clear that the Weald was under-developed by Coastal Fringe residents through a process which, consciously and historically repeated, resembled in miniature as it were, much the same process by which the Third World was under-developed by Europeans. And over a very long period of time we can see that a wide variety of landscapes, economies and communities were constantly converging and diverging, held together in a tension which involved the relations between the regional core (curiously inverted geographically here as a Coastal Fringe) and the periphery (at the geographical centre). The core would constantly seek to reassert its dominance politically, building cumulatively on past investment in land, political and cultural authority so that its inhabitants should remain wealthy. However, often growth within wider social spheres could only be obtained by investing in the peripheral Interior, where areas of 'free energy' awaited innovations, labour and capital. The constant interplay between centralising tendencies and centrifugal growth created the tension, but at no time did the Coastal Fringe, stultified and archaic though it might have been, lose its power over the vigorously growing Interior. Note also that the Interior's landscapes and culture did not evolve because it was *isolated* from the dominant culture (whether classical civilisation, feudalism, or capitalism) but through a process of *absorption* and exploitation. It was fully incorporated, but always subsidiary.

Historical and socio-political analyses such as this could perhaps be undertaken for many other regions within the country. Many places have patterns of early-settled country, and areas of later-settled wood-pasture claylands or uplands. As yet few attempts have been made.[17]

The pattern of contrasting communities in the early nineteenth century: 'open' and 'close' parishes

Having inspected the dynamics and processes involved in the evolution of the regional template, we may now examine how these differences had become manifest in the constituent village and hamlet communities by the nineteenth century. The existence of different types of community was noted as early as the seventeenth century, and although by the late eighteenth century the notions had becomed more refined, it was not until the 1840s that the words 'close' and 'open' were much used as descriptions of village 'types'. It should be noted that 'village' and 'parish' are not interchangeable in this context. The unit for Poor Law purposes since the Elizabethan period, endorsed by the 1662 Act of Settlement, was the parish, and decisions on the poor (on which the differences were grounded, at least in part) would normally be binding on all the settlements – village, hamlet, isolated cottage and farm – within that parish. Clearly therefore the parish had now for long been the theatre for power struggles together with the estate, rather than the older vill and manor. And how the parish dealt with its poor would reflect the social and economic history, geography and politics of that community.

The terminology from the 1840s and 1850s is inexact and there is neither a clear contemporary definition, nor any one agreed subsequent interpretation by modern scholars.[18] The 'close' parish was strictly speaking so termed because its vestry meeting (technically usually a 'select' vestry) was closed to all except a relative handful of its inhabitants. The meeting controlled the setting of a poor rate and how that rate should be spent, and it was therefore a very important aspect of country life. By contrast the 'open' parish functioned with a vestry meeting open to all ratepayers wishing to attend. To give the flavour of a vestry, we might take the example of East Hoathly, Sussex in March 1763. In his diary, Thomas Turner, village shopkeeper and overseer of the poor, noted that he along with seven others:

In the even went down to Jones's [the Crown pub] in order to make a poor rate ... We stayed until near 1 o'clock quarrelling and bickering about nothing and in the end hardly did any business. The design of our meeting was to have made a poor rate in which every one that was taxed was intended to be assessed to the racked rent, that everyone might pay his just quota (in proportion to his rent) of the money expended in maintaining and keeping the poor. But how do I blush to say what artifice and deceit, cunning and knavery there was used by some (who would think it cruel and unjust to be called dishonest) to conceal their rents, and who yet would pretend the justness of an equal taxation was their desire, But however great their outward zeal for justice appeared, that cankerworm of self-interest lay so corroding in their hearts that it sullied the outward beauties of their would-be honesty.[19]

At West Chiltington the vestry seldom included more than about four or five, out of a total of about 40 who were entitled to attend, but these contained by the early 1830s 'one or two violent men who are constant in their attendance and who keep the parish in continuous sqabbles'.[20] The character of the vestry, its size, composition and degree of self-interest were clearly key issues, which both gave to and derived from structures of local political power.

However, the 'close' parish, according to Dennis Mills' formulation,[21] hinged around rather more than the character of the vestry. For him the high degree of concentration of landownership was paramount, with much else flowing from that fact (fig. 2.3). Between one and three families might control virtually all the land in the parish, and from this there followed enormous power, exercised by a limited number of people. Such power might take the form of the squire as magistrate, as controlling the game; being MP or Peer; and having the power to enclose the land early thereby creating large farms or a park. He controlled cottage accommodation, and because he or his tenant farmers would have to face the problems if people fell on hard times, he would be minded to keep the poor rates low. He might therefore try to keep the population as small as possible by minimising the amount of cottage accommodation and therefore the amount of settlement. There are many feedback loops in such a system, but by minimising the available number of cottages, even by pulling some down if needs be, he might thus keep poor rates low.

The squire in the 'close' parish might also provide social and cultural facilities: the school might be erected at his expense, and his wife or daughter might visit the school, presenting prizes. He might provide almshouses and charity, and a reading room in an attempt to entice men from the pub. Education and charity were means of instilling moral and social discipline and so rewards would be given to those passing the test of paternalistic approval. He might also be patron

Causal links in the close village

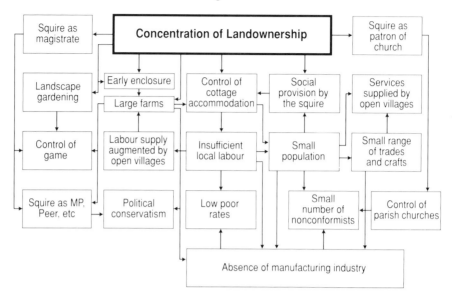

Causal links in the open village

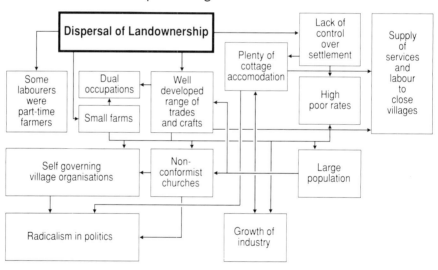

(after D. R. Mills. Open Univ., 1972, with minor amendments)

Fig. 2.3 The structures of Open and Close parishes: based on the original Dennis Mills formulation of 1972 (with permission from the author).

of the church, and through control of the advowson have virtual control over the parish church as well. Most such parishes were strongly conformist Church of England, with small numbers of nonconformists. Many clergymen might in addition be JPs (although this was not the case in Sussex), since about half the JPs in England were clergymen. Such parishes were politically conservative, with very little likelihood of manufacturing or industrial activity, and with few tradesmen or craft workers.

Many 'close' parishes were associated with estate or planned villages, often replacements for an original village removed from a newly imparked landscape. The fate of one such village, Newnham Courtenay, Oxfordshire, is documented through Goldsmith's *Deserted Village* (1770). Later model settlements arose for a variety of reasons – philanthropic, aesthetic or ideological – with social planning becoming all the while more sophisticated. The smithy's door came to have a horse shoe around it (as at Glynde in Sussex); and the cottagers of Old Warden (Beds) reputedly wore red clothes to match the estate paintwork on the cottages. Almshouse occupants were similarly obliged to conform to picturesque standards, and 'the stage [was] set with fittingly costumed, acquiescent "folk"'.[22]

Such concerns as these raise the point that 'close' villages not only came about through the character of the local vestry or through the degree of political, economic and social power attaching to landownership, but also through aesthetic or cultural considerations, which even at a time heavily influenced by Utilitarian philosophies, might have few tangible connections with practical concerns.

Such 'close' parishes are recognisable in both fact and fiction. Many are in areas of early depopulation: the north-east Midlands, western Norfolk or the East Riding of Yorkshire. In the 1791 *Select Views on Leicestershire* reference to Cotesbach we have:

The lordship contains 1,100 acres of land, old enclosure. Robert Marriott LLD owns the whole who is lord of the manor. You see but little of this village in your approach towards it, it being shaded by a number of large trees. It consists of a number of about 18 dwellings; there is no public house here, or tradesmen. The doctor, if he should choose to govern, may give laws to all that breathe in this place and indeed the cattle in the field are subject to his control, for not only all the lands owns him as its lord but every dwelling also. The patronage of the church and the living are all his own.[23]

In Trollope's *Framley Parsonage* the story is built around just such a village. Lady Lufton at Framley Court, Framley with its celebrated gardens, the Lufton Arms, the church opposite Framley Court, 'hardly a house otherwise in the parish, and as true blue a county as any in England'.[24] There are many such 'close' parishes also in the South East, and many in the Coastal Fringe in particular were 'governed from above'. In the Sussex Downland and adjacent areas West Firle was controlled by the Gage family; Stanmer by the Pelhams, Earls of Chichester;

and whole parishes were governed by the Duke of Richmond or Earl of Egremont.[25] And not all would agree with Bray on his visit to Edensor at Chatsworth that the Duke of Devonshire's munificence was well received so that:

The poor, the widow and the fatherless bless the providence which has bestowed such wealth on one so ready to relieve their wants.[26]

By contrast, the 'open' parishes might be denoted not only by a rowdy vestry, but by the dispersal of landownership, and certainly by the lack of any individual aesthetic. No great family dominated such parishes, and from these developments there followed certain consequences in the Mills version of the structure (fig. 2.3). Dispersed landownership could often mean that farms were small, with some so small that they were not viable full-time holdings. Many people were therefore part-time labourers or sought second occupations as carriers, innkeepers, craftsmen or shopkeepers. It could also follow from the dispersed pattern of landownership that no one individual had real control over incomers' settlement. So, large numbers of cottages might be erected, often poorly built, on the more abundant common land, on the waste and at the edges of the forests. Larger populations and higher poor rates followed as a consequence, with the latter falling precisely on those people who could least afford to pay them, the small farmers who were thereby deprived of capital for investment in their farming.

Various characteristics follow from such initial premises. Politically, these parishes might be more independent. It is surely no accident that from the 'open' parish of Tysoe, Warwickshire came the radical Joseph Ashby who was a union leader with Arch, as well as being a labourer, small farmer and Methodist lay preacher. The interaction of people and places such as these might encourage leaders of this sort: 'Real leaders of men, earning their support, rather than buying it.'[27] From them also came abundant labour, and they therefore supplied workers and services to the 'close' settlements, especially at harvest time. There were often many different trades and crafts represented, especially related to industries and woodworking; and frequently a relatively significant nonconformist element. Many of these parishes were large, with isolated corners allowing nonconformist ministries to challenge the hegemony of the Church of England, and to flourish in wayside chapels whose ministers, local men and farmers themselves, were perceived to be on a cultural level with their congregations.

Again, in the South East there were large numbers of these 'open' parishes, but they predominated in the Interior. In 1938 William Wood, harking back to the seventeenth century, noted that wealden men would range on the side of parliament in politics and no popery in religion, because they were not under any great 'territorial landowner'.[28] Following his 'pedestrian tours' through Sussex, Richard Heath wrote a series of articles in the 1870s and early 1880s which contains many interesting external perceptions of superstition, ignorance, immorality and poverty in the Weald of Sussex.[29] He noted the 'crabbed independence' of people in these 'open' communities, together with the petty jealousies among the builders, carpenters, wheelwrights and smiths. Many were 'just beginning to realise their power to think' and this, together with the greater independence, was turning people away from the Church of England, whose rural clergy:

as a class, have so closely identified themselves with the gentry as to give rise to the impression that they regard themselves as a sort of spiritual squirearchy ... At Buxted [a large wealden parish] the pastor of the chapel proved to be an ancient labourer in a dark smock, a truly simple-minded, good old man.[30]

On the edges of the Ashdown Forest in the heart of the Weald the woodlands and small fields held scatterings of cottages and hamlets as at Nutley or Fairwarp. Cobbett was enthusiastic about such communities. Travelling through them in the 1820s he wrote:

The labouring people look pretty well. They have pigs, They invariably do best in the woodland and forest and wild countries. Where the mighty grasper has all under his eye they can get but little.[31]

Agrarian capitalism was less obvious here than in many of the 'close' communities. In the poor Forest Ridges of the central Weald the abundant woodland, small fields, poor drainage, small farms and scatterings of buildings signalled piecemeal development on roadside waste. The ridges had been colonised in the late sixteenth and seventeenth centuries by a mixture of smallholders, tradesmen and craftsmen as well as by speculators in land. By the 1841 census hamlets such as Cade Street and Maynards Green had lost their pioneering origins, but farms here only averaged 45 acres, there was much by-employment, and the woods were the haunts of hurdle or implement makers – often itinerant families. Some small farmers fattened chickens and among farmer–labourers struggling to make a living, such activities were welcomed in the mid nineteenth century. The small farmers were able to get by in such ways as these, by looking beyond the large-scale farming methods of the downland areas. Many were essentially peasant cultivators, an 'awkward class' being neither large capitalist farmer nor rural proletarian, using family labour to a greater extent than hired labour, and having secondary jobs. This was the group largely expunged from the Coastal Fringe in the five centuries before 1800 but which remained important in the Weald, supplying goods, services and seasonal labour within the wider circle of south-eastern agrarian capitalism, and retaining barter and exchange for local business or even rents. The cash nexus was reserved for more distant business dealings.[32]

The implications of the differences

By whatever criteria one decides that a parish is 'open' or 'close', whether by the presence or absence of parochial settlement restriction, landownership dominance or some other definition, the contrasts in rural settlement are clear in South East England. Such parish definitions, it is shown here, are the mid nineteenth-century outcome of centuries of regional differentiation, which ultimately led to a greater preponderence of 'open' parishes in the Interior and more 'close' parishes on the Coastal Fringe.[33]

What are the implications of this pattern? On the highly farmed open chalklands of Southern England, communities had been decimated, and the remnants of those communities thereafter became very hierarchically ordered and dominated by the squirearchy. But the downland landscape had been stripped of its people in the search for agricultural profit. Seven hundred years ago the lower parts of these downland slopes were full of small peasant holdings, whose tenants, farming their land in strips, constituted a thriving community. But in later centuries, vitality gave way to shrunken and indeed deserted villages. Combinations of reasons can be advanced, ranging from French raids to the desertion of marginal high flinty downlands, the visitation of plague, and enclosure for sheep farming. In the long term after 1350 prosperity on the downland waxed and waned, but it was there only for the few: especially the landowners and their tenants, the yeomen and flockmasters. Society became increasingly polarised.

On the other hand the 'open' parishes, very densely populated, supplied labour and reproduced the workforce which was imported onto the downland seasonally to work. But peripheral status was maintained: the Interior's reserves of iron ore and timber were exploited by London capital; and cloth was produced in a proto-industrial system geared again to external exports. But from the mid seventeenth century, de-industrialisation left it 'overpopulated', with a large population now increasingly reliant on an under-capitalised farming and woodland crafts economy. With this latest episode in its history of under-development at the expense of regions beyond its boundaries, the Weald lapsed into eighteenth-century obscurity. Until its poorly developed infrastructure was seen as the essence of the picturesque, it was a place for genteel society to avoid.

However, the 'open' and 'close' parishes can also be seen as parts of an interlocking system,[34] and in the South East such a symbiotic relationship gave rise to movements of people, commodities and capital. Such movements between the two types of community may be characterised in three ways. Movement could be permanent, as for example when the downland parishes were enclosed 'by agreement' and families left, possibly to go into the Weald. Secondly it might be seasonal with organised gangs or otherwise large numbers of harvesters travelling to the downland and Sussex Coastal Plain from the Interior. George Bourne (Sturt) portrayed such movements at the turn of the last century from West Surrey down to the Sussex coast, with scythes and sickles sharpened over Hindhead to ward off footpads. Such movements might be over very long distances, as for example, with the Irish harvesters reported coming to the Lewes area in 1832:

The Irish labourers as the season advances are pouring in upon the agricultural districts. Several families have already infested this town annoying the inhabitants with their hourly calls and leaving their addresses. We hope we shall not have a recurrence of those scenes of which we were spectators several years ago.[35]

The third type was a daily movement, since shortage of accommodation in the 'close' parishes could result in long daily journeys to work. In the 'open' community of Bourne it was estimated by Sturt that by 1912 nine out of every ten men worked outside the parish boundaries (presumably meaning Farnham parish, in which Bourne was situated). In many parts of England, people would walk six to ten miles to work daily, and such long journeys were necessary if labourers had perforce to live in the 'open' communities. The large parish of Wye, a Kentish 'open' community, had many cottages lived in by labourers working on surrounding farms, all more than two miles away, and some going to 'close' parishes such as Little Chart or Egerton, the latter more than ten miles away. At Chailey, Sussex, there was a shortage of cottages as people held on to them but walked long distances to work. The rents were relatively low, and when they had been built people had 'swarmed in from all around'. By contrast the number of houses in the 'close' village of Glynde reputedly fell from 60 to 35 in the ten-year period before 1865. Evictions from 'close' parishes such as Kennington and Hothfield in Kent resulted in still more overcrowding in parishes such as Shadoxhurst.[36]

The difference between 'open' and 'close' villages was reflected also in the social interaction, or lack of it, between the two different types of community. The distances people moved on marriage, for example, demonstrates that many 'close' parishes of the Coastal Fringe had very limited horizons for marriage partners since they did not travel very far. In the Weald, however, many people travelled to seek work, with many wealden men visiting the downland, marrying local women, and taking their brides back with them into the Weald. This process was tempered, of course, by rumours and images; the Weald was perceived as a place both lawless and heathen, where neither the courts nor the established church had a strong presence. Many saw the Weald as a heathen place, so would a father let his daughter marry a wealden man? While some did, the spatial patterns of marriage indicate that very often it was a case of Weald marrying Weald, and downland marrying downland in an east–west direction.[37]

The difference also has very real implications for the pattern of class relations and class conflict in the countryside. For example, allowing that some conflict is inherent whatever the type of community, would we expect to find more or less discontent *shown openly* by working families in 'close' or 'open' parishes? Where would most dissent be shown? Would such dissent be likely to take the form of *covert* protest, in the form of poaching, cattle maiming or incendiarism? Or would it be more *overt*? Open demonstration such as a march along the main village road is one example, and the last of these on any large scale were the 'Captain Swing' protest marches of the 1830–31 winter, when agricultural workers joined with small farmers and tradespeople in attempts to bring attention to various grievances, including the absence of a living wage, tithes and taxes. Would we also expect a more horizontally linked class structure in the 'open' parish, which contained many smaller farmers and more tradespeople? These parishes might be more uniformly of a similar social class, although as Wells has demonstrated, this would not necessarily preclude groups of farmers or others from banding together to guard their own interests, as at Burwash. At Ewhurst, Sussex, the poor rate was reduced from 24s to 11s in seven years with the appointment of an assistant overseer, with effective decisions in vestry made by him together with the rector and churchwarden, others seldom interfering 'being generally chosen from the small occupiers, the men least likely to offer opposition'.[38] Nevertheless, such communities displayed social relations generally very different to the more vertically linked social hierarchies of the 'close' communities, where squire, tenant farmer and working people were more obviously set apart in class terms.

The pattern of 'open' and 'close' communities has not vanished. Although the rationale for the recognition of such differences based on the poor law was theoretically obviated by the 1865 Union Chargeability Act, which finally rendered a uniform parochial rate on all the constituent parishes of a union, landownership structures continued to vary from parish to parish, and although so many storms have battered the great estates, they have continued to exercise cultural and social power in many parts of England in the twentieth century. When the second Viscount Cowdray died in 1933 (his father Sir Weetman Pearson, an internationally renowned engineer, having purchased the 17,000-acre estate in about 1900 and been raised to a viscountcy in 1917) his funeral cortège left Cowdray Park and wound through neighbouring Easebourne watched and followed by respectfully bare-headed estate employees.[39] When the sixth Viscount Gage died in 1982 he had held the title since inheriting it from his father in 1912 at the age of 16. Estate workers lined the drive through Firle Park as his ashes were interred in the parish church adjoining Firle Place.

The social standing of such landowners is still high and in their capacities as chairmen of county councils, Lords Lieutenant, presidents of voluntary societies, university chancellors etc. their influence continues. In 1979 six million acres in England and Wales were held privately in estates of 5,000 acres and upwards, and although this was only half the amount of land so held in 1873, there were still about 1,200 landowners on this scale.[40] Some have sought to develop their estates commercially, bringing change to the constituent villages. In July 1983 the *Daily Mail*, under the heading 'Eviction stuns "feudal" village' reported the threatened eviction of ten Wiston (West Sussex) families as their jobs on an estate-managed turkey farm were being lost at a time when the owner took the attitude that 'my priority is to set up something which is sensible, workable and manageable'.[41] But in general such attitudes have been tempered by older traits of paternalism, and a general desire to move with the times only as a resort to hold the estate together for the future. Landscape change is usually resisted, and the wishes for the preservation of the status quo by landlord and residents in such villages have been strongly reinforced by modern planning interests and conservation pressure groups. In Sussex it is surely no accident that the highest landscape values and protection have been afforded to the downland area, which has been an Area of Outstanding Natural Beauty (AONB), an Environmentally Sensitive Area, and for which National Park status is currently being sought. Here too are the village conservation areas: villages which typify English country life as it is thought to be, and they are invariably former 'close' communities, guarded historically by a powerful family, now by the local state. More recently the High Weald has also been declared an AONB, but the Low Weald, the zone of 'bottomless' clay', and an area of nineteenth-century 'open' communities, has no such protection. There is, it would appear, a momentum which, once in motion, has led through time from a particular historical socio-economic structure to landscape formation, and thence to influence modern planning. Landscapes mirror society but in turn also influence the course and direction of future change.[42]

The complications

In practice, and upon more detailed investigation, it becomes difficult to categorise parishes as either 'open' or 'close'. They will rarely approach the 'ideal type' and might instead be placed somewhere along a continuum. A more overtly spatial emphasis to this has been added by Rawding, who sees the presence/ absence of the landowners and the distance of their prime residence from the parish in question to influence directly their degree of involvement and power. Again this would take the form of a continuum.[43]

It is also important not to tie the differentiation too closely with the environment. It has been noted that in the South East there is a preponderance of 'close' communities on the Coastal Fringe, and that most of the 'open' ones are in the Interior. But equally one can find spectacular examples of 'close' settlements in the Weald: places such as Ashburnham exhibited lordship and control equal to any on the downland. Parishes such as Hartfield and Withyham contain large

Fig. 2.4 The iconography of rural power: Withyham church, Sussex. The baroque monument is to Thomas Sackville (*d.* 1677, aged 13) by C. G. Cibber, but the Sackville Chapel dominates the church and is filled with family monuments, including one of 1962 to Vita Sackville-West. (Photograph by Denis Hutchinson.)

amounts of estate property, latterly belonging to the Sackville-Wests and controlled from Buckhurst Place, Withyham where the church contains splendid funerary monuments to the family equal to any church iconography on the Coastal Fringe (fig. 2.4). The same applies to the Abergavenny estate around Frant. So there are exceptions and although there are very few 'open' parishes noted on the downland, for example, it would nevertheless be hazardous to overemphasise a 'wealden-open', 'downland-close' dichotomy. Although the Weald had mainly 'open' communities largely as a result of its historical subordination, it also had 'close' ones; while the superordinate Coastal Fringe also harboured absentee owners and 'open' communities amongst its 'close' parishes.

The 'open–close' model may be looked at critically, from at least two broad positions. First, from an internal stance, one might accept the Mills formulation and the majority of the linkages in his 1972 proposal,[44] but nevertheless not accept the validity over time or over space of all the linkages. The model could be adjusted for regional variations and for change from one time period to another. Such modification would leave the parameters and variables essentially unchanged. Thus, for example, although there were certainly 'close' parishes where nonconformists among the tenantry would not be tolerated, there were others where the landowner held a rather pragmatic view of religion and might even help Methodist causes, although most of the other variables and linkages remain unchanged. On the Lincolnshire Wolds the Earls of Yarborough allowed chapels on their estate, and there are several examples of memorials in parish churches to large tenant farmers who were themselves Methodists. In North Lincolnshire as a whole, the Methodists, Wesleyan and Primitive, were generally stronger than the Church of England, and the linkages between landownership and social and ecclesiastical control would therefore need modification here. Again, the question of the 'close' industrial rural community should be addressed. At Swanscombe and Northfleet on the chalk coastline of north-west Kent, the parishes were dominated by the Portland Cement works of family-owned firms such as the nonconformist Whites, who housed and provided for their workers in communities gradually becoming more and more isolated behind the growing chalk quarries. Not for nothing was one of their children christened Robert Owen White![45]

Secondly and more radically, the model could also be critically examined from an external position, whereby one would look very searchingly at the very concept of 'open' and 'close' communities, arguing that the model, certainly as developed by twentieth-century historians and others misses the real essence of country living. It has been couched in explanatory and even predictive terms of positivist social science and says very little, for example, about the experience of human life or the consciousness of rural dwellers. Nor does it concentrate upon class relations and rural class conflict within the communities or between the communities, although most of the ingredients for a class-based analysis are there. Neither does it relate the internal structures of those communities to the wider socio-political-economic structures beyond its boundaries. They represent attempts to explain the community or locality from inside that community: to structure the community from within. There are very few attempts here to relate the community to the changes occurring in the contemporaneous British economy and society for example. The development of locality research has occurred since Mills initially prompted interest in the 'open' and 'close' concept, so it is really no surprise that his formulation was more concerned with internal structures *per se*. His was the outlook of regional positivism, explanatory and predictive social science, allied to an influence from local history. On the agenda for the future must be the cementing of that most important initiative into the insights of the regional analysis of the 1990s.

Finally, the model as conceived by Mills certainly reflects much of the original Mid-Late Victorian thinking but is overlain by a functionalist, static or at best partial-equilibrium approach. Its parameters interlock to keep the system adjusted and to keep the 'close' parish 'close' and the 'open' one 'open'. Feedback loops are not actually specified in his original diagrammatic rendering of the concept, but there is an implicit assumption that such a relationship exists between landownership, cottage control, population size, poor-rate payment levels, and rents paid to the landowner.

The asymmetry of power and the English rural community

The whole debate about 'open' and 'close' parishes ultimately revolves around the ageless issue of the wielding of power. Who had it and used it? Who had it but wasn't bothered about exercising it? Who was answerable to it? So instead of focussing either upon landownership structure or the manipulation of the Poor Law or any other convenient variable, the underlying structure needs to be assessed. The relationships between landownership and power should be seen as contingent: the two come together often, but either could exist independently of the other in the locality. Landowners exercised power, especially if resident, but often failed to exercise it if they were absentees. But others might also exercise power who were not landowners: large tenant farmers, for example, or the clergy (the 'squarsons'), or key employers such as rural industrialists. The coming together of power and landownership will depend on many factors, such as the owner's place of residence, his or her interest in the community, their religious persuasions, political interests, knowledge and involvement in agriculture and political economy. All may vary over time with the landowners' stage in their life-cycle, which has its own attendant fluctuations. By conceptually separating out landownership and power in this way, accommodation can be made for those parishes in which no resident landowner lived, but in which a small clique of farmers or others held sway (the Burwash case).

The exact local circumstances – the localised variation on this theme of power relations – brings us back to the main topic of rural settlement differentiation. The possible constellations of power relations, local economies and ecologies, changing either subtly or dramatically through time, yield infinite landscape variations, which mirror the rural society itself, and in turn help to give it shape. The landscape is derived from and takes on human meaning as layer upon layer of human activity shapes the setting, creating a 'sense of place' and a uniqueness and particularity which unfolds within the wider regional characteristic. Thus although by the nineteenth century it really no longer mattered as such whether a parish was located in the old core or periphery, and the political inter-relations were no longer meaningful for the everyday life of a parish, that older structure lingered on in skeletal forms sedimented from the past. The differences, accumulating over centuries, result in the pleasing diversity still to be discovered within and between village and region. Rather than describe such diversity of form, this chapter has sought to explain them in terms of the power relations between people, and the spatial structures to which such reciprocity gives rise.

> Where order in variety we see,
> And where, though all things differ, all agree.
>
>   (Alexander Pope, *Windsor Forest*, 13)

NOTES

1 Thomas Hardy, *Tess of the D'Urbervilles* (original edn 1891, Macmillan 1974) 39.
2 See for example the regional analysis of work published on nineteenth-century population studies in D. Mills and C. Pearce, *People and Places in the Victorian Census*, Historical Geography research series no. 23 (1989) 6.
3 See the chapters below by Joan Thirsk and Alun Howkins, and the work of Christopher Taylor in *Village and Farmstead* (1983) and in his edited edition of W. G. Hoskins *The Making of the English Landscape* (1988 edn); see also B. K. Roberts *The Making of the English Village* (1987).
4 A. Giddens, *The Constitution of Society: Outline of the Theory of Structuration* (Cambridge, 1984) 15–16.
5 Giddens, *Constitution of Society*, 16.
6 Oliver Rackham, *The History of the Countryside* (1986) xiii.
7 R. D. Blackmore, *Lorna Doone* (1893) 112.
8 P. Drewett, D. Rudling and M. Gardiner, *The South East to AD 1000* (1988).
9 R. Furley, *A History of the Weald of Kent* vol. 1 (Ashford and London 1871) 2–3.
10 M. Gardiner, 'The archaeology of the Weald: a survey and review' *Sussex Archaeological Collections* 128 (1990) 33–53; S. Needham, 'The Bronze Age' in J. and D. G. Bird (eds.), *The Archaeology of Surrey to 1540* (Dorking 1987) 97–137.
11 H. Cleere and D. Crossley, *The Iron Industry of the Weald* (Leicester 1985) 60–74. For a distribution map of the Romano-British South East see Drewett *et al.*, *The South East*, 181; and B. Jones and D. Mattingly, *An Atlas of Roman Britain* (Oxford, 1990) 241.
12 K. P. Witney, *The Jutish Forest: a Study of the Weald of Kent from 450–1350 AD* (1976); C. F. Tebbutt, 'A middle-Saxon iron smelting site at Millbrook, Ashdown Forest, Sussex' *Sussex Archaeological Collections* 120 (1982) 19–35. This outline is not intended to

deny the complexity of the process of settlement of the Coastal Fringe itself. For the more detailed exposition of the stages of Saxon settlement in the Coastal Fringe of Kent, see A. Everitt, *Continuity and Colonisation: The Evolution of Kentish Settlement* (Leicester 1986).

13 P. Brandon and B. Short, *The South East from AD 1000* (1990) 1–18.

14 R. A. Dodgshon, *The European Past* (1987).

15 East Sussex Record Office QR/E/33/2.

16 B. Short, 'The De-industrialisation Process: A Case Study of the Weald, 1600–1850' in P. Hudson (ed.), *Regions and Industries: A Perspective on the Industrial Revolution in Britain* (Cambridge 1989) 156–74.

17 See C. Phythian-Adams, *Re-thinking English Local History*, University of Leicester Department of English Local History (1987) 1–14. Work on 'linked territories' in Saxon and Medieval England is however, progressing, as evidenced by the work of Della Hooke and P. D. A. Harvey, building on the earlier work of Glanville Jones and Alan Everitt. See Hooke, 'Early medieval estate and settlement patterns: the documentary evidence' in M. Aston, D. Austin and C. Dyer (eds.) *The Rural Settlements of Medieval England* (1989) 9–30; and P. D. A. Harvey, 'Initiative and authority in settlement change' in *ibid.*, 31–43.

18 S. Banks, 'Nineteenth-century scandal or twentieth-century model? A new look at 'open' and 'close' parishes' *Economic History Review* 2nd series 41 (1) (1988) 51–73.

19 D. Vaisey (ed.) *The Diary of Thomas Turner* (Oxford 1984) 267–8. For Turner's overseer's accounts, see East Sussex Record Office PAR 378 and AMS 5841.

20 Report of Royal Commission on the Poor Law, *British Parliamentary Papers* xxvii, (1834), Appendix C, Questions 32 and 33.

21 D. R. Mills, *Lord and Peasant in Nineteenth Century Britain* (1980) chs. 2–5.

22 Gillian Darley, *Villages of Vision* (1978) 51–2.

23 Mills, *Lord and Peasant*, 27.

24 Anthony Trollope, *Framley Parsonage* I (1861) 19–24.

25 The social implications of living in such villages is explored in N. J. Griffiths, 'Firle: selected themes from the social history of a closed Sussex village 1850–1939', unpublished MA Dissertation (University of Sussex, 1976).

26 Darley, *Villages of Vision*, 84.

27 Mills, *Lord and Peasant*, 53–4. For a fuller account of the interactions between Methodism and trade unionism see N. A. D. Scotland, 'The role of methodism in the origin and development of the Revolt of the Field in Lincolnshire, Norfolk and Suffolk, 1872–1896', unpublished PhD thesis (University of Aberdeen, 1975).

28 William Wood, *A Sussex Farmer* (1938) 20.

29 Richard Heath, *The English Peasant* (1893, reprinted Wakefield 1978) 191–2.

30 *Ibid.*, 195–200.

31 W. Cobbett, *Rural Rides* (Penguin edn 1967) 173.

32 J. C. Kirk, 'Colonists of the waste: the structure and evolution of nineteenth century economy and society in the central Forest Ridges of the High Weald', unpublished MA Dissertation (University of Sussex, 1986); B. M. Short, 'The art and craft of chicken cramming: poultry in the Weald of Sussex 1850–1950' *Agricultural History Review* 30 (1) (1982) 17–30; M. Reed, 'Nineteenth-century Rural England: a case for peasant studies?' *Journal of Peasant Studies*, 14(1) (1986) 78–99; *ibid.* 'The peasantry of nineteenth-century England: a neglected class?' *History Workshop* 18 (1984) 53–76.

33 For an analysis of the distribution of landownership in South East England *c.* 1870 see

table 2 in D. R. Mills and B. M. Short, 'Social change and social conflict in nineteenth-century England: the use of the open-close village model' *Journal of Peasant Studies* 10 (4) (1983) 257; and P. Brandon and B. Short, *The South East from AD 1000*, 318.

34 S. J. Banks, '"Open" and "close" parishes in nineteenth-century England', unpublished PhD thesis (University of Reading, 1982) 11–14, 59.

35 *Brighton Gazette* 19 July 1832. I am grateful to Mr Geoff Mead for this reference.

36 G. Bourne, *Change in the Village* (1912) 2; Seventh Report from the Medical Officers of Health to the Privy Council, *British Parliamentary Papers*, xxvi (1865) Dr H. J. Hunter's Report, Appendix 6, 210–12; 273.

37 B. M. Short, *The Geography of Local Migration and Marriage in Sussex 1500–1900* University of Sussex Research Papers in Geography 15, 1983.

38 R. A. E. Wells, 'Social conflict and protest in the English countryside in the early nineteenth century: a rejoinder', *Journal of Peasant Studies* 8 (4) (1981) 514–30; and Report of Royal Commission on the Poor Law, *British Parliamentary Papers* xxxvii, (1834) appendix C, questions 32 and 33.

39 M. Beard, *English Landed Society in the Twentieth Century* (1989) 44–5 and figs. 6 and 7.

40 *Ibid*, 139; D. Massey and A. Catalano *Capital and Land: landownership by capital in Great Britain* (1978); D. Cannadine, *The Decline and Fall of the British Aristocracy* (Yale 1990); At the national level 102 out of the wealthiest 200 in Britain in 1991 derive their incomes mostly from their landed possessions (*Sunday Times Magazine* 14 April 1991, 24).

41 *Daily Mail* 16 July 1983.

42 B. M. Short, 'Sussex rural communities: contemporary perspectives' in Geography Editorial Committee, *Sussex: Environment, Landscape and Society* (Gloucester 1983) 192–207. For a study of planning applications, population growth and planning controls in Sussex see A. Rowswell, 'The influence of landownership on the growth/ decline of rural settlements in part of East Sussex', unpublished MPhil thesis (Brighton Polytechnic, 1986).

43 C. K. Rawding, 'The iconography of churches: a case study of landownership and power in nineteenth-century Lincolnshire' *Journal of Historical Geography* 16 (2) (1990) 157–76.

44 D. R. Mills, 'Has historical geography changed?', *New Trends in Geography* Unit 14, Open University (1972) 56–75.

45 Rawding, 'iconography'; G. Baker, 'Politics, pollution and the industrial development of a North-Kent parish: Swanscombe 1840–1910' unpublished MA dissertation (University of Sussex, 1990).

3 English rural communities: structures, regularities, and change in the sixteenth and seventeenth centuries

JOAN THIRSK

No present-day traveller through the English countryside can fail to notice sharp differences in the physical layout of villages in different parts of the country. That observation leads on to questions about their social structure. At one extreme are the estate villages, neatly composed, with a tidy arrangement of labourers' cottages, shops, post office and inn. At the other are the straggly villages, large and growing larger, having a mixture of imposing and modest houses. All have undergone many changes over the centuries, and some have been totally transformed in the last 200 years. Yet many bear traces of a form that was established in the sixteenth and seventeenth centuries, while some owe their shape to yet older patterns, imposed by their earlier experience of landownership and the search for a livelihood for all. Can we probe this subject more deeply, and reach a better understanding of the history of our villages and why they look as they do?

Possible investigations into the interlocking parts that make up one rural community are endless. Moreover, we also have to recognise that every place is different in some way from every other. The purpose of this essay is, therefore, limited to drawing attention to some of the regularities that emerge from the study of many communities in the sixteenth and seventeenth centuries. An acquaintance with many, rather than one or two, yields recurring patterns in structures and forms of change. Within the restricted compass of these pages, however, we have to omit from discussion some aspects of social structure, such as the religious and political sympathies of local communities. These associations have a literature that can be pursued elsewhere.[1] The main emphasis here is laid on the economic influences that shape social structure and the importance of landownership, while a brief reference is made at the end to the possibility of exploring special occupations in the composition of rural communities.

If once one claims to see regularities, of course, one invites the criticism of being a determinist. This is an ill-considered judgement, for the communities that deviate from the rules that we devise are as illuminating as those that conform. They broaden understanding, by inviting fresh questions, all of which have to be answered. The purpose of observing regularities in social structure is to help place individual communities in a context. This context then raises certain expectations, which, in turn, prompt precise questions to be put to the community under survey. These then often draw attention to associated regularities whose significance would otherwise have passed unnoticed. Thus the texture of evidence on social structures as a whole is thickened and enriched.

The very notion of a stable structure of interlocking parts also helps us to observe and comprehend change. When one element in a structure is gravely disturbed by changes of a radical kind, it is inevitable that tensions should show in the rest of the structure. Sometimes these lead to outbreaks of violence. At all events, the observer may reasonably expect adjustments to follow, and, having established a framework of normality, the historian is better equipped to understand the reasons for the subsequent transformation.

An obvious example of a change in the early modern period that wrought great tensions, and altered the social structure of many communities, was the enclosure of land and its conversion to pasture. Pastoral communities have one structure, arable communities have another. If arable land in large amounts is changed to pasture, it alters the amount of work available to labourers, future prospects of work for the young are changed, land values change, rents change. The consequences for a rural community, when this process is strongly under way, can be profound. We, as historians, can now generalise from many examples to show the likely outcome. Small villages were sometimes wholly depopulated, or, if much reduced in size, their class structure was changed. Indeed, they could be wholly transformed from substantial, and relatively egalitarian, peasant communities into estate villages, dominated by a squire.[2]

It is noticeable that regularities of social structure are sometimes described in other people's work, in studies where the authors are totally unaware that their descriptions match certain rules. Sometimes the regularities appear in the work of European scholars, describing developments in villages and hamlets in France, Spain or Germany. When that happens, one realises that this exploration could, indeed, encompass rural society throughout Western Europe, and not be confined to England.

A useful starting point for studying the diversity of social structures in rural England is the county of Lincolnshire. It had four distinctive farming regions, which also showed notable differences in their social structure, in the sixteenth and seventeenth centuries (fig. 3.1).[3] It proves to be a more fertile seedbed for the study of social structures than, say, Leicestershire, which was explored in a pioneering essay by W. G. Hoskins, and was judged to be one uniform region (though with our more refined perceptions of agricultural differences, it would nowadays be subdivided).[4] Lincolnshire farming systems and land use in the sixteenth and seventeenth centuries readily showed their connection with differing class structures. They also drew attention to the differing role of lords, for they were likely to be resident and influential under some systems, and

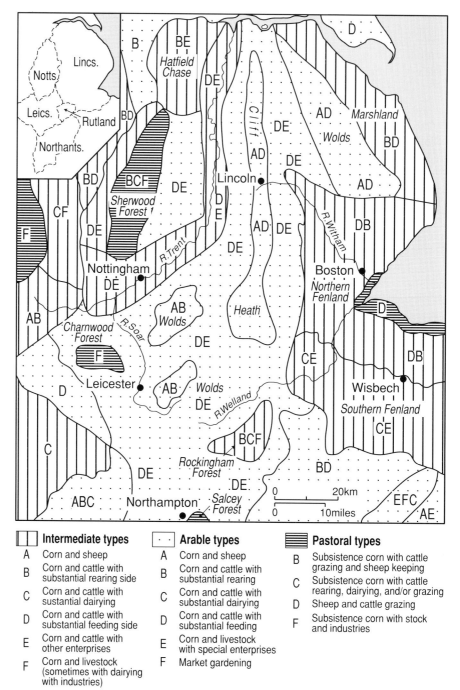

Intermediate types

- A Corn and sheep
- B Corn and cattle with substantial rearing side
- C Corn and cattle with sustantial dairying
- D Corn and cattle with substantial feeding side
- E Corn and cattle with other enterprises
- F Corn and livestock (sometimes with dairying with industries)

Arable types

- A Corn and sheep
- B Corn and cattle with substantial rearing
- C Corn and cattle with substantial dairying
- D Corn and cattle with substantial feeding
- E Corn and livestock with special enterprises
- F Market gardening

Pastoral types

- B Subsistence corn with cattle grazing and sheep keeping
- C Subsistence corn with cattle rearing, dairying, and/or grazing
- D Sheep and cattle grazing
- F Subsistence corn with stock and industries

Fig. 3.1 The Agricultural Regions of Lincolnshire and the East Midlands 1640–1750 (After Thirsk, *The Agrarian History of England and Wales V (i), 1640–1750*, Cambridge 1984, 91.)

absentee and negligent under others. As a result of these differences, communities had varying degrees of freedom for manoeuvre.

The first farming region to show a linkage between types of farming and types of social structure were the two clay vales, running from north to south, one lying on the west side, and the other in the middle of the county. They supported a corn-livestock system in the sixteenth and seventeenth centuries. This was the farming system of Leicestershire also, and it is the one that our textbooks in the past have treated as typical of the whole of England. It is associated with land in common fields, and a community life centred on a village, in which one or more squires lived in their manor houses, a parson lived next to the church, all exercising considerable authority in the place. Large farms were in the hands of a few yeomen, but the more numerous smaller ones belonged to husbandmen, and cottagers and labourers made up the base of a hierarchical structure.[5]

In addition to this textbook farming system, Lincolnshire possessed three others. The second characterised the chalk wolds on the eastern side of the county, and the limestone ridge, running up to and beyond Lincoln. Here lay sheep-corn country, where sheep were more important than cattle, and much enclosure had already taken place, or was under way. Populations were smaller than in the clay vales, farms were in fewer hands, and often only one gentleman owned the whole parish. Thus, he was lord over all, in contrast with the situation in the clay vales, where, if more than one manorial estate was accommodated in the parish, gentlemen had to share power between them.[6]

Different again was the system in the fenland round the Wash, and in the Isle of Axholme in north-west Lincolnshire, where pasture farming prevailed, supporting large populations. They lived in villages, because only limited areas of dry land above the wet fens could be used for settlement sites. The inhabitants occupied small pieces of arable land, but these were so fertile that a family could live off eight acres or even less, relying on access to hundreds of acres of pasture for grazing their animals. They had considerable numbers of dairy animals, bred horses, and caught fish and wildfowl in quantity. The authorities complained of the want of gentlemen there to inhabit, for the gentry owned the land, but did not live there. So the farming population had much freedom to run their own day-to-day affairs. Compared with the economy and social structure that characterised the two preceding corn-cattle, and corn-sheep systems, this was a totally different world.[7]

The fourth farming type in Lincolnshire was found in the marshland along the coast, running from the Humber to the Wash. Parishes here had superb saltmarsh grazings along the sea shore, but also large allotments of fertile arable inland. The villages were large, as in the fen, but they were populated by substantial farmers who, on average, were better off than anywhere else in Lincolnshire. An observer in 1629 said of this area that it was hard to find a poor man. Part of the reason was that marshland was being reclaimed from the sea, and all the time upgraded, from saltmarsh to salt-free pasture, and then to arable, so that parishes were gaining land steadily. This was in contrast with the experience of many regions where spare land was running short. The inhabitants bred and fattened cattle and sheep, and evaporated their own salt along the coast for salting down the meat. They also kept on average larger flocks of sheep than anywhere else in the county, even more than on the wolds and limestone. They had twice as much arable as fenland farmers, which enabled them to grow wheat for sale at the markets. These were readily accessible since grain could be shipped coastwise, notably to London. In short, the marshland enjoyed expanding, rather than constrained, land resources, and fine market opportunities. Its well-to-do farmers were not overawed by gentry or overwhelmed by the poor.[8]

Lincolnshire's four distinct farming regions, in short, were associated with four different social structures. They each exploited distinctive local advantages in their farming, even though three out of the four might loosely have been described as grain-livestock regions. Gentry were not equally influential in all cases, and between different classes of farmers the land was distributed in different proportions.

A similar diversity of local farming systems is seen in all other counties of the kingdom, and is well illustrated in *The Agrarian History of England and Wales*, volume IV, covering the years between 1500 and 1640.[9] It introduces yet more varied farming types, especially the pastoral ones in forests and on moorlands. It also draws attention to the role of rural industries, in some areas, but not in others, supplementing the living from the land. Here again regularities in the pattern obtrude, and have led to the proposition that industry as a by-employment of farming flourishes best in pastoral country, where lords are absentee and their control weak. Partible inheritance (i.e. the division of land between all sons, rather than inheritance by the eldest son only) often plays an influential role in reducing the size of holdings, so making the industries necessary. Moreover, pasture farming, which is not as labour intensive as arable farming, allows two or more different activities to be satisfactorily combined.[10] In *The Agrarian History of England and Wales*, volume V, covering the years 1640–1750, further insights have been gained into the connection between farming specialities and social structure. The introduction of special, industrial crops, and of market gardening, which were all unusually labour intensive activities, offered a new chance to small men who owned little land but could offer much labour.[11] The social structure was much influenced in particular places by these opportunities, for they enabled smallholders to survive at a time when elsewhere they were steadily losing ground.

The variety of England's farming regions has thus settled down into a pattern displaying some regularities.[12] A fundamental distinction has to be made between arable and pastoral systems of farming, i.e. places which were more concerned with producing grain for the market (the arable types) or animals (the pastoral type). Distinctions can then be made between different pastoral types: pastures in forests accommodated many horses and pigs, and cattle were more noticeable than sheep; moorland country had more sheep than cattle; valleys and lowland vales with high rainfall (as in the West Midlands), flourished as centres of dairying. Similarly, the arable systems varied between those that relied on sheep to fertilise their fields and grew barley as their main grain crop, and others which relied more on cattle (with some sheep, of course) and grew wheat. It is even possible to speculate whether the different market possibilities of these two grains affected social structures. Profitable wheat-growing required town markets in which to sell the crop, and best among these was London. The wheat-grower, in short, required longer-distance connections to make his most profitable sales. Barley, on the other hand, offered the grower more alternatives for the disposal of his crop. Barley was used for bread for the common people, and surpluses could thus be sold locally. Moreover, barley might also sell for beer that was again made locally, or might be used to feed livestock. Did this mean that middling farmers with a modest range of local markets around them survived better if they grew barley rather than wheat? It is a speculative proposition, but it illustrates another possible linkage between farming specialities and social structure, which deserves to be explored.

A firmer example of such linkages can be drawn from pasture-farming types. The breeding and rearing of cattle calls for substantial investment in animals that will not be fat enough for sale for several years; the farmer must wait for his returns. If he does not actually breed his young animals, he may buy them lean from others for fattening in the course of the summer, but he still requires considerable cash to buy them in spring, and wait till the autumn for the profit on sale. That kind of farming, therefore, comes into the hands of substantial yeomen farmers or gentlemen, and in a region like the Lincolnshire marshland, where the land favours that speciality, this class of person features conspicuously in the class structure. On the other hand, if dairying is the speciality, then small farmers find they can manage quite well financially because they can make cheeses and butter steadily through the summer and continually have something to sell. In parts of the West Midlands and in the fenlands, both of which regions developed dairying successfully in the seventeenth century, substantial clusters of small farmers survived in consequence.[13]

In arable areas generally, farms were of all sizes, for all classes needed grain for their households, but when grain growing became markedly profitable, as it certainly was in the sixteenth century when the population was growing fast, then the larger the acreage farmed, the greater the relative gains from economies of scale. Grain-growing for a greedy market, in short, shows an inbuilt tendency to demand larger units of production. So where grain was the leading speciality, and this means the lowland zone of England, in the east and south, where the rainfall and temperatures are more favourable to grain, farms increased in size, at the expense of the middling size farms. Those larger farms then demanded more wage labourers. Thus the tendency for change was almost inexorable in the social structure of such communities. More large farmers appeared at the top of the pyramid, more landless labourers at the bottom, and those in the middle were squeezed out. Margaret Spufford noticed this as a special feature of Chippenham, one of her three villages in Cambridgeshire, studied in her book on *Contrasting Communities*.[14]

In fact, the disappearance of the small farmer has tended to be formulated as a general trend in the seventeenth and early eighteenth centuries. It has become a convention to describe the rise of the large farmer, and the decline of the small, as though it were happening everywhere. But as our perceptions are further refined, we shall doubtless see it, not as a universal trend, but as a regional phenomenon, linked with the type of farming practised, or, more precisely, linked with grain farming for the market, and with cattle fattening. Large farmers needing capital for their enterprises were not forging ahead everywhere and eliminating all the rest.

While we may associate certain types of farming with certain types of social structure, we also have to recognise that no farming regime stands still. They all undergo steady change in response to outside forces. It is necessary, therefore, to consider the general changes in economic conditions that occurred in the period between 1400 and 1750, which spurred on change in farming specialities, and so wrought a gradual transformation in the social structure of villages. It is necessary to paint with a broad brush, but certain compelling events reacted strongly on almost all local communities.

The Black Death in the middle fourteenth century reduced the population by about a third, left fewer people wanting grain for bread, and fewer people to cultivate the arable. It is not surprising, therefore, that much land was put down to grass, and, because the textile industry was prospering in this period, it was mainly used to keep sheep. Many opportunities to enclose were offered, and seized, and hamlets, if not whole villages, were depopulated. The changing size of farms needs to be better studied regionally, but already some areas of country have been identified where husbandmen were accumulating larger units of land, and a yeoman class was expanding. The gentry's lack of interest in direct farming during the fifteenth century (shown in the fact that many leased out their home farms) means that in some places quite small men were acquiring land who in other times would not have had a chance to do so. Gentlemen even leased out parts, or all, of their home farms, to groups of local farmers, which suggests that small men got a chance of extra land in this way.[15]

A dramatic change occurred after 1500 when population began to rise again, more food was needed, food prices rose, and grain production became profitable. Gentlemen revived their interest in direct farming, and a great outcry arose at the amount of land which had been put under grass. The result was a return to grain growing, achieved by a more efficient integration of grain and livestock farming. In dedicated pastoral areas a more intensive livestock farming system developed, because the wealthier classes were eating better, and were demanding more meat. The general trend can hardly be summed up in a sentence, but economic pressures in the best grain-growing and the best meat-producing country encouraged the growth of large farms, the decline of middling husbandmen's farms, and an increase in the number of small farms and landless labourers.

In the seventeenth century and unmistakeably after 1650, the economic climate changed yet again. Grain was by then being successfully produced in such quantity that it was falling in price, and continued to do so for a hundred years. One branch of pasture farming that forged ahead was dairying, linked with the growth of industrial populations. Among arable farmers, a great variety of new crops was introduced, other than grain, beans and peas. Farmers earned far more profit from fruit, vegetables, hops, and industrial crops like dyeplants, rapeseed for oil and hemp and flax for canvas and linen. Many of these crops required hand planting, finicky weeding, and careful harvesting, so they created much work for labourers. This did not necessarily mean more wage labourers working for gentlemen and big farmers. Everything depended on the needs of the particular crop. It certainly happened where woad was grown, because a fairly large acreage was needed to make it worthwhile erecting a woad mill for the season, to grind the leaves. But successful vegetable-growing demands other skills. It was most efficiently performed by men with very small amounts of land, giving fastidious care to hand sowing, protecting their rows of plants against frost, tying up stems, weeding carefully and packing their produce with attention to every detail. In districts with suitably light land and access to a big town, or having some gentlemen residing locally who wanted such niceties, small farmers survived very successfully. Hence a social structure is discernible in places like Godalming in Surrey, Sandwich in Kent and Evesham in Worcestershire, which can only be understood in the light of the local farming system.[16] Among middling farmers, hops and fruit were chosen as good crops to supplement their basic grain-livestock farming with profitable extras. Hence in the West Midlands and in Kent a surprising number of farmers in the later seventeenth century were making new orchards and hop grounds. Many other sidelines found favour with them also, like pigeon-keeping (attention has recently been drawn to the many dovecotes that were built in the later seventeenth century, and county inventories of them have begun to be published, for they are attractive architectural features).[17] Pigeons brought in extra cash for little effort, and they were no longer frowned upon as consuming hard-won grain, for grain was sufficiently plentiful to be spared for this extra source of meat. Among the gentry, a different collection of new enterprises was favoured, notably activities that required the large areas of land which the gentry possessed. So gentlemen took a great interest in keeping rabbits in rabbit warrens, deer in deer parks for venison, freshwater fish in fish ponds, and wild fowl in decoys in the fens, where thousands of wild birds were caught every year to please the palates of the well-to-do.[18] Similarities with the present-day search for an alternative agriculture are striking. Small farmers who persisted with grain were hard hit, and it is not difficult to understand why they went under. Their misfortunes account for 'the decline of the small farmer' at this time, but it is important to be aware of the massive generalisations that are necessarily made when depicting one farming scene as typical.

Not until around 1760 did profitable grain-growing return, when populations began to rise rapidly once more. Enclosure started up again, after a definite lull, and a fresh wave of far-reaching changes in social structure occurred as grain-growing encouraged the renewed growth of large farms, gentlemen became more and more professional about planning the development of their estates and reorganising their land into larger tenant farms. They had land stewards at their elbow urging them to see this trend as being in their best interests. Increasingly landlords engineered other matters. They did not want more landless labourers on their estates than were absolutely necessary for their own farming needs, because their presence threatened to increase the poor rates. They pulled down unnecessary cottages, therefore.[19] But this watchfulness was most obvious and efficient when landlords lived on the premises; things were more lax where they did not.

Another significant change in the social organisation of rural communities between 1500 and 1700 is attracting notice, which has hitherto been overlooked. A noticeable increase occurred in the numbers of resident gentry in the countryside. In Somerset it has been calculated that there were 150 gentry in the county in 1569 and 352 in 1623, more than twice as many.[20] The county, in short, must have had many more villages with a resident gentleman or two in the early seventeenth century than in the mid sixteenth century. In Norfolk and Suffolk also the numbers of gentry living in the two counties reached a peak in the middle seventeenth century, declining noticeably after 1700.[21] It is necessary, therefore, to watch for the consequences of a gentleman coming to live in a village which previously had no resident gentleman; possibly we should watch for the effects in a whole district. Plainly certain areas were being gentrified one by one in the course of the seventeenth century.[22]

The ideal neighbourhood for a gentleman's house, according to the fashions prevailing at the end of the sixteenth century, was a village over which the lord presided, where he found servants and suppliers of foodstuffs to his household, and had sufficient land around the house to make gardens, orchards, and perhaps take in land for a park. To find such a well-placed village community meant searching in an arable farming area, which did not harbour an industrial occupation to give the inhabitants a living. But as gentry became more numerous in the seventeenth century, they were obliged to start colonising pastoral areas, and fit themselves into social structures of a different kind. The Northamptonshire forests, or parts of them, in the sixteenth century may represent one such example, where Arthur Throckmorton set up a new establishment in the later sixteenth century.[23]

Patches of the West Midlands offered potentially good sites to rising gentry. They offered land from which estates might be built up, even though the existing social structure was not ideal. Keele, in Staffordshire, is an example of a village that moved from being left to itself to being a gentleman's village. It originally belonged to the Crown, then from 1155–63 to the Knights Templars, a monastic order which simply leased out the land to tenants. It lay in woodland country, waiting to be tamed and brought under cultivation, and as the Templars enjoyed tax immunities, the lands were unusually attractive to tenants. Then in the early thirteenth century the Templars began to farm the land themselves, but their land was taken from them in the early fourteenth century (1313) and given to the Knights Hospitallers. Like many other landlords at this time, the Hospitallers ceased to farm the land themselves after the Black Death, so that by the 1370s it was all leased out and administered from the headquarters of the order in Clerkenwell, London. The local population was once again left free of interference until 1544 when the Sneyd family bought the estate after the Dissolution, decided to build a manor house in 1580, and lived there until the university bought the property in 1948 (fig. 3.2). For four hundred years it became 'a close village', closely supervised by its lord.[24]

Class differences in Keele under the new regime are revealed in the Hearth Tax return of 1666 when 75 per cent of the population lived in houses with one hearth or were too poor to be taxed. Only 5 per cent lived in two-hearth houses, while the Sneyd family dwelt in a house with 24 hearths. The social structure of Keele had changed radically since the Middle Ages. Yet it was not the archetypal 'close village' where the gentleman looked out over unspoiled countryside. The Sneyds had obviously not managed to mould the village and villagers into a community dependent wholly on farming for a living. The population procured part of its livelihood from coal- and ironstone mining; in fact, the parson, describing the place in 1705, omitted to mention the farming, and referred to the greater part of the population as 'poor labourers, colliers, and ironstone getters'.[25] Farming-wise its main business was livestock and especially dairying. So the dairying probably kept some small farmers on the land. But the gentleman in this case evidently accepted, or perhaps learned positively to welcome, industry as a means

Fig. 3.2 The Sneyd family residence at Keele Hall, Staffordshire, built *c.* 1580 (From Robert Plot's *Natural History of Staffordshire*, 1683).

of support for the local population. Other similar examples of this attitude are found in the West Midlands in the course of the seventeenth century. Circumstances moulded the attitudes of the gentry even while the gentry moulded their environment.

The Sneyds at Keele open up the question of the distribution of industries in rural areas in relation to resident gentry, and the changes that occurred in the course of the sixteenth and seventeenth centuries. The subject calls for more refined analysis, but the discussion needs to be opened here. It is not true to say that gentry always resisted the presence of industry. But generally speaking, as suggested above, industries flourished best in places where lords did not choose to live, and where ordinary folk were free to seize any opportunities for work that came their way. In practice, this meant that rural industries – and many new ones were arriving on the scene as more consumer goods were demanded, e.g. stocking knitting, lace making, pottery making, metalworking for pots, pans and so on – found a ready home in pastoral regions where few lords interfered, and farmers had time to spare to take up these by-employments. They set themselves to work in sheds and outhouses, keeping their animals and small pieces of land to supply their basic foodstuffs, but supplementing this with cash from industrial occupations. The evidence for this industrial expansion is particularly noticeable in the West Midlands and in parts of Yorkshire and Lancashire in the seventeenth century.[26]

The Keele example, however, alerts us to the existence of gentry with a different philosophical outlook from those who reigned supreme in arable parishes. Single gentry families, or even local clusters of gentry, could have different preoccupations and a different basic attitude towards their tenantry. We may even one day be able to label them regionally – in a very general way, of course, acknowledging all the many exceptions. The gentry of the Vale of Tewkesbury in Gloucestershire, for example, for two centuries at least, felt a strong sense of obligation to their tenantry and were active in setting up industries to employ the poor. It is more appropriate to speak of mutual aid between them and their tenantry, rather than describe them as overbearing gentry, requiring their tenantry to be dependent on them. The Newdigate family of Chilvers Coton in the coalmining area of Warwickshire also seems to have had a supportive outlook towards its tenants in the seventeenth century, and further investigation may show it to have been one of a group of local gentry with the same sympathies. At all events, they encouraged coalmining on their estate. Such clusters of like-minded gentry are not unimaginable in the sixteenth century, for a strong dedication to the commonweal characterised influential sections of political society, and produced a deep concern for helping the poor. That conviction retained its hold on gentry, among whom were some who were not securely established in the ranks of their class. Often they were younger sons, and were responsible for gentrifying districts where previously there had been few or no resident lords.[27]

Industry did not, however, remain forever confined to pastoral areas of country. Rural industry in the second half of the seventeenth century spread into another kind of countryside, where it was not at first congenially placed. Its most auspicious beginnings, as we have seen, were set in pastoral country without resident lords, where, among other factors, the population had time on their hands. But arable farming communities without resident lords, and presided over by freeholders, found the growth of population in the seventeenth century reaching such a level that land shortage became an insoluble problem. They lacked spare commons and waste land, but since, as freeholders, they ruled the roost, they tended to build cottages on their property in order to profit from the rental income. In other words, they positively encouraged newcomers. It was possible to continue in that mode only if industries offered work, and in Leicestershire we see that opportunity presenting itself with the spread of the framework knitting industry in the 1670s, 1680s, and later. W. G. Hoskins' study of Wigston Magna is a good illustration of this opportunity being seized.

Knitting had arrived in the neighbourhood, in pastoral forest country next door, a generation before. Now it offered a lifeline to village communities in arable farming country, and it was taken.[28]

When industries found a congenial habitat, it is tempting to think of them spreading indiscriminately in the area, when once they had taken hold in a particular parish. Perhaps that is how many at first began. Subsequently, however, their locations underwent a refining process. Evidence is found of a certain specialisation developing between rural communities, after the first phase of disorderly growth. In north Worcestershire, for example, a remarkable expansion of metalworking, scythemaking, knife-making, and lockmaking took place, but after the first boisterous phase, some villages withdrew from dual employment, i.e. the coupling of farming with industry, in order to pursue agriculture alone. This probably meant more intense industrial specialisation in other places, thus making the industrial workers more dependent than hitherto on the farming villages for their food. But it involved a dovetailing of effort, that could settle into a mutually beneficial and long-enduring relationship.[29]

More will be learned about this trend, when attention is paid to the integration of economic and social structures in a local context before the onset of the eighteenth-century Industrial Revolution. It calls for fresh investigation into the way neighbouring communities set up new, interlocking connections with each other, as their specialities and the skills of their inhabitants deepened, and different forms of cooperation hardened into long-term patterns. A historian of Leicestershire farming villages around Lutterworth uncovered a dovetailing of land-use between communities having enclosed land for pasture, while neighbours retained their common fields and an interest in grain growing. The common field farmers supplied the grain needed locally, and sometimes when the pasture farmers in enclosed parishes needed to revitalise their grasslands by a spell under the plough, they leased them to common field farmers, who then returned them in improved condition.[30] The pasture farmers themselves would not have had the labour and the routines to undertake the ploughing and cultivations themselves. Amid all this lies the hint of economic restructuring, and the dovetailing of effort, which doubtless left its mark on the social structure. Some of those arable villages with common fields, whose economy was stabilised by their beneficial relationship with neighbours, can be shown to have accommodated increasing numbers of labourers and cottagers, not by increasing the number of houses, but by subdividing them. The deeper one delves into a local community with the notion of a structure that is constantly changing, the more facets appear that influence the final outcome.

Yet another aspect of social structure that is worth exploring concerns those occupational groups which did not make up large numbers of people, but which had to find a home in some village or other. Did they gravitate to villages with one type of structure rather than another? Such a question might have been expected to find an answer in the case of chapmen and pedlars, whom Margaret Spufford investigated in her book on *The Great Reclothing of Rural England*. They had to be licensed, and so had to give notice of their place of residence. But, in fact, the licenses usually show the name of a town, and Margaret Spufford did not analyse the villages from which some of them came.[31] A thought-provoking example has emerged from looking at the role of partnerships between humble men in business in the seventeenth century, among whom were horse traders, investigated in a recent book by Peter Edwards.[32] One might have expected to find them in the more lawless places, in hamlets on the frontiers between parishes, for example, for horse traders were generally dismissed as men of low reputations. Instead, they are found living in close villages where the squire dominated the scene and was a great lord. An example, cited in Peter Edwards' book, shows a partnership of four men in Northamptonshire and Warwickshire, all of whom appear to have lived in squire-dominated villages.[33] But Peter Edwards possesses a much better example in Shropshire, at Lilleshall, where some important horse traders of the West Midlands lived alongside the rich, landowning Leveson–Gower family. On second thoughts, it is obvious that horse traders found their best clients in manor houses. Household accounts of the gentry show them entertaining innumerable friends and kin who needed hay, oats and stabling for their horses. Such guests were always on the lookout for more horses to borrow or buy and take home. In short, we seem to have alighted here on an occupational regularity, that justifies our posing a precise question whenever we encounter a village with resident horse traders: did it have a resident squire, who gave copious hospitality to guests? We are also entitled to pose the general question whether more occupational regularities are waiting to be uncovered; and, by way of a suggestive possibility, we could propose that when market gardeners are found in villages that have no easy access to a town market, the explanation lies in the presence in the same place of resident gentry with appreciative households, encouraging the development.

At different periods contemporary observers have commented on the structure of rural communities, without realising how neatly their remarks fit into the larger framework which we are here attempting to construct. By way of conclusion two illustrations are offered. A parson in the Vale of the White Horse in Berkshire in the eighteenth century wrote as follows: 'If there is one inconvenience that often attends a great venison country [and that obviously meant country with deer parks belonging to grand resident gentry], it is generally overstocked with proud nobility and overbearing commoners' ('overbearing commoners' meaning large farmers with more than their reasonable share of livestock claiming common grazing; this came about because the proud nobility favoured letting their land to large farmers with resources to stock it). Then he went on: 'And as we are without these sore plagues in our neighbourhood, I can very well dispense with the rent of venison and rest contented with Ilsley mutton.' Ilsley was a great local sheep market to which sheep were brought from west and east to this spot on the chalk downlands. The writer himself was living in a clay vale where a mixture of village structures is found, some with resident gentry, some dominated by freeholders. He was evidently living in an area where the gentry were not conspicuous.[34]

A second writer who wrote with great precision about farming types and their corresponding social structures was William Cobbett. The schematic regularities in his observations greatly enrich a text that might otherwise be read simply as flat description of different tracts of countryside. He constantly drew attention to the fact that the grain-growing areas were populated by rich farmers and desperately poor labourers, while in the pastoral country, and particularly in what was left of the forests, smallholders, and cottagers still had a multitude of different resources that helped them to eke out a living. As we have seen, the differing structures of corn country and forest were clearly visible in the sixteenth and seventeenth centuries, but 200 years later the contrasts had deepened. Here are Cobbett's remarks on some of the great corn fields of north-west Kent, on the Isle of Thanet:

All was corn around me. Barns I should think two hundred feet long, ricks of enormous size and most numerous crops of wheat . . . The labourers' houses all along through this island beggarly in the extreme. The people dirty, poor looking, ragged, but particularly dirty . . . what a difference between the wife of a labouring man here and the wife of a labouring man in the forests and woodlands of Hampshire and Sussex. Invariably I have observed that the richer the soil, and the more destitute of woods, that is to say, the more purely a corn country, the more miserable the labourers. The cause is this, the great, the big bull frog grasps all. In this beautiful island [i.e. Thanet] every inch of land is appropriated by the rich.[35]

At Cricklade, in Wiltshire, lay more corn country on which Cobbett wrote in the same vein:

The labourers seem miserably poor. Their dwellings are little better than pig-beds, and their looks indicate that their food is not nearly equal to that of a pig. Their wretched hovels are stuck upon little bits of ground on the road side where the space has been wider than the road demanded. In many places they have not two rods to a hovel. It seems as if they had been swept off the fields by a hurricane, and had dropped and found shelter under the banks on the roadside.[36]

In contrast, in the forests, this time in the Forest of Dean:

Here their cottages are very neat and the people look hearty and well . . . every cottage has a pig or two. These graze in the forest. Some of these foresters keep cows, and all of them have bits of ground (for growing grain) cribbed, of course, at different times from the forest. How happy are these people compared with the poor creatures about Great Bedwin and Cricklade, where they have neither land nor shelter, and where I saw the girls carrying home bean and wheat stubble for fuel.[37]

One final comment on Cobbett should be made, however, to warn against too facile and simplistic contrasts between arable and pastoral country as Cobbett portrayed them. More subtle differences in the sixteenth and seventeenth centuries have been identified in this essay, and the same need to be explored, and explained, in later periods. In particular, we should look for some long-lasting effects upon social structure of the colonisation and gentrification of pastoral country that occurred in the sixteenth and seventeenth centuries for it occurred at a time when many gentry felt a deep responsibility to help the poor, and allowed, or even promoted labour-intensive occupations, whether in arable farming, dairying or in industries. Where the colonisation of land went hand in hand with that philosophical outlook, the stark contrasts that Cobbett painted were modulated in the sixteenth and seventeenth centuries, and may have remained so into the nineteenth century. A modified version of the hierarchical social structure of estate villages may thus have persisted as a deep underlying tradition, in places which Cobbett did not visit or did not choose to describe. Thus, in calling for a sensitive appreciation of subtle nuances in the economic and social structure of regions, we return full circle to the beginning of this essay. We may see regularities and make rules, but the irregularities are equally significant and informative when measuring and classifying regional diversity.

NOTES

1 On religious sympathies, see the tentative suggestions in Joan Thirsk (ed.), *The Agrarian History of England and Wales, IV, 1500–1640* (Cambridge 1967) 112, 463. For a more searching examination, see A. Everitt, 'Nonconformity in country parishes', in Joan Thirsk (ed.) *Land, Church and People. Essays presented to H. P. R. Finberg, Agricultural History Review,* 18, 1970, *Supplement,* 178–99. For political sympathies, see David Underdown, *Revel, Riot, and Rebellion* (Oxford 1985).
2 Joan Thirsk, *Tudor Enclosures* (Historical Association, General Series, 41, 1987).
3 Joan Thirsk, *English Peasant Farming. The Agrarian History of Lincolnshire from Tudor to Recent Times* (1957, reprinted 1981), chapters 1–8.
4 W. G. Hoskins, *Essays in Leicestershire History* (Liverpool 1950).
5 Thirsk, *English Peasant Farming,* chapters 4 and 8.
6 *Ibid.,* chapters 3 and 7.
7 *Ibid.,* chapters 1 and 5.
8 *Ibid.,* chapters 2 and 6, p. 57.
9 Thirsk, *Agrarian History, IV,* 1–160.
10 Joan Thirsk, 'Industries in the countryside', in Joan Thirsk (ed.), *The Rural Economy of England. Collected Essays* (1985), 217–33.
11 Joan Thirsk (ed.), *The Agrarian History of England and Wales, V, 1640–1750,* part I (1984); part II (1985), chapters 18 and 19.

12 Joan Thirsk, *England's Agricultural Regions and Agrarian History, 1500–1750* (Cambridge 1987).

13 *Ibid.*, 15–17.

14 *Ibid.*, 16; Margaret Spufford, *Contrasting Communities. English Villagers in the Sixteenth and Seventeenth Centuries* (Cambridge 1974), 58–92, especially 90–92.

15 Christopher Dyer, *Warwickshire Farming, 1349–c.1520. Preparations for Agricultural Revolution* (Dugdale Society Occasional Papers, no. 27, 1981) 4–8.

16 Thirsk, *Agrarian History*, V, (II), 570–71, 579–81.

17 M. W. Barley, and Peter Smith, in Thirsk, *Agrarian History*, V (II), 647–8, 808–9. For an example of a county survey, see John Severn, *Dovecotes of Nottinghamshire* (Newark 1986).

18 Thirsk, *Agrarian History* V, (I), 575–8.

19 Christopher Clay, in Thirsk, *Agrarian History*, V, (II), 237.

20 The evidence on the Somerset gentry was gathered by Michael Havinden, but has not yet been published. Its significance is discussed in Joan Thirsk, 'The Fashioning of the Tudor-Stuart Gentry', *Bulletin of the John Rylands University Library of Manchester*, 72, no.1 (Manchester 1990) 75–6.

21 Nigel Wright, 'East Anglian Gentry Homes', in *Centre of East Anglian Studies Newsletter*, July 1988, 3.

22 Thirsk, *Agrarian History* V, (II), 74–8.

23 *Ibid.*

24 Christopher Harrison (ed.), *Essays on the History of Keele* (University of Keele 1986) 5–21, 31–7, 41–2, 51–62.

25 *Ibid.*, 56, 58–9.

26 Marie B. Rowlands, *Masters and Men in the West Midland Metalware Trades before the Industrial Revolution* (Manchester 1975), chapters 1–3; Lorna Weatherill, *The Pottery Trade and North Staffordshire, 1660–1760* (Manchester 1971) 46–9, 109–29; Norman Lowe, *The Lancashire Textile Industry in the Sixteenth Century* (Chetham Society, Manchester, Third Series, XX, 1972) 26–55; G. H. Tupling, *The Economic History of Rossendale* (Chetham Society, Manchester, New Series, 86, 1927) 161–77.

27 Joan Thirsk, 'Projects for Gentlemen, Jobs for the Poor: Mutual aid in the Vale of Tewkesbury, 1600–1630)', in Thirsk, *The Rural Economy of England. Collected Essays* (1985) 287–307; Joan Thirsk, *Economic Policy and Projects. The Development of a Consumer Society in Early Modern England* (Oxford 1978) 1–2, 18–22.

28 W. G. Hoskins, *The Midland Peasant. The Economic and Social History of a Leicestershire Village* (1957) 95–115, 212, 227–8.

29 Large, 'Urban Growth and Agricultural Change in the West Midlands during the Seventeenth and Eighteenth Centuries', in P. Clarke (ed.), *The Transformation of English Provincial Towns, 1600–1800* (1984) 173–86.

30 John Goodacre, 'Lutterworth in the Sixteenth and Seventeenth Centuries. A Market Town and its Area', unpublished PhD thesis (University of Leicester, 1977), III, 130–34, 137, 155–65, 189–90, 197–9.

31 Margaret Spufford, *The Great Reclothing of Rural England. Petty Chapmen and their Wares in the Seventeenth Century* (1984) 15, 23–31.

32 P. Edwards, *The Horse Trade of Tudor and Stuart England* (Cambridge 1988) 81–5.

33 Edwards, *The Horse Trade*, 82. The provisional identification of these villages as 'close', i.e. squire dominated, is discussed in Joan Thirsk, 'Seventeenth-Century Village Life in Old England' (Plimoth Plantation, Mass., USA, forthcoming).

34 Donald Gibson (ed.), *A Parson in the Vale of White Horse. George Woodward's Letters from East Hendred, 1753–1761* (Gloucester 1982) 47.

35 W. Cobbett, *Rural Rides* (1853 edn) 320.

36 *Ibid.*, 21.

37 *Ibid.*, 34.

4 Population movement and migration in pre-industrial rural England

MALCOLM KITCH

Pre-industrial society is often contrasted with our own restless, individualistic world. Our ancestors are believed to have lived in supportive communities, alongside their kin in extended families that included grandparents, parents and children. In recent years, however, studies of rural society have established that this view is largely a myth. Most people spent the greater part of their days in nuclear families; only a minority died in the place where they were born and people often moved several times during their lives. When movement involved a long-term change of residence it is described as migration, in contrast to personal mobility – short-term movement such as seasonal travel in search of work.

Considerable personal mobility existed from the later Middle Ages. From the mid fourteenth century the loosening of seigneurial bonds allowed English people to become even more mobile.[1] Landlords complained that tenants were deserting their holdings for better land elsewhere and that servants and labourers were seeking higher wages from other employers.

Sources for the study of rural migration

From the sixteenth century, migration and personal mobility becomes better documented. A study of tax records for Towcester in Northamptonshire showed a considerable turnover of the population between consecutive years. In 1525 47 of the 278 men taxed in the previous year had left. This unusually full source shows that six of 47 had died and 41 had migrated. This represents a turnover rate of 16.9 per cent a year – higher than other communities in pre-industrial England.[2] Professor Rich, using the Muster Returns of 1575 and 1583, had already drawn attention to the mobility of males in sixteenth-century England. These Returns listed men aged between 16 and 60 who were eligible for military service. On comparing the lists of names he observed a surprising amount of discontinuity. 'After a lapse of less than ten years' he wrote, 'the men who answered the musters had changed by over 50 per cent.' This represents a turnover rate of 5 per cent a year, in line with other evidence. This study, however, did little to erode the established idea of the stability of rural communities, though as Professor Rich noted, contemporaries were fully aware of the foot-looseness of sections of their society. He quotes Captain Dawtry who commented from Hampshire on 'servants and artificers which change and remove . . . their dwellinges dailye'.[3]

From the 1530s parish registers also show the mobility of the rural population. The continuity (and discontinuity) of surnames over a period of time indicates the movement of individuals and of families with the same surname in and out of the community. The small 'close' village of Glynde (population 216 in the 1801 census) lies three miles from the East Sussex county town of Lewes. Between 1558 and 1812 out of 444 different surnames that appeared in the parish register (excluding people whose only connection with the village was to marry in its church) 261 surnames (58.8 per cent) occurred only once and 71 per cent were found only during a period of 25 years or less. Within a hundred years, 91 per cent of the surnames had disappeared. Only 38 surnames recurred over more than a century, including four that survived over two centuries. The turnover of surnames in the nearby village of Berwick during the same period was remarkably similar: 70 per cent of the surnames had gone within 25 years and 91 per cent within one hundred years.[4]

Evidence from a later date and another county shows a similar picture. In Nottinghamshire 84 per cent of surnames of non-freeholder tax-payers in one division of the county disappeared between 1544 and 1641, a rate of turnover close to that of Sussex. A century later an unusually detailed survey of Cardington in Bedfordshire made in 1782 revealed that only one-third of the heads of households were natives of the village. Though there are local and regional variations in the rate of turnover, no community studied has shown a stable population.[5]

Other types of listings, notably the contemporary seventeenth-century surveys of two Midlands parishes, provide more detailed evidence on the mobility of the rural population. At Clayworth in Nottinghamshire 60.8 per cent of the community living there in 1676 were no longer resident in the village in 1688 – a turnover rate of 5 per cent per year. In the Northamptonshire village of Cogenhoe 50 per cent of the 1628 population had arrived during the previous ten years. About a fifth of this turnover was due to mortality – in Towcester 16.7 per cent, a very similar proportion, disappeared. The extent of such well-documented mobility over short periods of time did much to erode the notion of the stability of English rural communities.[6]

Though listings of the population demonstrate the mobility of the population they rarely reveal whether some sections of the community were more mobile than others or where and how far people travelled.

Not until 1841 do the national decennial censuses permit a detailed examination of the mobility of the population. The first three censuses had listed parish numbers and in 1841 the county of birth was included. From 1851 onwards the census enumerators recorded the parish of birth. The census, however, provides only a ten-yearly snapshot, ignoring movement between censuses. Anyone who had left a community and returned by the time of the following census would not be recorded as having moved at all! For families with children born in the intervening decade the children's place of birth may indicate intercensal movement. But does the 1851 census provide reliable evidence for traditional migration patterns? In 1851 the rural population of England was near its peak. In counties that had experienced industrialisation and urbanisation, traditional migration patterns were changing, though in the handful of counties, such as Sussex, that were less affected by these processes migration patterns had changed little.

Another source available from the sixteenth century is marriage registers, though only a small minority recorded the residence of the bride and groom. For people who married by special licence the place of residence of each party was almost always given. Marriage licences were relatively expensive and therefore usually taken out only by people of some substance so patterns derived from this source may not be typical of society as a whole.

The tens of thousands of documents produced by the operation of the Old Poor Law – settlement certificates and removal orders and examinations – also allow the historian to see poor men and women on the move in the eighteenth and early nineteenth centuries. Settlement Certificates were documents that migrants took with them to prove their home parish would be responsible for them if they became indigent. Removal orders were issued by magistrates requiring indigents to be returned to their home parish.

Urban apprenticeship registers reveal the annual movement of thousands of boys, mostly in their teens, from the countryside to towns as apprentices – even larger numbers left their rural homes to become urban servants or labourers but their movement was rarely recorded before the census.

For the eighteenth century rural apprenticeship registers too – the Country Apprenticeship Books – exist. From 1710 a variable duty was payable when a master or mistress received a premium for taking a 'Clerk, Apprentice or Servant', except for poor children bound apprentice by their parish. The problems of enforcement were considerable and the number of recorded indentures is clearly too low, even allowing for the fact that where no premium was paid, as in the case of most domestic servants, no duty was levied and consequently no details were recorded. By the later eighteenth century the yield had fallen considerably though the Act was not repealed until early in the following century. Even if only a minority of indentures were recorded the information provides a unique insight into the movement of boys (and a small number of girls) from villages and small market towns to other villages and market towns, as well as to London and the provincial urban centres.

Deposition Books are the last major source for the study of personal mobility. They record statements made by witnesses in church courts. Witnesses stated their age, occupation or social status, place of birth and their present residence and often listed moves they had made since birth.

Unfortunately none of these sources provides a complete picture of migration in pre-industrial England. Court depositions are the only one that should reveal lifetime migration (all the movements that a person had made since birth). Witnesses in church courts were, however, not a true sample of the whole population: women, the poor and the richest members of society were under-represented. Another limitation is that the information given was not always complete because witnesses sometimes failed to list all the moves they had made. The only source that provides information about the whole population, not just groups such as apprentices and the poor, is the census. But as has been noted this omitted movements made between censuses.

Other sources give only partial information. Poor Law documents show where the person had moved and where he or she had a legal settlement, though this was not necessarily the place where they were born or even the place where they had last been living. Marriage licences and registers record where the partners were living at the time of the marriage, not where they were born or how recently they had moved into the community. Apprenticeship indentures list the apprentice's present home, not where he (only occasionally she) had been born or moves made since birth. Combining the various sources reveals much about the forms and direction of internal population movement. But more local studies, particularly those that combine the sources and examine a community or a district over a long period, are needed before confident generalisations will be possible.

Who were the rural migrants?

In pre-industrial England individual, as opposed to family or household, migration often began when children left home to enter service as a domestic servant if they were a girl, or as a 'servant in husbandry' if they were a boy. These were youths taken on by farmers to gain experience.[7] A spell as a servant was a phase in the life cycle of a large proportion of the population. In the seventeenth century about one-third of all households employed domestic servants. Domestic servants were mostly young, female, unmarried and living-in. In the eighteenth century some girls left home to be apprenticed to female trades such as mantua making and seamstressing. Service, including service in husbandry, was for most people a temporary phase. Except for his sex the typical farm servant resembled the domestic servant: he too was young, unmarried and lived-in with his master. The term was generally twelve months so servants in husbandry usually saw service with several farmers. When their term expired, generally in the autumn, they found a new master, often, like domestic servants and agricultural labourers, at hiring fairs. When in 1825 Abraham Edwards left his home in Sussex at the age of 12 to go into service he began a lifetime of travelling as a labourer that never took him more than a few miles from his starting point. Even marriage at the age of 30 did not enable him to find a permanent home. Though in most parts of England the era of living-in servants was over by the early nineteenth century the practice continued well into the century in some areas, particularly pastoral districts.[8]

Servants were, as Captain Dawtry noted, a highly mobile section of society. Three-quarters of those who left Towcester between 1524 and 1525 were assessed on wages, i.e. they were servants or labourers. Three centuries later in the Kent parish of Brenchley a comparison of the population in 1851 and 1861 shows that domestic servants were still the most mobile part of the village community. Only 9 per cent of the servants living there in 1851 were still resident ten years later, compared with over 30 per cent of the farmers, labourers and craftsmen.[9]

The age that boys and girls left home to become servants is typical of the age that most children left home in pre-industrial England. Though some left as young as 10 or 12 the most common ages were 14 and 15. However, differences between the sexes in the age of leaving home are apparent, as are differences between communities. Though almost a quarter of boys in the Devonshire village of Colyton left between the ages of 10 and 14, 40 per cent aged under 25 were living with their parents and 25 per cent of the 25–29 age bracket were still resident in the parish. In Swindon in 1697 two-thirds of 15–19-year-olds were still living with their parents but in Cardington in 1782 64 per cent of the boys and 57 per cent of the girls living in the parish had left home (but not necessarily the parish) by the age of 15. The differences are probably explained by local economic conditions such as employment opportunities in the village and nearby communities. It seems likely that in all communities economic necessity compelled the children of the poor to leave home at an early age.[10]

The poor of all ages were a highly mobile section of the population. In an economy characterised by structural as well as seasonal unemployment, endemic underemployment and periodic economic depressions, jobs were often hard to find, especially from the mid sixteenth century when population growth outstripped economic growth. As a consequence vagrancy became more common (fig. 4.1). Vagrants were regarded by the ruling classes as a threat to law and order and to social stability. They were harshly treated under a series of statutes, culminating in the post-1662 Settlement Acts. Many arrested as vagrants were, or claimed to be, unemployed people moving around the countryside in search of a job, not long-term, professional vagrants. In Salisbury between 1598 and 1638 about one-ninth of the vagrants apprehended claimed to have a trade. Others were itinerant by their trade – chapmen and pedlars. Nevertheless, there were some long-term vagrants who, in spite of the risks, preferred life on the road supported by petty crime. Dr Beier has argued that, 'Vagrants ... lived in a state of almost

Fig. 4.1 William Henry Pyne 'Travellers reposing' from his *Microcosm* (1806) vol. II. 'Rustic travellers', itinerants and gypsies (seen bottom left, cooking) were favourite subjects for both poet and painter.

perpetual motion.' Their numbers were swelled by long-term, economic and demographic trends and short-term crises such as bad harvests and trade slumps. The 1590s and the years between 1620 and 1650 were particularly bad. Three Midlands parishes recorded a fourfold increase in the number of 'poor travellers' they relieved in the early seventeenth century, many of whom were only temporary vagrants whose ultimate destination was London or some large town. In the countryside vagrants were literally a passing problem and they should be distinguished from poor people who, having become destitute, were removed to the parish where they had a legal settlement.[11]

Studies of vagrants in early seventeenth-century England have argued that, at least before the mid seventeenth century, vagrants were predominantly young, single and often travelled long distances. Analysis of the data, however, shows that the young did not predominate: the percentages of migrants cited in Dr Clark's study aged between 10 and 19, between 20 and 29 and between 30 and 39 are in fact much the same – 21.5 per cent, 18.2 per cent and 19.9 per cent respectively. Indeed many vagrants were middle-aged and even elderly. The percentage aged over 40 (19.95 per cent) is high, bearing in mind that in pre-industrial England the expectation of life at birth was only about 40.[12] The argument that whatever the age, most migrants were unmarried males is less contentious. Fifty one per cent were single males and only 25 per cent were unmarried women.[13]

Labourers were another highly mobile sector of adult English society, often sliding into temporary or permanent vagrancy. They were forced to move around in search of work, though married labourers with a cottage, (perhaps a high proportion of labourers in 'close' villages) were less likely to move permanently. A study of mobility in nine communities in the Vale of York and one in the Yorkshire Dales in the late eighteenth and early nineteenth centuries showed that only one-third of the labourers were living in their native parish. This low proportion is also found in many places in the 1851 census. Thus in Ropsley, Lincolnshire, in 1851 35 per cent of farm workers were born inside the parish. Some other studies, however, have suggested higher figures – 48 per cent in the case of 15 Derbyshire townships and up to 70–80 per cent in the Oxfordshire 'close' villages of Bletchington and Middleton Stoney. In Bolton Abbey and Sprotbrough in Yorkshire 48 per cent of farm workers were natives. In the Sussex village of Newick the figure was lower. Under 25 per cent of the farm labourers were natives compared with over 49 per cent of all males. There is evidence then that in 'close' estate villages the labouring population was less mobile. The computation of national averages is simple but produces artificially uniform figures. Economic and social historians are increasingly emphasising that pre-industrial England was a land of strong regional and local differences. Differences in wage levels, different forms of agriculture (arable or pasture), the existence of by-employment and the 'open'/'close' dichotomy were some of the factors that determined the mobility of farm labourers.[14]

In constrast with agricultural labourers, servants and the poor the better-off members of society were more likely to remain in one place, though rarely over several generations. In Yorkshire farmers were the least mobile section of society in a group of ten communities. Fifty four per cent of them were natives, compared with 47 per cent of tradesmen and only 30 per cent of labourers. Nevertheless, long-term stability was rare and few farms remained in the same family for more than two generations.[15]

Myddle in Shropshire provides a unique insight into the mobility of all sections of a rural community. In the early eighteenth century one of its inhabitants, Richard Gough, wrote a history of Myddle which noted the movement of people and families. It was not an isolated community. Visits to London, 190 miles away, were not uncommon. Yeoman and gentlemen families moved away less often than the poor and middling sections of the parish. Even they, however, were not rooted to the soil. Gentry and yeoman families did leave, though less frequently than those below them in the social scale. Balderton Hall farm, Gough noted, had changed hands five times in 100 years. There was more continuity at Sleape Hall farm until John Groome, the last in a line of Groomes who had leased the land, proved an inefficient farmer who having 'wasted the most part of his stock, he parted with this farme, and tooke a less place'. A few Myddle farmers lost their land for other personal failings. Thomas Hall became impoverished and quit as a result of riotous living. Others departed to take up land elsewhere that had come their way through inheritance or marriage. The usual sources tell us who moved but not the reasons why people left.[16]

The mobility of farmers was influenced by such factors as landownership and tenure. Substantial freehold-farmers were less mobile than tenant farmers who often left their holding when their lease expired. Successful tenants, as on the nineteenth-century Ashburnham estate in Sussex, moved to a better property. The unsuccessful presumably risked falling into the ranks of farm labourers.[17] But even freehold farmers, a minority in most areas by the eighteenth century, were not rooted to their farms. The deep attachment to family holdings that was characteristic of many parts of rural Europe seems not to have been part of the culture of rural pre-industrial England. Except for the tiny county elite long-term stability over several generations was rare. A study of the Northamptonshire Subsidy Returns showed that in the 31 years between 1597 and 1628 about 27 per cent of the freeholders disappeared from the Returns. As one would expect the mobility of non-freeholders was even higher at between 40 and 60 per cent.[18] From the late sixteenth century in many parts of the country smaller arable farmers, the husbandmen of early modern England, were especially vulnerable to economic and demographic trends. Though a considerable number of small freeholders survived into the nineteenth century, in many communities a large proportion of the middling peasants were forced from their land as England moved towards a system of agriculture characterised by large landowners, tenant farmers and labourers with only a small number of small freeholders. Freeholders who were squeezed out became tenant farmers or labourers, in either case a more mobile group than substantial freeholders. Small farmers in pastoral regions survived better.[19]

Why did the rural population move?

Alongside long-term movement there was a good deal of seasonal mobility in rural England. This was usually short-distance and temporary. Many communities, especially 'close' villages, needed additional labour at harvest time. This form of movement was allowed under the otherwise restrictive Settlement Laws. It has not been much studied before the nineteenth century though Everitt noted the

Fig. 4.2 William Henry Pyne 'Mowers' from his *Microcosm* (1806) vol. I. The composite figures are depicted working and travelling. In his commentary on the drawings, C. Gray noted that 'the crops of hay about London, which are uncommonly abundant, are so forward, as to enable the mowers to complete the work around the metropolis, and return to their respective counties in time for their hay-harvest.'

seasonal mobility of rural labourers from the forest areas of England in the sixteenth and seventeenth centuries.[20] In Sussex a wealden labourer might work in Sussex or Surrey for the hay harvest; in the Downland Zone for the corn harvest; back into the Weald of Sussex or Kent for the autumn hop and apple picking and wood-cutting in the winter.

Other crops too required seasonal labour. In the late sixteenth century the woad harvest at Wollaton in Nottinghamshire employed 387 people per day, a figure larger than the total population of the average Midlands village at the time. These temporary workers came from neighbouring villages. In Milcote, War- wickshire, in 1626 the woad harvest employed weeders and pickers from nine different local communities.[21] Other labour-intensive crops too, such as flax and

Fig. 4.3 Luke Fildes, 'the Village Wedding', 1883 (Bridgeman Art Library). The village of Aston Tirrold provided the setting for what the first Lord Russell of Liverpool referred to as 'a rustic wedding party returning from church through a snugly thatched and pleasantly wooded Berkshire village' (L. V. Fildes, *Luke Fildes, R.A.: A Victorian Painter* 1968). Although the models were based on domestic servants and the soldier was based on a trooper in the Life Guards at Knightsbridge Barracks near Melbury Road, Kensington, Fildes' home, the picture conjured up much of the rural spirit as it was believed to exist, and was especially popular as an engraving which sold throughout the British Empire.

tobacco, required temporary outside labour. Well into the late nineteenth century groups of specialists – sheep-shearers and the like – moved from farm to farm plying their trade. Such men were, however, only a small group amongst the larger body of migrant seasonal labourers (fig. 4.2).

Seasonal labour migration usually involved temporary movement. Marriage meant a permanent change of residence for one partner, usually the woman (fig. 4.3). Though the incentive to find a partner from outside might have been strongest in small communities, men and women in communities of all sizes often looked elsewhere for a spouse. A study of Sussex marriage licences and parish registers between the late sixteenth and the early nineteenth centuries examined the extent of exogamous marriage, that is marriages in which one of the partners came from a different community. One might expect that during this period greater literacy and easier communications would have increased personal mobility and that more people would marry outside the community. Yet in Ardingly between 1558 and 1812 the percentage of marriages in which one partner came from outside the parish fell steadily. In the nearby parish of Horsted Keynes too between 1590–1690 and 1700–1836, though the proportion of such marriages was lower, there was also a fall from 37.9 per cent to 23.4 per cent. The difference might be attributable to the sources used – the parish register for Ardingly and marriage licences for Horsted Keynes – but geography, economic conditions and population size also had an effect. More generally, differences were apparent between the movements of the inhabitants of the High Weald and the inhabitants on the Downland and Coastal Plain.[22]

Studies of marriage migration exist for many other parts of England. Marriage registers and licences show that in 25 to 40 per cent of marriages one partner, and sometimes both, came from outside the parish in which the marriage took place.

In the case of 52 per cent of the married couples living in the north Kent village of Shorne in 1851 one or both partners were newcomers. The figure for Newick, 55 per cent, was very similar. Non-native wives were more common than non-native husbands, as is usually the case – 2.5 times more common in Newick. Three-quarters of the men born and still living in Newick in 1851 had found a wife from another village. In Colyton in the late eighteenth century marriage mobility was less: 55 per cent of men in this Devon village were married to women who had been born outside the village.[23] In pre-industrial rural England one may generalise that about one person in two was married to someone born in a different community and that about 50 per cent of married couples lived in a place where neither of them had been born.

The basis for figures derived from parish registers may be less firm than it appears. A comparison of information derived from the marriage registers and the unusually detailed baptismal registers that recorded the names and place of residence of grandparents for the East Yorkshire village of Pocklington between 1773 and 1782 shows that many people described as residents in the marriage register had parents living elsewhere. Unless their parents had moved since their children married these 'residents' might not have been long-term residents of Pocklington. The percentage of brides from the village falls very considerably, from 91 per cent to 43 per cent, when calculations are based on the baptismal register rather than the marriage register. In the Berkshire village of Binfield too, many brides and grooms listed as 'of Binfield' were only temporary or recent residents.[24]

In marriage migration usually only one partner actually moved, though the direction of movement as indicated by parish registers is often misleading. In many if not most marriages that took place in the bride's home village the couple subsequently resided where the husband lived and worked. Many brides had, as has been already been shown, left home before they married. Though mobility declined after marriage, couples still moved in search or work or betterment. In

Binfield only about one-third of the 104 couples who married between 1779 and 1801 are identifiable as householders in the years immediately following their marriage. It has been suggested that in rural communities, such as Shepshed, that were experiencing industrialisation, immigration after marriage became less common than in other types of community. In the agricultural community of Bottesford one measure of stability was remarkably steady from the seventeenth to the early nineteenth centuries. Throughout this period about 37 per cent of the families that can be reconstituted from the parish register had at least one child who remained in the community until he or she married.[25]

Though there have been many studies of the relationship between marriage and migration, marriage in fact was only a small component of the total mobility of the population. Marriage was responsible for only 7 per cent of annual in-migration in Clayworth and 5 per cent in Cogenhoe. A more substantial element in these places was the movement of whole families, sometimes whole households including servants. In Clayworth one-third of the total movement may have been the result of family or household migration.[26]

How often and how far did people move?

As has been seen, most people moved at least once during their life. The turn-over rate in communities was usually of the order of 4–6 per cent per annum. The sixteenth century Muster Returns and the late seventeenth-century Clayworth listing show rates of 5 per cent. Between 1851 and 1861 the Kent village of Brenchley showed an annual turnover rate of 6 per cent.[27] The biographical details recorded in court depositions should provide the best source for the frequency of individual moves but unfortunately they under-state the amount of movement. Witnesses sometimes omitted some of the moves they had made and even occasionally gave an incorrect birth place. In late sixteenth- and early seventeenth-century Sussex and Buckinghamshire only 17 and 9 per cent respectively of the witnesses deposed that they had moved more than twice, probably too low a figure, especially for Buckinghamshire. When the recorded moves are plotted against age it seems that moves made during people's most mobile years, that is between the mid-teens and the mid-twenties, were often left out. Deponents were mainly concerned to record moves made as adults.[28] Apart from the census the other sources only capture one move that people made. Although the census recorded the place of birth and address at the time the census was made, it did not list all moves made since birth, though some of them can be glimpsed by tracing the birth-places of successive children. More research needs to be done before a clear picture of the frequency with which the population of pre-industrial England moved emerges, but it is clear that many people moved more than once in their life.

There is better evidence for how far people travelled in search of a spouse or an apprenticeship, or in the case of the census, since birth. The clear pattern that emerges is of predominantly short-distance mobility, though a minority of people moved long distances, especially before the mid eighteenth century, to London and other large towns. All sources show the familiar 'distance-decay' effect, with the number of migrants falling as distance from the place studied increases. Why travel further than was necessary to find a job, further than was necessary to find a spouse or further than was necessary to earn higher wages? Most moves, whether to marry or to find a job, were within about ten miles, no further than a neighbouring village or local market town in most parts of England. Cumulatively some people moved many miles in their life-time but rarely in a straight line and they often ended up not far away from their native parish. In the Leicestershire village of Shepshed in the eighteenth century, though the 239 people who settlement papers and removal certificates show moved into it came from 96 different places, 94.5 per cent of these places were within 15 miles. In Sussex a century and a half before, two-thirds of the deponents claimed to have travelled only ten miles during their life and only 13 per cent more than 20 miles. In Buckinghamshire at the same period mobility seems to have been higher, though the sample is small. Forty per cent gave evidence of travelling less than ten miles and 17 per cent more than 40 miles. Most of the servants who left Cogenhoe only moved to a neighbouring parish, sometimes returning later. Many were probably local young people who preferred not to travel too far from their family. In the Essex village of Moreton between 1796 and 1812, 90 per cent of the grandparents of children baptised in the parish lived within ten miles.[29]

Inherent differences in the sources make comparisons between figures derived from more than one source an uncertain exercise. Table 1 shows the proportions of people born and still living in rural parishes derived from the 1851 census. Parishes close to industrial towns have been excluded. Where separate figures for males and females are available they usually show a higher percentage of native-born males than females. Apart from Thornborough and Sprotbrough the values are very close with an average of 51.5 per cent.

The 1851 census also provides information about lifetime migration. Figures for five rural parishes are given in table 2. The percentage of migrants who had travelled more than ten miles ranges from a fairly small minority of immigrants (24 per cent) to a majority (54 per cent). A detailed study of these localities might account for the wide range and why Sprotbrough in particular attracted a larger proportion of people from over ten miles than the other four parishes.

Marriage distances too were usually short. The observation 'Cupid may have wings but apparently they are not adapted for long flights' made by a writer on the geography of marriage in the U.S.A. in the 1930s is also valid for preindustrial

Table 1 *Percentage of population born in rural parishes, 1851*[30]

Place	Number	Percentage born in parish
Bentley, Hants	768	59
Canon Pyon, Hereford	714	53
Dart Valley, Devon	5453	56
Newick, Sussex	968	47
Plumpton, Sussex	277	41.8
Ropsley, Lincs	686	54
Shorne, Kent	984	53
Sprotbrough, W. Riding	200	33.5*
Thornborough, Bucks	715	67
Average		51.5

Note: * figures for adult population only

Table 2 *Lifetime migration distances travelled by rural migrants, 1851*[31]

	Distance in miles		
Place	0–5	6–10	over 10
Bentley, Hants	42	16	42
Newick, Sussex	54.5	18.6	26.9
Plumpton, Sussex	54.3	21.7	24
Shorne, Kent	44	17	38
Sprotbrough, W. Riding			54

England.[32] Though mean distance calculations will differ according to the nature of the source used – marriage registers, marriage licences and the census – they agree in showing that most people found a spouse from a nearby community, often a neighbouring village. As in Myddle, most partners came from within ten miles – in some studies around 90 per cent of non-native spouses lived within this distance of their future partner. Over 70 per cent of brides in Newick had been born within ten miles. In late eighteenth-century Colyton, slightly longer distance movement was the norm: only 44 per cent of non-native wives came from within ten miles. For Pocklington, when calculations are based on the baptismal register rather than the marriage register the proportion of brides who travelled more than ten miles increases but even so the great majority, almost 70 per cent, still came from within this distance.[33]

As in other forms of migration, occupation and social status had an influence on average distances. In nineteenth-century Shorne farm workers were more inclined to restrict their choice to local girls than were the better-off members of the community. The detailed study of marriage migration in Sussex between the late sixteenth and the early nineteenth centuries found that as in other forms of migration, there was a positive correlation between wealth and distance. Yeomen found partners from outside the village and from further afield more often than labourers. The mean distance travelled by all marriage partners was only 2.9 miles with a maximum of 4.9 miles for the wealden village of Burwash. On average 86 per cent came from within ten miles but there were significant differences between distances travelled by spouses in the various geographical regions of the county. Distances were greater in the Weald than in the Scarpfoot Zone. Accessibility too, determined by the geography and ecology of the area, had an effect. Partners did not come in equal numbers from all directions and mean distance statistics give a misleading impression of symmetry – migration was not uniform in all directions. The geography of Sussex that made travel easier east–west than north–south is reflected in the migration fields of parishes. Travel was easy along the Scarpfoot and the Downs, notoriously hard in the Weald. The latter was an area of small, poor farms and weak social control, characterised by greater personal mobility. Other geographical features also affected the quest for a spouse. Ashdown Forest, to the north of the county, acted as a watershed. The inhabitants of parishes to the north of the forest looked north for partners; those living south of it looked to the south. There was a distinction too between the small, often 'close' villages of the Downland and the large, often 'open' villages of the Weald. It was amongst 'close' villages with the greatest amount of social control and limited in-migration that most of the places with lower median distances are found. These factors also affected marriage patterns and population mobility in general in all parts of England.

Differences in geographical and occupational structure seem to account for different migration patterns for villages in different parts of Yorkshire in the late eighteenth and early nineteenth centuries. Comparison of three parishes in the Yorkshire Dales with nine from the Vale of York which had fewer farmers and agricultural labourers showed a higher percentage of migrants from over 10 miles in the case of the inhabitants of the Dales – 23.2 per cent compared with 17.1 per cent for the Vale of York villages.[34]

A study of dynasties of rural families has argued that though substantial shopkeeping or farming families rarely remained long in one place, movement over several generations tended to be within a group of parishes. The same holds for other groups in society.[35]

As an exception to the generalisation that most movement was short-distance it has been argued in a well-known study that in the late sixteenth century and early seventeenth century many poor migrants to a group of Kentish towns had travelled long distances. A later and larger study of 2,651 vagrants apprehended in several parts of England also showed considerable long-distance migration on the part of many vagrants. Just over 50 per cent had travelled more than 40 miles. Of these 22 per cent were from over 100 miles away and almost 5 per cent from over 200 miles. However, these figures include urban vagrants whose migration patterns were not necessarily the same as for other groups of poor or even for all vagrants. By the late seventeenth century long-distance migration by the rural poor had become exceptional. By then fewer poor were travelling long distances, because of the Settlement Laws after 1662, or because of economic growth or a combination of both factors. A study of Derbyshire removal orders between 1720 and 1724 found that 67 per cent of those removed had travelled less than 11 miles. In eighteenth-century Nottinghamshire too, eight miles was the median distance.[36] Long-distance movement of poor vagrants therefore seems to have become less common after the late seventeenth century. Settlement Papers and Removal Orders did not record any intermediate stops the vagrants might have made, although other sources reveal that (except for apprenticeship migration) long-distance movement often occurred in stages, with the ultimate destination unplanned. Some of the long-distance migrants in the earlier period might have moved in stages from their place of birth or of legal settlement over a long period of time before being apprehended.

Dr Clark's study of migration based on 7,047 church court depositions from 7 areas between 1660 and 1730 found that three-quarters of the rural deponents had moved by the time they made their deposition. But there was a good deal of variety within and between counties and between the sexes. Fifty-nine per cent of male rural deponents had moved less than ten miles, compared with 64 per cent of females. Nine per cent of males but only 6 per cent of females had moved more than 40 miles. Only 3 per cent of males and less than 1 per cent of women had travelled more than 100 miles. This study too highlighted economic and social differences in migration patterns. Professional people and gentlemen travelled further than servants but even so usually less than 25 miles. For servants in husbandry in most of the hirings for which evidence exists the youths had rarely travelled more than nine miles. Eight to ten miles was a comfortable day's journey on foot. This distance was the average market area of most communities in lowland England.[37]

The distances travelled by Sussex rural apprentices in the eighteenth century also conformed to the pattern of predominantly short-distance movement, with a sizeable minority of long-distance movement. The moves of 1,023 apprentices (985 males and 38 females) have been analysed. They came from 248 of the 280-odd parishes in Sussex and travelled to 239 places, including London and towns and villages in the neighbouring counties of Surrey, Hampshire and Kent. Analysis of the occupations of the masters to whom they were apprenticed shows that most, including those apprenticed to masters in rural communities, were destined to non-agricultural jobs. The average distance travelled by those moved to places in the county, other than the ten chief market towns, was 8.5 miles. When migrants to places in the neighbouring counties (excluding London) are included the migration area increases and the average figure rises to 10.9 miles. Other evidence shows that few Sussex apprentices would have travelled outside their own and neighbouring counties, except for those who went to London. Both figures are in line with the average distances travelled by other types of rural migrant.[38]

The close ties between villages and market towns are reflected in migration flows. Though this survey concentrates on movement within the countryside, migration to and from county towns and larger regional centres was an important part of the migration pattern of the rural population. Villages were not self-contained communities, isolated from urban life. Indeed before the late eighteenth century many urban dwellers worked outside the town. Large towns needed people from the country to maintain their population and to enable it to grow. Late seventeenth-century Norwich received over 400 immigrants while London annually attracted about 8,000 immigrants of all sorts. The newcomers to both these cities came predominantly from the countryside. The larger the town, the wider its migration field. Small towns, like those in Sussex and Maidstone and Faversham in Kent drew most of the migrants (apart from the poor) from places within ten miles, only a handful from long distances. For middling sized towns such as Worcester the catchment area was larger, up to 30 miles. For provincial centres such as Bristol and York the area was larger still. These latter types of town also attracted a larger minority of migrants from much greater distances.[39]

Why did the rural population move?

Whether a spouse or a job was the objective, knowledge of the opportunities open was necessary. Distance was an important factor in communications. If personal knowledge was absent others could advise – family, friends or neighbours. The longer the distance, the fewer the contacts and the weaker the communications network.

In the case of marriage the reasons for moving are obvious. In marriages where both partners did not come from the same community one partner, usually the wife, had to leave home. Migration after marriage was prompted by the same factors that obliged most people to leave their homes: the quest for a job or higher wages. Though the quest might have proved to be in vain the motive was the anticipated job or higher wages. Employment therefore was the key element in the decision to migrate, whether made by an individual or by a family. Much adult migration can be explained as a relocation of labour from areas that were economically backward or where there was a labour surplus to areas where there was a scarcity of labour. A study of the impact of new employment in Mid-Wharfedale in Yorkshire shows a clear correlation between the expansion of local industries in the early eighteenth century (lead mining and then clothmaking) and the reduction in movement of people from an area that had previously experienced a considerable exodus. The creation of jobs meant that fewer people had to move to obtain work. For those with a job, migration might be motivated by the pursuit of a better-paid or more secure job.

An illustration of the part played by economic factors in migration can be seen in late seventeenth-century Norfolk where migration patterns differed between the poor sheep-corn areas of the county and the richer wood-pasture area. Migrants from sheep-corn areas were more likely to move to places in wood-pasture areas than to other sheep-corn-areas.[40]

By the late seventeenth century a regional pattern of rural England was emerging. Some areas were coming to specialise in pasture or arable farming and new rural industries were springing up, notably in parts of the Midlands.

The decision to migrate was usually voluntary. Compulsory relocation was rare, though from the mid eighteenth century in the area between the Cotswolds and the Humber, labourers' cottages were sometimes destroyed and labourers driven out.[41]

The 'push/pull' explanatory model stresses two complementary forces in the decision to migrate. The 'push' element was especially strong in 'close' communities and where employment opportunities were poor, where wages were low and where the prospects of inheriting a farm were slight. The poor were most vulnerable to the 'push' factor. The 'pull' was exercised by places, especially towns, where it was believed that wages were higher and that better employment opportunities existed. Wage rates for the same job varied considerably in the early eighteenth century. They were highest in the South, lowest in the North. Not surprisingly, there was a distinct North to South migration flow. From the mid eighteenth century relative wage levels changed as, due to competition from industry, agricultural wages rose faster in the North than in the South.[42]

Before the railway age getting a job in a new place meant moving home. For the freehold farmer and the skilled artisan migration after marriage was possibly less common than for the poor and farm labourers. Unfortunately comparisons are made difficult by the fact that many studies of migration do not differentiate between the occupation or social status of migrants.

The decision to migrate was not always economic. The desires to live in a better place or close to one's relations are not purely characteristics of the modern world and the pre-industrial equivalent of the 'bright lights syndrome', the attraction of migrants, especially the young, to towns should not be dismissed, though the motives of poor migrants in quest of subsistence were presumably more basic.

One study that has tried to determine trends across the whole country noted regional differences – migration rates were lower in the West of England than in the East, although there were some exceptions and differences even within counties.[43] These were caused by such factors as employment opportunity, inheritance patterns and density of population. Some historians have argued that the severe Settlement Laws after 1660 had an important effect in reducing the mobility of the poorer members of the population.

Trends in rural migration

This survey has emphasised the significance of local factors in promoting migration and the existence of local differences in migration patterns. The quest for long-term trends is further complicated by a paucity of studies that investigate a locality, let alone a region, over a long period of time. Comparing communities located in different places and at different times is risky. Even within a limited time-span there were differences in the average distances that people moved, consequences of the different geography and socio-economic structure of communities and regions.

During the sixteenth century migration and personal mobility increased, prompted by population growth and, in the case of urban apprenticeship migration, a modest degree of economic expansion. Woodland, fen and pasture areas, usually less-populated than areas of arable farming, were relatively open to in-migrants, especially if they were also areas of partible inheritance. But the Elizabethan and early Stuart economy did not grow sufficiently to provide jobs for all the ever-increasing population. Real wages began to decline and vagrancy grew, swelled in some places by local factors such as depopulation resulting from the enclosure of land for pasture. Though pastoral areas with their range of employment and easy entry were attractive to incomers such areas were, as Dr Beier noted, vulnerable to bad harvests and trade slumps. In these conditions pastoral areas too experienced an outflow of population.[44]

From the seventeenth century one factor in the long-term changes in rural mobility was the evolution of the 'open' and 'close' villages. Also, from the seventeenth century the rise of by-employment – part time or occasional jobs that provided additional income – reduced the economic pressure to move. In some areas, however, such as the Sussex Weald, rural industries declined. Local developments in agriculture and industry affected both the 'push' and the 'pull' factors in the period before the Industrial Revolution. As a recent writer has noted, the development of two forms of rural industry had a different impact on rural migration. By-employment stimulated less in-migration that the development of single industries.[45]

In the mid seventeenth century population growth slackened. Consequently there was less pressure on land and jobs, and therefore less incentive for people to move. In consequence both the frequency of migration and distances travelled by some types of migrants seem to have diminished. When the population began to rise again in the early eighteenth century, demographic growth was accompanied by agricultural and industrial growth. The economic development of hitherto economically backward areas that began even before the era of industrialisation stemmed the long-established flow of migrants from the highland zones of the West and, above all, the North. Men and women from the upland areas of Cumberland, Northumberland, Durham, north Yorkshire and Lancashire who had for generations made their ways south to the Midlands and beyond, often as far as London, now had employment opportunities either locally or in the developing northern towns. In the eighteenth century the growing industrial towns of the North and Midlands recruited most of their population from neighbouring counties not, as was once believed, from southern and western counties.[46] They mopped-up migrants who might previously have travelled to local market towns or other rural communities in search of work. Industrialisation did not make the population of England more mobile.

There is a good deal of evidence that the range of population movement by the poor and urban apprentices declined from the late eighteenth century, possibly earlier. For the poor one reason may be the post-1662 Settlement Laws, though this view has been disputed ever since it was first put forward in the early nineteenth century. Economic and demographic changes also had a part to play.

Even though in many parts of England traditional migration patterns had changed and even if the poor travelled shorter distances than their Elizabethan predecessors, the 1851 census shows that rural communities in the mid nineteenth century were scarcely less mobile than they had been in the sixteenth century. Though living-in servants in husbandry had become rare by 1851, few of the agricultural labourers who replaced them enjoyed long-term employment so that they too had to move in search of work. Marriage distances too seem to have changed little, as studies of Colyton and Moreton between the late eighteenth and mid nineteenth centuries have shown.[47]

Early Victorian rural England was still predominantly a land of small villages and modest market towns in which people still had to travel outside their community in search of spouses and jobs, though possibly slightly shorter distances and less often than before.

The social world of the inhabitants of pre-industrial England was not restricted to their native village. But it was geographically confined. Throughout this period it embraced the area within a 10–15 mile radius, an area wide enough to include surrounding parishes and the local market town. Its shape was determined by the physical and human geography of the locality. Within it most people found employment and a spouse. Pre-industrial rural England was then a geographically mobile society, not a land of self-contained communities populated by men and women rooted to their native soil.

NOTES

1 P. McClure, 'Patterns of migration in the late Middle Ages: the evidence of English place-name surnames', *Economic History Review* 2nd series, 32 (1979) 167–82 and A. Macfarlane, *The Origins of English Individualism* (Oxford 1978) 152–3.

2 J. Sheail, 'The distribution of taxable population and wealth in England during the early sixteenth century', *Transactions of the Institute of British Geographers* 55 (1972) 123.

3 E. E. Rich, 'The population of Elizabethan England', *Economic History Review* 2nd series 2 (1950) 259 and 260.

4 W. de St. Croix, 'Names from the Parish Register Books of Glynde, from 1558–1813', *Sussex Archaeological Collections* 24 (1872) 99–114; E. B Ellman, 'Family names in Berwick from 1606 to 1812', *Sussex Archaeological Collections* 22 (1870) 22–9.

5 R. Schofield, 'Age-specific mobility in an eighteenth-century rural English parish', *Annales de Démographie Historique* (1970) 261–74; S. Peyton, 'The village population in the Tudor Lay Subsidy Rolls', *English Historical Review* 30 (1915) 247.

6 P. Laslett, 'Clayworth and Cogenhoe' in P. Laslett (ed.), *Family Life and Illicit Love in Earlier Generations* (Cambridge 1977) 65–72.

7 A. Kussmaul, *Servants in Husbandry in Early Modern England* (Cambridge 1981) and 'The ambiguous mobility of farm servants', *Economic History Review* 2nd series, 34 (1981) 222–35.

8 B. Short, 'The decline of living-in servants in the transition to capitalist farming: a critique of the Sussex evidence', *Sussex Archaeological Collections* 122 (1984) 147–64; M. Reed (with a rejoinder by B. Short), 'Indoor farm service in 19th-century Sussex: some criticisms of a critique', *Sussex Archaeological Collections* 123 (1985) 225–41. On farm service in its late nineteenth-century form, see Alun Howkins, chapter 5 of this volume.

9 B. Wojciechowska, 'Brenchley: a study of migratory movements in a mid-nineteenth century rural parish', *Local Population Studies* 41 (1988) 34.

10 R. Wall, 'The age of leaving home', *Journal of Family History* 3 (1978) 181–202.

11 A. L. Beier, *Masterless Men. The Vagrancy Problem in England 1560–1640* (1985) 29–37; P. Clark, 'Vagrants and vagrancy in England 1598–1664' in P. Clark and D. Souden (eds.), *Migration and Society in Early Modern England* (1987) 54.

12 E. A. Wrigley and R. S. Schofield, *The Population History of England 1541–1871* (Cambridge, 2nd edn, 1989) 252.

13 Clark, 'Vagrants and vagrancy', 54.

14 B. Holderness, 'Personal mobility in some rural parishes in Yorkshire, 1777–1822', *Yorkshire Archaeological Journal* 42 (1967–70) 445; S. Caffyn, 'The social structure of mid 19th-century Newick', *Sussex Archaeological Collections* 125 (1987) 162–3; M. Birch, 'Bolton Abbey, West Riding of Yorkshire, 1851–81: population turnover in a 'static' community'; B. Hazelwood, 'Ropsley, Lincolnshire 1851: in-migration and occupations', 2; R. Hall, 'Occupation and population structure in part of the Derbyshire Peak District in the mid-nineteenth century', *East Midlands Geographer* 6 (1974) cited in A. Stanbridge, 'Sprotbrough, West Riding of Yorkshire, 1851 and 1881; in-migration and occupations', 10; A. Webster, 'Bletchington and Middleton Stoney, Oxfordshire, 1851 and 1881; in- and out-migration and occupations'; in D. R. Mills (ed.), *Victorians on the Move* (Mills Historical and Computing, Branston, 1984).

15 Holderness, 'Personal mobility', 453–4.

16 R. Gough, *The History of Myddle*, (ed. D. Hey 1981) 91, 221, 226.

17 B. M. Short, 'The turnover of tenants on the Ashburnham Estate, 1830–1850', *Sussex Archaeological Collections* 113 (1975) 157–74.

18 Cited in Rich, 'The population of Elizabethan England', 261.

19 J. Thirsk, 'Seventeenth-century agriculture and social change' in J. Thirsk (ed.) *Land, Church and People* (Reading 1970) 157.

20 E. J. T. Collins, 'Migrant labour in British Agriculture in the nineteenth century', *Economic History Review* 2nd series 18 (1976) 38–59; A. Everitt, 'Farm labourers' in J. Thirsk (ed.) *The Agrarian History of England and Wales, IV, 1500–1640* (Cambridge 1967) 434.

21 J. Thirsk, *Economic Policy and Projects. The Development of a Consumer Society in Early Modern England* (Oxford 1978) 5.

22 B. M. Short, *The Geography of Local Migration and Marriage in Sussex 1500–1900*, University of Sussex Research Papers in Geography 15, 1983.

23 W. Grimmette, 'Shorne, Kent 1851–1861; age- and sex-related migration and family formation' in D. R. Mills (ed.), *Victorians on the Move* (Branston 1984) 18; S. Caffyn, 'The social structure of mid 19th-Century Newick', 163; E. A. Wrigley, 'A note on the life-time mobility of married women in a parish population in the late eighteenth century', *Local Population Studies* 18 (1977) 26.

24 M. Escott, 'Residential mobility in a late eighteenth century parish: Binfield, Berkshire 1779–1801', *Local Population Studies* 40 (1988) 24.

25 Escott, 'Residential mobility', 24; D. Levine, *Family Formation in an Age of Nascent Capitalism* (New York 1977) 40 and 41.

26 Laslett, 'Clayworth and Cogenhoe', 70.

27 B. Wojciechowska, 'Brenchley', 30.

28 J. Cornwall, 'Evidence of population mobility in the seventeenth century', *Bulletin of the Institute of Historical Research* 40 (1967) 143–52; H. Hanley, 'Population mobility in Buckinghamshire, 1578–83', *Local Population Studies* 15 (1975) 34.

29 Cornwall, 'Evidence of population mobility'; Hanley, 'Population mobility', 35; D. Levine, *Family Formation*, 36; Laslett, *Family Life*, 73; C. Davey, 'A note on mobility in an Essex parish in the early nineteenth century', *Local Population Studies* 41 (1988) 64.

30 Figures from D. R. Mills (ed.), *Victorians on the Move*, table A; Caffyn, 'The social structure of mid 19th-century Newick', figure 2; B. Short (ed.), *Scarpfoot Parish: Plumpton 1830–1880* (University of Sussex Centre for Continuing Education, Occasional Paper 16, 1981), table 16.

31 Figures from D. R. Mills (ed.), *Victorians on the Move*, table D; Caffyn, 'The social structure of mid 19th-century Newick', table 5; Short (ed.), *Scarpfoot Parish*, table 16.

32 J. H. S. Bossard, 'Residential propinquity as a factor in marriage selection', *American Journal of Sociology* 38 (1932–33) 222 quoted in Short, 'The Geography of Local Migration', 1.

33 R. A. Bellingham, 'The use of marriage horizons to measure migration. Some conclusions from a study of Pocklington, East Yorkshire in the late eighteenth century', *Local Population Studies* 44 (1990) 55; Caffyn, 'The social structure of mid 19th-century Newick', 163; E. A. Wrigley, 'A note on the life-time mobility of married women', 26.

34 M. Long and B. Maltby, 'Personal mobility in three West Riding parishes, 1777–1812', *Local Population Studies* 24 (1980) 23.

35 A. Everitt, 'Dynasty and community since the seventeenth century' in his *Landscape and Community in England* (1985) 321.

36 L. Bradley, 'Derbyshire Quarter Session Rolls: Poor Law Removal Orders', *Derbyshire Miscellany* 6 (1971–3) 98–114 cited in P. Clark 'Migration in England during the late seventeenth and early eighteenth centuries', *Past and Present* 83 (1979) 73.

37 Clark 'Migration in England', 68–9; A. Everitt 'The marketing of agricultural produce' in J. Thirsk (ed.), *The Agrarian History of England and Wales, IV*, 498; H. Rogers, 'The market area of Preston in the sixteenth and seventeenth centuries' *Geographical Studies* 3 (1956) 46–55.

38 My calculations from R. Garraway Rice (ed.), *Sussex Apprentices and Masters 1710–1752*, Sussex Record Society, 28 (1924). I am currently engaged in a more extensive analysis of the County Apprenticeship Books.

39 P. Clark and P. Slack, *English Towns in Transition* (Oxford 1976) 86; E. A. Wrigley, 'A simple model of London's importance in changing English society and economy 1650–1750' *Past and Present* 37 (1967) 46.

40 M. F. Pickles, 'Mid-Wharfedale, 1721–1812; economic and demographic change in a Pennine dale', *Local Population Studies* 16 (1976) 32; Clark, 'Migration in England', 78.

41 Holderness, '"Open" and "Close" parishes in England in the eighteenth and nineteenth centuries', *Agricultural History Review* 20 (1972) 30.

42 E. W. Gilboy, *Wages in eighteenth-century England* (Cambridge, Mass., 1934) 220; and E. W. Hunt and F. W. Botham, 'Wages in Britain during the industrial revolution' *Economic History Review* 2nd series, 11 (1987) 380–9.

43 Clark 'Migration in England', 66.

44 Beier, *Masterless Men*, 38–9.

45 A. Kussmaul, *A General Review of the Rural Economy of England 1538–1840* (Cambridge 1990) 142.

46 For example E. J. Buckatzsch, 'Place of origin of a group of immigrants into Sheffield 1624–1799' in P. Clark (ed.), *The Early Modern Town. A Reader* (1976) 292–6.

47 Wrigley, 'A note on the life-time mobility', 28 and Davey, 'A note on mobility', 64.

The English farm labourer in the nineteenth century: farm, family and community 5

ALUN HOWKINS

The physical world of landscape and place profoundly affected the ways in which those who lived on and worked the land experienced their work and their lives. At one level the English countryman or countrywoman of the second half of the nineteenth century inhabited a world structured by their relationship to economic and social power. The landlord, who owned the land, the farmer who used his capital and sometimes his labour to exploit it, and the labourer who literally worked the land all had precise relations to social and economic power.

Yet this power was mediated through their locality and through very different regional socio-economic systems. As a result there was not one set of experiences which characterised the lives of labouring people in the nineteenth century but many, and these differences cannot simply be reduced to minor or 'superstructural' variations. What it meant to be a labourer in different areas of England was literally to live in different worlds.

The parameters of these worlds are both clear and almost impossible to trace. A nucleated village settlement, the standard unit of much historical work on the rural areas is perhaps unproblematic and there is certainly a good deal of evidence that village identity was strong. Yet many boundaries are much more difficult to deal with and obscured to the historian even where contemporaries saw them clearly. The Northumberland shepherd had a world that was defined clearly by the lines of the hills which marked the sheep walks from the arable lands of the coastal regions. George Murray, interviewed in the early 1970s, was born in Scotland. His father was an itinerant farm worker but mainly a shepherd. When Mr Murray started work he left Northumberland, where his parents were living, and went across the border into Scotland for six months as a 'boy'; then he came back:

After I finished there I had just to dodge about and do what I could until the beginning of April again. [April was the hiring time for shepherds.] I went into Kielder and I put in a lambing at Kielder, and I did three years then on a hirsel at Kielder Head Farm.[1]

Less obvious were divisions associated with regions which simply had different characters. Here the fens are a good example. Even Norfolk fenmen looked West to Cambridge and Wisbech rather than East to Norwich for the centre of their *pays*. There were certainly differences in the productive system between the high farming of West Norfolk and the often small-scale farming of the fens. But it was culture, which the idea of the fen-tiger enshrined in folk-tale, which was the real divider. Similarly in east Norfolk and Suffolk those who looked after cattle on the marshes, the 'marshmen' were seen as, and saw themselves as quite different 'breeds'.[2]

In some areas of England though the local world was yet smaller, defined perhaps by a farmhouse or farm settlement in the first instance. Mr John Coleman who was Commissioner charged with investigating Northumberland for the Royal Commission of 1881 explained the farms of the county for an audience raised in village England. Here was a very small local world:

> The whole management of a Northumberland farm must appear very peculiar to a southern farmer. Each farm is, to a large extent, a colony in itself. No doubt, owing to the scarcity of the population, and to the absence of villages, this was a necessity in the original laying out of the land . . . but there is a sort of clannish feeling between the labourer and his employer, from their living together on the farm . . .[3]

There was a further set of defining elements which operated through these local systems but also crossed them – those of age and gender. What stage of the life cycle a man or woman was at crucially determined his or her experience of being a 'farm labourer' at any point in the nineteenth century. More important still was the difference between the position of men and women within the workforce, the family and the broader social structure.

Locality, age and gender need bringing together not as variables ranked in order of importance, but as different aspects of determinacy articulated within a broader system of economic power. Only by seeing them in this way can we begin to get at the enormous difference in experiences of labouring people throughout England. Yet such a task is huge and, except in the most general terms, well beyond the scope of this essay. I want therefore to take one aspect only – hiring practices – which were enormously different throughout the regions and throughout the nineteenth century, as a way into these problems. The reasons for this are simple enough. How long a worker hired for, where he or she lived as result and what socio-cultural system came out of that hiring were clearly central in the experience of labouring life. To simplify still further, I want to see those hiring practices as 'farm' hiring, 'family' hiring and 'community' hiring.

In 1894 Arthur Wilson Fox wrote the 'Summary Report' for the agricultural labour section of the Royal Commission on Labour.[4] As he pointed out, he was especially suited since he had looked at three northern and two eastern counties and therefore had experience of different farming and social systems. As in the case of Mr Coleman on Northumberland some years earlier, differences in regions were based as much on culture as on economic realities. Before summarising his findings on difference he wrote:

Many causes may be suggested for the distinctions observable in the general condition and affairs of the inhabitants of different localities, but I venture to think there is one which may be especially noticed, and that is the difference in the system of domestic life which the agricultural necessities or customs of each district demand or create.[5]

In 1900 and 1905 Wilson Fox produced two further national reports on the labourer and returned to the questions of regionality.[6] Wilson Fox's broad areas are shown in fig. 5.1, although given scale and Wilson Fox's own imprecision on occasion, any graphic representation is approximate. Wilson Fox chose to distinguish four areas in England essentially based upon hiring practices. Area 1 was the North of England and comprised Northumberland, Durham, Cumberland, Westmorland, North Lancashire and Yorkshire. Although this was not a unified region it had in common (with the exception of Northumberland) the practice of hiring by the year or half year with single men living in the farm house, with the foreman or occasionally in 'barracks'. Northumberland was totally different in that although hiring was by the year, and those hired lived 'on the farm', they usually lived in cottages and were married with the whole family being hired. In this sense single men were seldom hired at all, especially in North Northumberland which was the main arable area. We shall return to Northumberland shortly.

Area 2 in Wilson Fox's classification comprised those counties where there was 'some' living in the farm house, with the farmer, or occasionally in 'barracks'. The counties in this group were north Lincolnshire, north Cambridgeshire, Rutland, Nottinghamshire, Derbyshire, Cheshire, West Herefordshire, Staffordshire, Shropshire and parts of Devon and Cornwall. Area 3 was the most mixed. Here said Wilson Fox 'the systems vary' from family hiring in Dorset to weekly, even daily, hiring in many parts of Oxfordshire. This group consisted of Kent, Warwickshire, Worcestershire, Oxfordshire, Gloucestershire, Wiltshire, Berkshire, Hampshire and Dorset. Finally, in area 4 were those counties where, by 1900, according to Wilson Fox 'weekly engagements largely prevail for all classes of farm servants'. These were Bedfordshire, Buckinghamshire, Huntingdonshire, Middlesex, Northants, Norfolk, Suffolk, Essex, South Cambridgeshire, Hertfordshire, Surrey, Sussex and Somerset.[7]

Obviously these are only generalisations, as Fox himself showed in his own detailed reports done on various areas in 1892–94, but I think they are a good basis to work from although some aspects of the pattern may have been different even less than 30 years earlier. For example the Sussex Weald would probably have been moved from area 4 to area 3 as would have parts of the Surrey sands had Fox's survey been done in 1870. Similarly five years on, when Wilson Fox did his next survey in 1905, a number of the counties in group 2 were showing a decline in living-in compared with 1900.[8]

If we superimpose these areas over a farming regions map, broadly

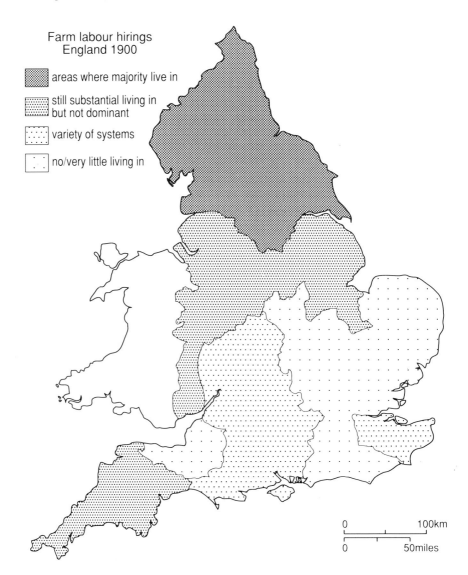

Fig. 5.1 Farm Labour hirings in England *c.* 1900.

distinguishing arable/pastoral/intermediate areas, what is most striking is the lack of congruence in many respects. Living-in was a feature, for instance, of northern and western agriculture as a whole, not of a particular crop. Conversely day labour was present in the South and the East as a whole not simply in areas of arable production. With the exception of Kent the 'mixed' areas shade off from living-in towards the South.

This suggests that the broad distinctions between living-in/yearly or half yearly hiring and living-out/weekly or daily hiring had little to do with pastoral/ arable divisions and that we should look elsewhere for the basis of Wilson Fox's areas. The first and most striking correlation is between areas which are broadly settled in 'clachan' type settlements, i.e. isolated farmsteads around which a limited amount of housing grew, and living-in; and village settlement and living-out although, of course, this is not an absolute correlation. Nor is it very surprising. John Coleman immediately made the connection as we saw above, between remoteness from villages and the need to house a workforce. Secondly there is the correlation between living-in and labour shortage largely because of direct competition with industry. Again this is not surprising at one level since the 'perks' of living-in were unlikely to be granted where labour supply was plentiful. Living-in service in all its forms was, as the nineteenth century went on, associated not with a particular farming system but with a particular settlement pattern and hence a particular social structure. Similarly day labour, the opposite end of some continuum of labour was also associated with a different settlement pattern and social structure.

Let us now return to our three categories of hiring and look at the first of them, 'farm hiring' or living-in farm service. The first thing to say is that even within this much narrower structure there were significant differences, for living-in farm service was not the same thing across even the same county let alone England and Wales as a whole. It is conventional to see living-in farm service as part of the life cycle. This is the position taken by Anne Kussmaul and Keith Snell on the pre-modern period and put clearly by Ian Carter in his study of the North East of Scotland:

For most men farm service was not a career in itself but a stage in a career that started outside farm service and would finish outside . . . Individual peasants circulated through family labour, farm service, day labouring and peasant farming in the course of a life's work.[9]

In parts of Lancashire, Westmorland and other areas of the North West this 'older' system of hiring by the year survived, as it did even in the marginal lands of the South and East. Here a system of small farms preserved the older model of farm service much more clearly than elsewhere. In the Garstang area of Lancashire for example, small farmers hired one or occasionally two labourers who lived in the house and ate with the master and mistress who did much the same work as the labourers. A Lancashire farmer told Wilson Fox in 1894, 'I go to work with my men and show them how. My wife and I dine with the servants. They have the same food as we have.'[10] Crucially there was possibility of social mobility. Many North Lancashire labourers were the sons and daughters of small farmers and expected to get farms of their own when they had saved enough to

marry and rent a holding. As Mr Dobson of Upper Rawcliff near Garstang told
the 1890 Commission on the depression:

> I was a labourer up to 22 years ago. I worked very hard when a labourer and so did my wife,
> who was a servant at the farm where I was employed ... We had not a sixpence when we
> married, but then we began to save a bit.[11]

Farm service seen in this way, essentially an exchange of households among
equals as part of the life cycle, was probably declining from the seventeenth
century. By the mid nineteenth, despite its widespread existence, where it appears
it is inevitably seen as a 'survival' of an earlier system and the mark of a more
'primitive' stage. This view is supported by some contemporaries who saw
'living-in' with a farmer's family as an ideal and usually lost, golden age. In this
version the similarity in social origins between master and man, the fact that they
worked and lived together sharing the same food and often dressing the same
gave a coherence and unity to agricultural society as well as enabling the farmer to
train and control the young servant.

However, this was not the only form of living-in service. Crucially, the arable
agriculture of the North and North East of England could not harbour the
'survivals' of an older system since it was itself in many respects new. Very
basically, the East Riding of Yorkshire, the Wolds of Lincolnshire and large areas
of Northumberland and Durham were not under the plough until the end of the
eighteenth century at the earliest and it was only in the first 50 years of the
nineteenth century that widespread agricultural colonisation led to a demand for
new labour. Given that the area was sparsely inhabited, some form of living-in
was the ideal solution as it was in apparently very different, but in some ways
similar, areas like the 'new' farming regions of America or New Zealand.
However, unlike Lancashire or the North East of Scotland, because these new
farms were large and required considerable capital investment, their workforce
was never part of the traditional chain of agricultural service where they could
become farmers themselves, nor were they, for the same reason, farmer's sons. As
a result a 'new' system of living-in emerged in these areas, some of whose
characteristics were common to the old system but which in crucial ways were
fundamentally different.

The basis of this system was outlined by Mr Jonathan Dunn who farmed just
over 500 acres in the Vale of York, two-thirds of it arable in 1881. He told the
Richmond Commission:

> We do not divide our labourers. We have a class of young, unmarried men that we board
> and lodge in the house, and those we make our carters. There is what is called the foreman,
> the seconder, the thirder and the fourther and perhaps the lad. Those we hire by the year,
> and board and lodge them.[12]

Although the precise names might change this structure held good for most of the arable North, with the exception of North Northumberland and parts of Wales.

However, even within this there were minor, but important distinctions. First where men lived in the farmhouse with the farmer's family; secondly, where they lived with a married foreman and thirdly where they lived in a 'barracks' or separate building of some kind. Finally, and not strictly, living-in was the system in North Northumberland where family hiring dominated but the family lived on the farm in 'hinds' cottages'. All these systems, with the exception of Northumberland, applied overwhelmingly to unmarried and usually young men. Very occasionally married men lived in, but it seems likely that these were unusual and temporary arrangements and seem mainly to have been restricted to North Wales.

It is important to stress here that the relationship between master and men in all these situations was not that of pure farm service. Different masters may or may not have been good, the food or accommodation superior or inferior, but there was never a sense of equality which was in theory present in pure living-in service. Even when ploughboys lived in the house, as they did according to Wilson Fox in Durham, Yorkshire, South Northumberland and North Wales, the system was more that of the Scottish 'chaumer'. In the Lleyn peninsula in the 1890s, for example, young servants lived in the 'lloft-stabal' (stable loft) a room over the horse stable, 'a rudely finished room over an open shed'.[13] Hugh Owen, a small farmer, told the Royal Commission on the Land of Wales in 1893, 'generally they were boarded in the kitchens, had their meals in the kitchens, and mostly slept in the hayloft, I mean the stable loft outside'.[14] Where the hired man ate in the kitchen he was, according to some, allowed to sit until 9 o'clock. Sometimes they were even denied that, as Mr Evan Parry told the Royal Commission on Labour, 'thousands of times did I suffer from cold as a servant; I was not allowed to go near the fire, and though I was fond of reading I had no place to go except the stable loft'.[15] Fred Kitchen says the same. 'Opposite the window was a wide fire place ... There George, the missus and Laddie the sheep dog warmed their toes; but never the toes of the hired lad.'[16]

On the larger farms even this form of living-in was gradually being replaced from at least the 1850s by the second form where the unmarried workers lived in the house of the foreman or his equivalent. This system was present in Yorkshire, North Cambridgeshire, Lincolnshire, Nottinghamshire and Rutland. In Nottinghamshire the young men 'live in the houses of the married labourers, usually waggoners [head horseman] or bailiffs, who are paid for their board and lodging by the farmers ...'.[17] In North Lincolnshire in the 1880s it was said, 'the young single men [who look after the horses] ... in former time lived in the farm house and shared the farmers meals, but now they are usually boarded with the foreman and rarely live in the farmhouse'.[18]

This form of living-in, living with a foreman or bailiff, shades off into the third form, probably the most unusual in England and Wales, that of young men living in 'barracks' or separate farm buildings. In England this seems to have been restricted to the East Riding of Yorkshire and possibly parts of Nottinghamshire and north Lincolnshire although there are scattered references to 'barracks' on some large estates elsewhere even in the Midlands and South East. It was also present in some parts of North Wales. On the Yorkshire Wolds, the Richmond Commission noted in 1881:

Day labourers are scarce and often reside at long distances from the farm; hence the system of hiring team and cattle men by the year is universal, and barracks under the eye of the hind, who is practically their master, are necessary. Formerly the hired servants boarded at the tenant's house, and were more immediately under his control and supervision; but on large occupations this practice has given place to that which I am describing for reasons which it is quite easy to understand.[19]

The ploughboy of the north then emerges as a very different figure from the classic hired servant. He was young, outside the control of family, earning reasonably good money and, perhaps most importantly, from a very young age, perhaps even 16, he was involved in horse work, the most prestigious of all work on an arable farm. By 20 or 21 he stood at the top of the farm hierarchy in terms of status at least. Service here was not part of an economic/life cycle pattern in which living-in was a step towards becoming a farmer but simply one form of wage labour. When the ploughboys of the Lleyn Peninsula or the Yorkshire Wolds married they became day labourers not small farmers like their compatriots in parts of Lancashire or Westmorland.

In the area we have just looked at 'farm' hiring reigned supreme. The isolation of the steadings, labour shortage and the late development of fully capitalist relations of production created a particular kind of workforce, often young, male, single, and living-in. Elsewhere the farm as a workplace came into relationship with the family and created a hiring system based on the hiring of the whole family. For example it was noted in Dorset in the late 1860s:

When a labourer is engaged by the year, the size of the family and the vigour of his wife and sons, becomes an important element for consideration as they are expected to go out to work when required. If the wife cannot go, she must send a daughter or [as I found in at least one parish] she must provide a substitute.[20]

This insistence on family labour persisted in many counties of southern and eastern England in an informal way into the twentieth century as an elderly labourer remembered in the 1970s. '... [a boy] had to go sometimes, they'd even compel them to. Boys have got a job at, like a builders at Stalham, and they've had to leave and come on the farm or they'd turn them out of their house.'[21]

The system of family hiring was at its most advanced and firmly entrenched in

Northumberland and other northern counties. Here again well into the twentieth century hiring contracts specify what was effectively family hiring:

I James Nixon do hereby agree to serve Sir Edward Blackett Bt. as Hind at Hatton for one
year from the 13th day of May next . . . My boy James to have constant employment for the
Summer half year . . . and my two daughters to work when wanted and to be paid at the
discretion of the farm steward.[22]

Family hiring was reinforced by the fact that every hind (living-in regular
worker) had to provide a female worker to work with him even if he was
unmarried. As Mrs Brown who was born in 1876 near Wooler in Northumberland said, 'Anybody that hadn't a woman it was hard to get hired . . . and if they
had no woman workers, well they could hire one and take her to live with
them'.[23] Francis and Christopher Storey hired with Sir Edward Blackett in
March 1865 as hinds, 'House and garden rent free and coals led [i.e. brought to
house].' However, these two brothers were unmarried and so had 'no woman'
and turned therefore to the extended family, 'our niece to work when wanted and
to have 10d per day in summer and 1/6 a day during harvest'.[24] Women hired in
this way were sometimes known as 'bondagers' although the term seems to have
been less used actually in Northumberland than later writings, and indeed
contemporary outsiders would suggest. In 1881 Mr Coleman's report to the
Richmond Commission went as far as to say that women workers were 'formerly
styled a bondager, a term which is now most strongly objected to because it was
supposed to denote a degraded condition of servitude' (fig. 5.2).[25]

These farm accounts of Northumberland farms, especially those in Glendale to
the north and east of the Cheviots show the family as a working unit up until the
Great War. Not only were these workers hired as families, they were paid as a
group. For example, the account books from Castle Heaton Farm near
Coldstream record each worker's earnings individually but also show that they
were paid monthly as a group to the 'head' of the household, usually the father, a
practice which was only abandoned, on this farm at least, in 1916.[26]

If we look in a little more detail at Castle Heaton Farm we see a unit bound
together by close ties of proximity and family. In 1881 Alexander Mckay lived in
'Castle Heaton Farm Hind's Cottages No. 1', he had three daughters aged 19, 18,
and 15, all of whom are described as farm labourers. At no. 2 lived James
Harrington a domestic coachman and his family while at no. 3, as in other cases,
the 'head of household' was a widow Mary Sprat who is described as 'housekeeper', a full-time job as she had two daughters and three sons all described as
'agricultural labourers'. At no. 4 the head of household was also a woman, Sarah
Tully who again was a 'housekeeper' with two sons and a daughter described as
'agricultural labourers'. These women were what Wilson Fox called 'cottars', 'a
single woman or widow who is hired direct by the farmer and lives in a cottage by

Fig. 5.2 A remarkable picture *c.* 1870 from the Alnwick area of Northumberland showing part of the workforce on a north Northumberland farm. The picture is especially striking since it shows bondagers and child labour, both of which were central to the Northumberland system. My thanks to Judy Gielgud for identifying this picture.

herself on the farm'.[27] There were women on these kind of agreements also at nos 5 and 6. At no. 7 was Ralph Jackson a hind with two sons and two daughters all labourers, and at no. 8 lived the farm steward and his family. His wife did not work and his children were too young to hire. A little way away were two other cottages. In one lived the shepherd and his family, all of whom were employed on the farm, in the other another cottar with two sons and a daughter working on the farm.[28]

This general situation continued at Castle Heaton up to the Great War although there were probably changes which were not obvious to this kind of comparison. In 1890 there were 11 'family' groups employed on the farm, only one apparently headed by a woman. In 1913 there were ten groups, none headed by a woman. Whether there actually was a decline in the numbers of women on 'cottar' hirings is difficult to judge but it seems unlikely. What is certain is that the group around a farm changed regularly. In 1889 there was not a single family employed on Castle Heaton Farm that was there on the 1881 census. By 1913 the entire workforce has changed again.

The relationships between family, workplace and household shown on the large Northumberland farms show just how complex the experience of farm labour could be. Family hiring enabled widows to exist as wage earners with independent status as cottar tenants, nieces and nephews were hired by and lived with uncles, the family remained undivided by generation since sons and daughters were a real economic asset. The home and the workplace also remained almost the same place and strong bonds grew up between families, and between master and workers on the same farm.

Northumberland provides perhaps an extreme example of the variety of social structures covered by a notion of 'family hiring' but even where living-in was not the dominant system, in the South and Midlands for example, the family still provided a key element and structuring principle of the workforce. Leafield in Oxfordshire, for example, shows that even if the normal 'nuclear family' was the dominant 'type' of household relationship, it was not the only one. The census enumerators' books for the village in 1871 show the range of possibilities within family and household types.[29] The majority of family and household types in the village conform to the nuclear model – that is father, mother, children living in the same house with father as bread winner. However, it is equally clear that as well as domestic work a large number of women worked at wage labour which seriously modified the internal structure of the household even if its external appearance remained the same.

In Leafield, a combination of outwork and woodland trades produced a range of family and household structures. Central here was outwork gloving which employed most of the women as outworkers, with mother and daughter(s) in many families employed on this basis. The possibility of work of this kind showed how important family was as a unit of production in various ways even in the late nineteenth century. At 'the Row' in Leafield for example lived Elizabeth Eels, a spinster, Martha Eels, her niece, John Eels her nephew and another niece, aged five, Mary Anne Hopkins. Martha worked at the gloving and John, aged 18, was a farm labourer. Gloving also kept 19-year-old Maryanne Pratley, an unmarried mother and her one-year-old son out of the workhouse and enabled Jane Shayler a widow of 31 to support her ten-year-old and three-year-old daughter. The woodlands which surrounded Leafield also provided a variety of family employments. Several women worked at chairmaking which enabled Phoebe Dadd to raise her family although she was a widow.

Here also we can see the importance of children's work. The gloving industry enabled (or forced) daughters to work and contribute to family income from 12 or 13 years of age. Informally children probably contributed even more. School log books show constant involvement of children in the agricultural process throughout the agricultural year. In Sussex in the 1860s and 1870s they went hop pole shaving, flint picking, beating, shepherding, hop pole tying, barking, flower selling, hay making, weeding, hopping, harvesting and gathering acorns, as well as endless versions of 'helping father'.[30]

The situation in Leafield and East Sussex is shading out into our final category, 'community' hiring. By this I mean essentially hiring by the day from within a separate, if frequently occupational community. This is the classic form of capitalist hiring with the labourer having nothing to sell but his/her labour power and all relationships being based on a cash nexus.

Pure day labour, literally hiring by the day, was uncommon. Throughout Wilson Fox's area 3, Bedfordshire, Buckinghamshire, Huntingdonshire, Middlesex, Northamptonshire, Norfolk, Suffolk, Essex, South Cambridgeshire, Hertfordshire, Surrey, Sussex and Somerset, terms of hiring were enormously varied with only 'true' casuals being hired by the day. Many workers may have been paid by the day but most were effectively hired by the week or longer. In most areas horsemen and cattlemen were hired by the year even in those areas like North West Norfolk where arable/capitalist agriculture was at its most advanced. The roads on Old Michaelmas Day (October 11th) were, according to Mrs Moy of Yaxham in Norfolk, 'thick with Dicky [donkey] carts' as those hired by the year changed their places.[31] Certainly the numbers of cases under the 'master and servant' legislation, though nothing like as high as in Yorkshire, suggest that many, both farmers and workers, thought in terms of yearly hirings.

The key difference was not simply length of hiring but its social and cultural relations created by where hired workers lived. In the Maldon district of Essex, for example, as in most southern and eastern areas in the 1890s; 'most farms have one or two farm cottages belonging to them, inhabited usually by horsemen and stockmen, but in the majority of cases the labourers live in cottages hired from independent owners'.[32] The village settlement pattern created social groups which were both male and female, of different ages and included those who were outside agriculture. Crucially there was no break point in their early twenties when marriage automatically changed the work, living and status of workers. Again in some ways this was a new system although it lacked the suddenness which seems to have marked the transformation in northern agricultural service. What seems to have happened in southern areas was that living-in, having lost the notion of service among equals from the seventeenth century onwards, remains (and remained) as an inferior category for the very young male – the 'copper-hole Jack' or 'backus boy' of southern farms. Charlie Barber didn't 'live-in' but filled many of the jobs of young males:

I left school, I passed the fourth standard . . . I went as copper-hole-Jack, or houseboy . . . we used to do anything, any sort . . . weed the flower garden . . . house work, looking after ponies all that sort of thing.[33]

Right from the word go different categories applied. Certainly a boy's first hiring in the North was often negotiated by his father but in the South the pressure was much greater than that – a son was expected to follow his father onto the farm, and thereafter family ties remained much more important than in the North since most young men lived at home until marriage.

Although the term of hiring in the South was nominally very short, male workers at least tended to stay with one employer for much longer periods than this. As Wilson Fox wrote in 1893, '. . . it is remarkable that in the Eastern counties . . . the men frequently stay for years with the same employer'. This was, as we have seen, in direct contrast with those areas where farm hiring dominated:

The hiring system in the North seems to be responsible for a constant changing of the labourers from one employer to another . . . There being a definite period of engagement, at the end of which the employer has to ask his men if they intend to remain for a further time unsettles them and puts the possibility of change into their heads . . . (Also) . . . their only associates being their fellow workmen on the farm . . . the monotony of such a life is irksome, and can only be relieved by seeking fresh scenes and new employment.[34]

By staying in one place, the 'community' hired labourer, especially if working with animals, grew in skill and knowledge of 'his' farm. As Jack Leeder who spent his life as a Norfolk team-man said:

Farmers have made their money on team-mens brains . . . they knew more about the land and how to plough it than ever the farmer did . . . and they were never paid a quarter of what they were worth.[35]

This pride in work and its recognition by both peers and employers was reinforced by the village structure. If the northern ploughboy was isolated the horseman, team-man or even labourer in the South was integrated within the village structure. Although migration is often underestimated, a worker like this frequently remained attached to his family, beginning work with his father for example, and on marriage was likely to settle. This made the world of the village with its different influences and particularly its contacts with a wider sphere very important. 'The village', noted Wilson Fox of Norfolk and Suffolk:

creates a community among which there is a constant interchange of ideas, one consequence of which is the frequency of early marriages . . . Another is the facility for organisation by means of unions, and the third is the tendency for relations between employers and employed to become confined solely to business matters.[36]

Except on estate villages and perhaps those completely dominated by one landlord or farmer there was the space within these communities for the worker to organise and socialise for himself. The pub, the chapel, the friendly society, the allotment and the trade union were all products of a settled and permanent structure of social relations.

Much of this really only functions for male workers. We have already seen how in parts of the North and elsewhere family hiring gave a key role to regular

Fig. 5.3 Potato picking on Shankhouse Farm, eastern Northumberland. A gang of probably casual women workers of the kind referred to in this chapter; it seems likely that the picture was taken in 1914 or 1915 because of the soldiers.

women workers hired as part of a family. Here, shortage of labour because of the isolation of many of the more remote farm settlements meant that farmers had to employ relatively more workers all the year round as the 'residual army' of the southern villages simply did not exist. Nevertheless extra workers were employed at key seasons. The farm accounts of Castle Heaton farm show women family members hired for the cereal harvest along with migrant Irish workers. For the harvest period in 1913 four Irish migrants were hired along with five women family members and two 'boy' family members.[37] In parts of the North and more so the West there were groups of women workers though who stood outside the family hiring system altogether. On the smaller farms of Northumberland where family hiring was not economically viable, or where there were off-farm sources of women workers as on the coastal plain, women were hired by the day for key harvest operations. The farm books of a 202-acre family farm near Dinnington in Northumberland show that most work was done by the two brothers who ran it plus three hinds. At hay, and especially potato harvest though, casual workers, mainly women, were brought onto the farm (fig. 5.3). The small cereal harvest seems to have been taken entirely by regular workers. The numbers involved were relatively large. At potato harvest in 1908 16 'girls' were employed over two weeks 'taking up potatoes'. Women workers were also brought onto the farm, to plant potatoes in the spring, to spread muck, also in the spring and for threshing on and off throughout the winter and spring.[38]

It is not clear from the records precisely who these women were, since names seldom appear, but there are no obvious family relationships between these women and the male workers, unlike the situation on the bigger farm at Castle Heaton. One assumes they were from the nearby mining settlements at Seaton. A few miles away Bob Thompson, a farmer, remembered:

there used to be a lot of women came out at harvest time ... lot of bottle makers wives, and they used to have a stretch same as they used to get stretches for potatoes, they had so many yards, where they had to make the band, tie the shef [*sic*] up and put it out of the way of the machine ... they all had their stint to do.[39]

Slightly further south in County Durham it was noted in the 1860s that there was no shortage of casual workers 'extra women being easily procured from the numerous pit villages'.[40]

In the mainly arable areas of the South and East women workers tended to be more and more casual, brought into the production processes at particular times from the wives and daughters, widows and spinsters of the village-based community, and paid by the piece for particular tasks. In the West Grinstead area of West Sussex for example women helped their husbands at hay harvest, and young girls were employed in 'dropping peas after a dibbler'. A few miles north at Rusper they worked at hay harvest, corn harvest and weeding. At Hailsham in East Sussex women found seasonal working tying hops 'at so much an acre'.[41] In North Cerney in Gloucestershire women were employed throughout the farming year on a casual basis:

They are useful for a variety of occupations: stone-picking, picking, drawing and cleaning turnips for sheep and cattle, weeding corn, hay-making, hoeing root crops, picking, raking and burning couch, harvesting, pulling, topping and tailing turnips, pulling straw for the thatcher, cutting chaff, untying the sheaves for threshing machine [*sic*] mending corn sacks etc. etc.[42]

It was in eastern England, in the great wheatlands, especially Norfolk, Cambridgeshire and Lincolnshire, that the casual employment of women seems to have been both most widespread and organised. It was in these areas that the infamous 'gang system' developed. This was basically a system of sub-contracting where a 'gangmaster' took a particular job for a price from a farmer and then employed women and children, boys and young men as well as girls, to do the work for day rates. For his 'trouble' the gangmaster took as much as a third of the wages of those he 'employed' making, according to one estimate in the mid 1860s, as much as 15s–£1 a week on a gang of 15–20 persons. The Rev. W. T. Beckett, the

Diocesan Inspector of Schools for Norwich, who made that estimate summed up the system neatly. For the farmer, 'it enabled him to dispense with a certain number of labourers, as were it not for this system he would be obliged to keep a greater number of regular labourers ...'. It also enabled him to do without a foreman or bailiff to supervise the work, this being done by the gangmaster. For the labourer though they 'are deprived of part of their fairly earned wages ... [and] have often, to use a Norfolk phrase, "to play", that is remain unemployed on wet days, or when the weather is not altogether suitable for the kind of work required.' Most simply of all 'to the poor man it displaces labour and renders it less'.[43]

Agricultural gangs were usually based in the larger and 'open' villages, and went out day by day to work for the farms around. Occasionally they stayed away over night although this practice was uncommon. They undertook a range of agricultural tasks on a seasonal basis which, added together, covered much of the year. As a Norfolk gangmaster said in the mid 1860s:

There is work of some kind for my gang during most of the year, even in winter, except when there is frost or snow. Then the only work is perhaps for half a dozen or so of the bigger boys in topping and tailing turnips for food for sheep etc. From now, October, to March the work will be chiefly pulling and topping and tailing mangolds and turnips, forking twitch, and stone picking; then picking and burning twitch, puddling thistles and docks, weeding corn and other kinds of weeding, and this with singling mangolds and turnips, and so on, will last up to harvest ... after harvest comes forking and clearing the land, and so work goes up to now again.[44]

Travelling from place to place, 'immodestly' dressed, young men and young women 'indiscriminately' mixed together, but above all public and visible the agricultural gang embodied all that the Victorian elite attacked in women's field work. Unlike the 'dairymaids' of the pastoral regions hidden in the dairies and with their echoes, no matter how absurd, of Meissen figurines, the field woman would be seen everywhere in the huge fields and open places of the wheatlands. Bent double, clad in 'rags', heavy boots, short skirt and with a sack around her shoulders she was the antithesis of the ideal of the 'angel at the hearth' and a constant reproach to those who sought an ordered paternal idyll.

Yet their work, given the nature of farm organisation, was vital. They stood 'outside' the system which projected a model of a settled, regular, deferential and male workforce but without them the system with its demands for periodic and massive labour inputs would have collapsed. Yet the 'casual', especially the woman casual, could be and was marginalised. They were perceived as 'temporary' even if as with many women workers that was clearly nonsensical, they came into the village and went again, their threat to order was soon gone.

There was some work in rural areas which was considered 'fit' for women – essentially that which centred on the 'indoor' work of the dairy and the farmhouse. As this work was hidden, in the sense that it was to an extent out of public view, and because of the long-term links between the house and the dairy, it was accepted. As dairying and cheese making became commercial, as it did in many areas after the 1850s, women were replaced by men. In Derbyshire for example it was said in the 1880s that there '. . . are fewer dairymaids and girls employed about the farmhouses than was the case formerly. In consequence of cheese making at home having about died out maid servants are no longer required'.[45] The keywords here are 'at home' for cheese making was actually increasing – but in 'factories' run by men on the 'American system'.[46]

However, if the work of the dairymaid was acceptable to even refined Victorian opinion, that of the field worker was usually not. The very difference in name is significant – the dairy*maid* and the field*woman*, the one with its stress on innocence and the rural idyll, the other with its connotations of experience and harshness. Hardy knew the distinction well when he made Tess a dairymaid at Talbothays in her period of innocence and love for Angel Clare, and a field-woman at Flintcombe Ash when she was deserted and truly 'a maiden no more'. Those men who reported on the employment of women in agriculture in 1843 and 1867–70 often felt the same. The Hon. E. B. Portman, for example, who reported on the three ridings of Yorkshire, Cambridgeshire, Hants, Devon and Cornwall made an absolute distinction between 'indoor' farm service and outdoor farm labourer and concluded, 'girls should not . . . be employed in the fields at all'.[47]

Field work was, as the century progressed, regarded more and more as unsuitable and unnatural for women. Portman was only being more extreme than most of the other investigators when he wrote that as a result of field work 'such sense of decency' that girls have is 'entirely broken down' and that it made them 'entirely unfit . . . for their duties in the future as wives and mothers'.[48] By making these girls rough in manner and appearance, as it was stated field work did, it put them physically outside Victorian society and its model of womanhood which demanded delicacy of features, pale skin and elaborate dress. The Rev. James Fraser who investigated Norfolk, Suffolk, Essex, Sussex and Gloucestershire for the same report wrote of fieldwork:

Not only does it almost unsex a woman, in dress, gait, manners, character, making her rough, coarse, clumsy, masculine; but it generates a further very pregnant social mischief by unfitting or indisposing her for a woman's proper duties at home. Some of the work on which women are frequently employed . . . is work to which, on physical grounds, they never ought to be put at all. Exposure to wet or cold, from which no farm labour can claim exemption, is likely, owing to the greater susceptibility of the female constitution, to be especially injurious to them.[49]

Whatever working women thought, and there were many who accepted some versions of the 'unfit work' argument, there were many who clearly did not really see what the fuss was about and saw women's work not as unnatural or especially degrading but simply as necessary and inevitable. Fraser was told in Linton in Gloucestershire by a 'group of labouring women', 'that it would be a hardship if the law were to lay restrictions upon the employment of women in the fields',[50] and fieldwork for most working women was seen in these terms. The overwhelming sense that comes through this material though is its inevitability. Elizabeth Dickson, a widow from Norfolk, put the case eloquently and simply. 'My children were obliged to work very young, some before they were 7 years old. If you have nothing except what comes out of your fingers' end, as they say, it's no use, you must let them; they want more victuals.'[51] The women of Linton who spoke to Fraser made the same point, 'their families would often have gone to bed hungry had they not earned their money in that way'.[52] The village elites, when they could overcome their moral fears about women working at all, saw the problem in the same way. The Rev. Thurtell of Oxburgh in Norfolk put it bluntly when he said 'The females of very large families *must* [*sic*] be permitted to work, in order that they may live.'[53]

It was not simply, though, a case of demand from labouring families, but demand from farmers. As the number of casual workers from other sources began to decrease from the 1850s the labour of women and children became more and more important and it seems likely that women's employment in agriculture reached its peak. The Rev. W. G. S. Addison of Hartparry in Gloucestershire put this double demand clearly to Fraser, 'Female labour is absolutely required by the farmers, and the additional wages are as greatly needed by the labourers families.'[54] James Freezer who farmed 1,000 acres in Norfolk required 'about 16 women all through the year to cultivate this quantity of land properly'. Crucially for him, as for so many others, 'the farm can be worked much cheaper with women than without them . . . For weeding a woman can do the work not only cheaper but better than a man.'[55]

To many contemporaries and, until recently, to most historians the English farm labourer of the nineteenth century was an unproblematic figure. He had escaped labour and social history's concerns with a differentiated workforce and was portrayed as a single type. Unskilled, or at best semi-skilled, doomed to day labour and poor pay. Yet the picture which emerges here is a very different one. The uneven development of capitalist labour relationships, which grew from quite different regional farming and hiring patterns, produced a complex variety of experiences for those who worked the land. Equally important was gender. The work experiences of men and women, although broadly circumscribed by the productive system, were significantly different even within the same dominant system. None of this is to overturn economic relationships as a major determinant of work experience but simply to argue that within the 'whole' of agrarian capitalism regional variety remained, at least until the Great War if not later, a key element in how ordinary people lived their lives.

NOTES

For more detail of the material in this essay see the author's book *Reshaping Rural England. A Social History 1850–1925* (Unwin Hyman 1991).

1 Northumberland Record Office (hereafter NRO) NRO Trans. 62.

2 George Ewart Evans, *Where Beards Wag All. The Relevance of the Oral Tradition* (London, 1970) chapter 14.

3 *British Parliamentary Papers*, (hereafter *PP*) XIV (1882) Royal Commission on the Depressed State of the Agricultural Interest, 392.

4 *PP* XXXV (1893–94) Royal Commission on Labour. The Agricultural Labourer. Summary Report.

5 *Ibid.*, 5.

6 *PP* LXXXIII (1900) Earnings of Agricultural Labourers. Report by Mr Wilson Fox on the Wages, Earnings and Conditions of Agricultural Labourers in the United Kingdom; *PP* XCVIII (1905) Second Report by Mr Wilson Fox on the Wages, Earnings and Conditions of Employment of Agricultural Labourers in the United Kingdom.

7 *PP* LXXXIII (1900) 582–3.

8 *PP* XCVIII (1905) 361.

9 Anne Kussmaul, *Servants in Husbandry in Early Modern England* (Cambridge 1981); Keith Snell, *Annals of the Labouring Poor* (Cambridge 1985); Ian Carter, *Farm Life in Northeast Scotland 1840–1914: A Poor Man's Country* (Edinburgh 1979) 109–11.

10 *PP* XXXV (1893–94) Royal Commission on Labour. The Agricultural Labourer . . . the Poor Law Union of Garstang, 167.

11 *PP* XVI Pt I (1894) Royal Commission on Agriculture. England, 63.

12 *PP* XVII Pt I (1881) Minutes of Evidence Taken before Her Majesty's Commissioners on Agriculture Part II, 171.

13 *PP* XXXVI (1893–94) Royal Commission on Labour. The Agricultural Labourer. Wales . . . Pwllheli, 151.

14 Quoted by D. Roy Saer in notes to recording *Caneuon Llofft stabal*, Welsh Folk Museum, St. Fagans, 1980, 3.

15 *PP* XXXVI (1893–94) 147.

16 Fred Kitchen, *Brother to the Ox* (1940, new edn Firle 1981) 54–5.

17 *PP* XXXV (1893–4) Royal Commission on Labour. The Agricultural Labourer . . . the Poor Law Union of Southwell, 117.

18 *PP* XV (1882) Royal Commission on the Depressed State of the Agricultural Interest, Reports of the Assistant Commissioners, 374.

19 *PP* XVI (1881) Royal Commission on the Depressed State of the Agricultural Interest. Assistant Commissioners Reports. Digest of Evidence, 143.

20 *PP* XVII (1867–68) Royal Commission on the Employment of Children, Young Persons and Women in Agriculture First Report, 4.

21 Interview AJH/Jack Leeder, Norfolk. Tape in author's possession.

22 NRO ZBL/ 78 Hiring Agreements, Hatton Hall Estate.

23 NRO T. 98, NRO 1208.

24 NRO ZBL/ 78.

25 *PP* XV (1882) 6.

26 NRO Woods MS.

27 *PP* xxxv (1893–94) Royal Commission on Labour. The Agricultural Labourer ... Glendale, 102.

28 NRO, Enumerators Books. 1881 Census, Berwick on Tweed Union. Cornhill District.

29 Public Record Office, Census Enumerators Books 1871, R.G.9/889.

30 Extracted from the School Log Books of Bishopstone, Falmer and Stanmer, Laughton, Udimore and Waldron Schools. I am grateful to Diana Hitchen for this material from her own work.

31 Interview AJH/Mrs Moy, Norfolk. Tape in author's possession.

32 *PP* xxv (1893–94) Royal Commission on Labour. The Agricultural Labour ... Maldon, 702.

33 Interview AJH/Charlie Barber, Norfolk. Tape in author's possession.

34 *PP* xxxv (1893–94) Summary Report, 13.

35 Interview AJH/Jack Leeder. Tape in author's possession.

36 *PP* xxxv (1893–94) Summary Report, 5–6.

37 NRO Woods MS.

38 NRO 479. Farm Diaries of J. W. and J. E. Rutherford.

39 NRO T.34. NRO 103.

40 *PP* xiii (1868–69) Royal Commission on the Employment of Children, Young Persons and Women in Agriculture. Second Report, 58.

41 *PP* xvii (1867–68) xvii, 78–81.

42 *Ibid.*, 102.

43 *PP* xvi (1867) Royal Commission on the Employment of Children in Trades and Manufactures not regulated by Law, Sixth Report, Appendix (Agriculture), 83–5.

44 *Ibid.*, 86.

45 *PP* xvi (1881), 941.

46 *Ibid.*, 942.

47 *PP* xviii (1868–69), 49.

48 *PP* xvii (1867–68), 95.

49 *Ibid.*, 16.

50 *Ibid.*, 132–3.

51 *PP* xvi (1867), 89.

52 *PP* xvii (1867–68), 132.

53 *Ibid.*, 137.

54 *Ibid.*, 140.

55 *Ibid.*, 167.

Sportive labour: the farmworker in eighteenth-century poetry and painting

6

JOHN BARRELL

Landscape with clowns

At some time in the 1730s William Hogarth added some figures to a landscape painted by his friend George Lambert; the result was the picture now known as *Landscape with Farmworkers* (fig. 6.1).[1] It shows a small piece of enclosed ground beside a farmhouse, and in the distance a winding river and a wooded hill. The figures added by Hogarth have been mowing the hay in the enclosure, and are now raking it up into haycocks ready to be loaded on to a wagon and carted away. Or rather one of them – the woman on the right – is doing that, but the shirtsleeved man in the foreground has for the moment found something more enjoyable to do. He prefers making hay to haymaking, and has tumbled with a woman into the central haycock where he is feeling her up, his hand under her skirt. How the woman herself feels about this is not clear. Another woman – again, it isn't clear whether she is amused or angry – is attempting to separate them; a second man, watching all this, is certainly amused. It seems clear enough that we are invited to share his amusement: the horseplay in the haycock may be fun for all involved or it may be an assault, but either way it is meant to be fun for us, to spy on these farmworkers precisely when they think they are unobserved.

About 50 years later, in 1785, George Stubbs produced a very different painting of the hay harvest (fig. 6.2). The workers here are loading hay on to a wagon with a statuesque dignity. The five figures standing in the foreground look as if they had been copied from a sculpted frieze, and the two men in this group are doing their work with the same kind of gravity with which, in Italian Renaissance paintings, serious-minded archers shoot arrows at St Sebastian. The man standing on the wagon is pitchforking the hay with the patient concentration St Michael shows when dealing with rebel angels. If Hogarth's haymakers thought that no one could see them, these know they are being watched, are on show. Everyone is neat, unruffled, composed, the women especially, and most especially the woman in the centre, looking at us looking at her. This is the image of a disciplined workforce; or workers disciplined enough, at least, never to take a break when a member of the employing or the picture-buying classes might be watching.

Fig. 6.1 George Lambert and William Hogarth, *Landscape with Farmworkers, c.* 1730–40(?). Oil on canvas 101.5×127 cm., Yale Center for British Art, Paul Mellon Collection.

These pictures are rather extreme examples of two different images of the eighteenth-century farmworker, too extreme to be in any straightforward sense 'representative' of the periods in which they were produced. I cannot think of any other painting of a rural subject from the decades before 1750 which is as ribald as Hogarth's and Lambert's, and there is no other painter of the 1780s who represented agricultural work with the elaborate dignity of Stubbs. Each painting is an extreme version, however, of what was certainly the dominant image of the farmworker in polite culture at either end of the 50-year period that separates them. In that 50 years the character of the farmworker as it was represented in poetry and painting changed dramatically, from comic to serious, drunken to sober, sensual to chaste, idle to industrious. This essay is an attempt to look at

Fig. 6.2 George Stubbs, *Haymakers*, 1785. Oil on panel 89.5×135.2 cm. London, the Tate Gallery.

some examples of these two opposed images, and to suggest how the change came about.

It is important at the outset to establish that such images as these are never simply faithful representations of the world, of the way things are, and equally that they are never simply conjured up out of the imagination of the individual artist. Pictorial images always have a history, they always belong to a tradition of representation, however much they may also depart from that tradition. They belong – to put it another way – within specific genres and modes, which appear to set limits to how things are to be represented, even though those limits are continually crossed. If we are to attempt to understand the difference between these two paintings, an essential first step is to try to understand where each belongs, in terms of the various genres of representation, and in terms of the history of those genres and their relation to each other.

Throughout the eighteenth century we come across a concern that the representation of rural life in literature and painting should be able to represent more and more of the actuality of rural life in England. This concern is most clearly expressed in relation to poetry, and especially pastoral poetry, the genre which pretended to describe the lives and loves of shepherds. The argument went something like this. English pastoral poetry was too limited in what it could represent by the conventions it had inherited from Greek and Latin literature. The classical writers of pastoral had themselves attempted to represent something of the actuality of rural life in the classical world. In doing so they had established a set of poetic conventions which had been passed down to the poets of the eighteenth century with all the authority, of learning and precedent, that attached to every aspect of classical culture. But the more carefully and dutifully the conventions of classical pastoral were observed by English poets, the more they would depart from its spirit: to dress the rough shepherds of England in the flowing drapery of Greece or Rome would not just be to classicise them, it would be to idealise them. The same would be true of the other main genre of poetry used for the representation of rural life, the georgic. The georgic, invented by Virgil on the model of a poem written by the Greek poet Hesiod, was supposed to be used to instruct farmers in the duties of their profession, and to instruct an urban audience in the crucial importance of agriculture to the well-being of a nation.[2]

Unless the conventions of pastoral and georgic were questioned, therefore, English poets would have no means of producing a more local, a more contemporary image of rural life. They would also find it difficult to perform what was coming to be seen in the early eighteenth century as one of their primary functions: the celebration of the growing importance of Britain among the nations of the world, and the creation of a sense of British national identity.[3] Rural life was seen as a crucial aspect of that identity for a number of reasons, among them that British agriculture was believed to be more advanced and productive than the agriculture of its competitor nations, and it was an item of faith among the polite classes, at least, that in Merry England the relations between landlord and tenant, farmer and worker, were believed to be more harmonious, and to approach more nearly to equality, than anywhere else in the world. A poetry tied to the conventions of classical poetry – or too much tied, for no one imagined that the classical inheritance could or should be simply wished away – would be unable to represent either the progressive nature of British agriculture or the relaxed character of social relations in Britain.

The first solution found to the problem of how to represent the actuality of rural life in early eighteenth-century Britain was to represent the farmworker as a comic character: as a rustic, as a 'clown' – the word has a long history of being used to describe the comic idiocy of rural life. This was a more complex solution than might at first appear, because it was not thought that to represent someone or something in terms of comedy was necessarily to represent it with the primary aim of provoking laughter. The comic was believed to have at least two functions, which were not easily disentangled but which were certainly not identical. The painting by Hogarth and Lambert is a comic painting, and it was certainly intended to provoke a reaction of condescending good humour in those who look at it. But it uses the comic mode also to indicate that this is an image of rural life as it really is in England, and not as it once was in Greece or Rome. The comic mode is the only mode in which the life of the poor, the vulgar, can be represented 'realistically': to use the resources of the comic is to claim to offer a realistic image of 'low life' – although in fact, of course, that image is as conventional as any other.

A 'rustic' or a 'clown', therefore, or his female equivalent, could certainly be an object of mirth, but could also be – and at the very same time – an object of sympathy. In 1714 the poet John Gay, author of *The Beggar's Opera*, wrote a series of comic pastorals about contemporary English rustics, *The Shepherd's Week*, in which he intended to resist the drift of the argument I have been rehearsing, and to show that the attempt to anglicise and up-date the pastoral by an infusion from the comic would result in a poetry of rural life that was merely ridiculous, merely vulgar. But the poems were greeted as accurate and not at all as ridiculous representations of rural life; they were even felt to be moving, in their account of the emotions experienced by the 'vulgar'; and the fact that they were amusing does not seem to have meant that they could not also be very affecting.[4] As we shall see, this ambiguous nature of the comic mode would eventually become one of the factors which appeared to make untenable this comic solution to the problem of how to represent the farmworker.

As I have already suggested, the comic could perform very much the same function for the painting of rural life. Broadly speaking, English painters of the period of George Lambert and William Hogarth had inherited two main traditions in which rural life could be represented. On the one hand there was the classicising tradition of the seventeenth-century French landscape painters, especially Claude Lorrain and Nicolas Poussin, who when they depicted the work of the countryside, always represented it as being done by olive-skinned youths, lightly clad in flowing drapery, and evidently very much at ease in a perpetual Mediterranean spring. On the other hand there was the image of rural labour offered by the Dutch landscape painters of the seventeenth century: Hobbema, Ruysdael, Wijnants, whose rural workers were sometimes, but not always, overtly comic and boorish but who were always dressed in a recognisably more contemporary costume, and one more adapted to the uncertainties of a northern climate. English painters of the 1730s and 1740s were thoroughly eclectic; George Lambert was happy to paint in both the French and the Dutch styles, even in the same picture. The closer they came to the Dutch style, however, the more comic the image they produced of the farmworker, and the more that image was to be understood as a representation of rural life in contemporary Britain.

Sportive labour, laborious sport

I have suggested that the comic mode was especially of value in the image it could offer of social relations in the countryside. For most of the eighteenth century the contemporary farmworker is shown in poetry and painting as enjoying a thoroughly agreeable life, in which labour is not especially arduous and is continually interrupted by periods of relaxation and by moments of what poets described as 'jocund mirth'. Such images are as much a representation of the polite as of the vulgar – of the employers of rural labour, of the landowners of Britain, and of all those whose incomes were derived directly or indirectly from agriculture. For to represent labour as continually interrupted by leisure, in paintings commissioned by and in poetry read by the polite classes, is to suggest that the polite chose to represent themselves as thoroughly tolerant and good-humoured in their relations with the vulgar. Whatever the reality of work-discipline and of the relations of master and servant in agriculture, for much of the eighteenth century, and especially in the period 1720–60, the art and literature of rural life was concerned to assert that England was Merry England, that Britain was Happy Britannia, and that the freedom, prosperity and independence enjoyed by the polite were the privilege of all Englishmen, haymakers especially.

In George Lambert's *View of Boxhill* of 1733 (fig. 6.3), a group of gentlemen lie at their ease on the slope of Box Hill and watch a pair of haymakers making love on a loaded haywain; in the dark left foreground another rustic may be stopping a fox-earth or netting the mouth of a rabbit burrow. In Thomas Gainsborough's *Peasant with two Horses* of 1755 (fig. 6.4), some haymakers are loading hay on to a wagon in the background, while the foreground is taken up with an image of relaxation: a young clown has led the horses into the shade and is dozing until the wagon is ready to be driven away. In the same painter's *Landscape with a Woodcutter courting a Milkmaid*, also of 1755 (fig. 6.5), there is a ploughman in the distance trundling his plough effortlessly through the soil, while in the foreground a young man gathering sticks has taken a few minutes off work to chat up a girl milking her cow upon the common[5] – she is interested or flustered enough to have taken her eye off the animal, who has just kicked over a full pail of milk. Work is always going on somewhere; everywhere there is evidence of work having been done, but there is always time to break off, to stretch, to look around, to make love, even to sleep.

Much of this is true of the extraordinary and anonymous picture of haymaking at Dixton Manor in Gloucestershire (fig. 6.6), painted around 1730 apparently by a local artist.[6] The painting uses the conventions of the panoramic battle-painting to display a wide meadow in which every process involved in the hay harvest is being carried on simultaneously. Left of centre the mowers are advancing in

Fig. 6.3 George Lambert, *A View of Boxhill, Surrey, with Dorking in the Distance*, 1733. Oil on canvas 89×134 cm.. Yale Center for British Art, Paul Mellon Collection.

crescent formation across the meadow, away from the viewer (fig. 6.7); to their right another group, mainly women, are 'tedding' the mown hay – turning it over with their rakes to help it dry in the sun (fig. 6.8). At various places in the meadow other groups are raking the tedded hay into haycocks, or loading it onto wagons – there are two wagons leaving the meadow fully laden, two in the process of being loaded, and a fifth has just returned empty having already discharged its load. In the shade of a distant hedge yet another group of haymakers is relaxing (fig. 6.7) – perhaps awaiting the arrival of two women approaching from the distance apparently with refreshments. The squire and two women members of the family are riding across the meadow to inspect the progress of the hay harvest. In the bottom right-hand corner, in a field which (as the ridge and furrow marks make clear) was formerly arable land but is now pasture, a group of morris men are dancing in their full regalia (fig. 6.8).

It is the simultaneity of the representation of all these different activities which relates this picture to the images of rural labour we have looked at by Hogarth, Lambert and Gainsborough. I do not mean just that mowing, tedding, making

Fig. 6.4 Thomas Gainsborough, *Peasant with two Horses*, 1755. Oil on canvas 92.1×102.2 cm. By kind permission of the Marquess of Tavistock, and the Trustees of the Bedford estates.

hay-cocks, loading and carting the hay are all taking place at the same time, but that the lunch-break is happening at the same time as well; and that the morris men, whose performance presumably celebrates the end of the hay harvest, are doing their dance when a good half of the work is still to be done. It is possible I suppose that their genial master has given them an hour off from the haymaking to practise their performance, but I don't think we need be too literal-minded about this: what matters is that work, rest and play are all represented together, as all part of a harmonious image of the work of the farm. Indeed, those morris men are quite crucial to the picture: without them the relations of labour and leisure in the picture might have been too unbalanced to be represented. They establish the genre of the picture as comic, and they establish Dixton Manor as a properly merry corner of Merry England.

The comic mode, however, could do more than just represent the life of the

Fig. 6.5 Thomas Gainsborough, *Landscape with a Woodcutter courting a Milkmaid*, 1755. Oil on canvas 106.7×128.2 cm. By kind permission of the Marquess of Tavistock, and the Trustees of the Bedford estates.

eighteenth-century farmworker as a balance of labour and leisure. Its peculiar alchemy was to convert labour itself into leisure, pain into pleasure. Here is the poet James Thomson's description of haymaking, from *The Seasons*, a long georgic poem which Thomson began in the mid 1720s and which he continued to revise until the mid 1740s.[7]

Now swarms the Village o'er the jovial Mead:
The rustic Youth, brown with meridian Toil,
Healthful, and strong; full as the Summer-Rose
Blown by prevailing Suns, the ruddy Maid,
Half naked, swelling on the Sight, and all   355
Her kindled Graces burning o'er her Cheek.
Even stooping Age is here; and Infant-Hands
Trail the long Rake, or, with the fragrant Load
O'ercharg'd, amid the kind Oppression roll.   360
Wide flies the tedded Grain; all in a Row
Advancing broad, or wheeling round the Field,

Fig. 6.6 Artist unknown, *Countryside around Dixton Manor, Gloucestershire, c.* 1725–35. Oil on canvas 113×287 cm. Cheltenham Art Gallery and Museums.

> They spread the breathing Harvest to the Sun,
> That throws refreshful round a rural Smell:
> Or, as they rake the green-appearing Ground,   365
> And drive the dusky Wave along the Mead,
> The russet Hay-cock rises thick behind,
> In order gay. While heard from Dale to Dale,
> Waking the Breeze, resounds the blended Voice
> Of happy Labour, Love, and social Glee.   370
>
>   James Thomson, *The Seasons*, 'Summer', lines 352–70

That this is to be a comic image of rural work is established straight away by the phrase 'jovial Mead'; it may be too much to claim that the villagers, prior to a day of back-breaking toil, are jovial, but no one will bother to deny that the meadow may be, and much the same might be said later in the passage about the haycock (lines 367–8), whose gaiety somehow rubs off onto the haymakers whether or not they feel gay themselves. The image of the 'ruddy Maid' – such descriptions of nubile women and girls stripped for action soon became *de rigeur* in representations of the hay harvest – continues this comic vein, making the same

association between haymaking and rustic sensuality that Hogarth makes in *Landscape with Farmworkers*. The comedy does not exactly conceal or deny the hard work involved in getting in the hay: it continually acknowledges the strength necessary to the task, the energy and activity of the haymakers, but it still manages to suggest that the labour of haymaking is all 'happy Labour'. It does this partly by emphasising the sharing of work, the communal and therefore festive atmosphere: 'social Glee'. All the village is involved; and so the fact that the aged are obliged to spend the day painfully 'stooping' to their tasks is offered as an instance of happy labour. The children, similarly, may be tasked beyond their strength – but because a load of hay, however heavy, is never dangerously so, the 'kind Oppression' of their burdens seems to wish away the less genial oppression which requires their day-long presence in the meadow. In this picture, especially, of children rolling and laughing in the hay, labour loses all its arduousness, and the relation of master and servant all its coercion.

The alchemy of the comic is rather less effective, however, in Thomson's description of the corn harvest.

Fig. 6.7 Detail of left hand side of fig. 6.6.

Soon as the Morning trembles o'er the Sky,
And, unperceiv'd, unfolds the spreading Day;
Before the ripen'd Field the Reapers stand,
In fair Array; each by the Lass he loves,
To bear the rougher Part, and mitigate   155
By nameless gentle Offices her Toil.
At once they stoop and swell the lusty Sheaves;
While thro' their chearful Band the rural Talk,
The rural Scandal and the rural Jest
Fly harmless, to deceive the tedious Time,   160
And steal unfelt the sultry Hours away.
Behind the Master walks, builds up the Shocks;
And, conscious, glancing oft on every Side
His sated Eye, feels his Heart heave with Joy.
The Gleaners spread around, and here and there,   165
Spike after Spike, their sparing Harvest pick.
Be not too narrow, Husbandmen! but fling,
From the full Sheaf, with charitable Stealth,
The liberal Handful. Think, oh grateful think!

Fig. 6.8 Detail of right hand side of fig. 6.6

> How good the GOD of HARVEST is to you;   170
> Who pours Abundance o'er your flowing Fields;
> While these unhappy Partners of your Kind
> Wide-hover round you, like the Fowls of Heaven,
> And ask their humble Dole. The various Turns
> Of Fortune ponder; that your Sons may want   175
> What now, with hard Reluctance, faint, ye give.
>
> James Thomson, *The Seasons*, 'Autumn', lines 151–76

In this delightful fantasy of agricultural work, all the reapers are sorted into courting couples, an arrangement equally conducive to love and labour: the man reaps the corn, the 'Lass he loves' binds the 'lusty Sheaves' – once again the comic adjective is transferred to an inanimate object. Nothing could exemplify the alchemy of the comic more clearly than the lines which describe the conversation of this 'chearful Band': the long day's labour is indeed tedious, these lines acknowledge, and the weather is indeed sultry; but the magical effect of the rural talk, jest and scandal ensures that what would otherwise have been felt as arduous and exhausting is not felt at all. The master follows his reapers across the field, building the sheaves into stooks, and rubbing his hands at the thought of how the harvest will cram his barns to overflowing. His interests may not be precisely the same as the reapers', but all are joyful, one way or another, and so far this seems another perfect image of 'social Glee', of the perfectly harmonious relations of master and servant.

Enter the gleaners, who are compared with 'the Fowls of Heaven' in such a way as seems to naturalise their appearance in the harvest-field, as if they follow the reaping-hook as surely as the seagull follows the plough. The husbandmen – Thomson uses the word, here as elsewhere, to mean farmworkers, or those at any rate in a subordinate position to an agricultural employer – are now urgently enjoined not to be selfish; they should consider the interests of others as well as themselves, and with 'charitable Stealth' should leave 'the liberal Handful' to be picked up by the gleaners. This injunction is extraordinary, and in the lengths to which it goes to preserve the illusion of a common interest uniting the master and his employees it has the effect of entirely subverting that illusion. For gleaners of course are not birds, they are 'the unhappy Partners' of the human race, the relations no doubt – parents, children – of the loving couples who are doing the work of reaping. It is not the 'husbandmen' therefore who need to be reminded of the need to leave something for the gleaners, it is the master: and it is his greedy anticipation of plenty which necessitates the 'charitable Stealth' of the reapers. A very different picture of the harvest is beginning to show through this jovial comic georgic: a picture of reapers attempting to leave as much corn as possible to be collected by the gleaners, and between the two the master, not sure which way to look, at the stealthy reapers or the pouncing gleaners, not certain whether to be delighted at the abundance of the harvest, or angry at the amount that is eluding his grasp.

This point is made much better than I can make it by Stephen Duck, a Wiltshire farmworker who in his poem 'The Thresher's Labour' (1736) chose to imitate Thomson's description of the corn harvest so as to reveal this other, subversive picture of the relations of master and servant. This is from Duck's account of the corn harvest:[8]

> The Morning past, we sweat beneath the Sun:
> And but uneasily our Work goes on.
> Before us we perplexing Thistles find,   240
> And Corn blown adverse with the ruffling Wind.
> Behind our Master waits; and if he spies
> One charitable Ear, he grudging cries,
> 'Ye scatter half your Wages o'er the Land.'
> Then scrapes the Stubble with his Greedy Hand.   245
>
> Stephen Duck, 'The Thresher's Labour', lines 238–45

For Duck, who has practical experience of reaping, the harvest is not quite the jolly occasion it is for Thomson; the tedious hours, the sultry heat, are not at all 'unfelt', and are made still harder to bear by small irritations that found no place in Thomson's poem: thistles that sting the hand and entangle the reaping hook, wind that blows the corn away from the hook. 'Behind the Master walks', wrote Thomson; 'Behind our Master waits', writes Duck, and the change of verb catches exactly the suspicious look of the Master, anxious to prevent his employees from performing exactly that act of surreptitious charity which Thomson's reapers for some reason had to be persuaded to perform. In his description of the hay harvest, Duck begins by acknowledging the spirit of jovial and eager emulation with which the mowers approach their task, which makes labour a game, a sport; he points out also, however, the futility of such an attitude to work. 'At first our Labour seems a sportive Race', he writes (line 115):

> But when the scorching Sun is mounted high,
> And no kind Barns with friendly Shade are nigh;
> Our weary Scythes entangle in the Grass,
> While Streams of Sweat run trickling down apace.
> Our sportive Labour we too late lament;
> And wish that Strength again, we vainly spent.
>
> Stephen Duck, 'The Thresher's Labour', lines 120–5

Duck, like Thomson, saw only what he wanted to see in the hay and the corn harvests, and like Thomson there was much that remained invisible to him. At one point in his account of haymaking he writes that one day the grass is mowed, and 'Next Day the Cocks appear in equal Rows' (line 202). Mary Collier, the author of a poem entitled 'The Woman's Labour', a sequel and a rejoinder to 'The Thresher's Labour', points out what Hogarth and Thomson had noticed but Duck had not, that the hay-cocks had not simply made themselves:[9] after describing a group of women haymakers at their mid-day meal, taken in the meadow, she writes:

> ... soon we must get up again,
> And nimbly turn our Hay upon the Plain;
> Nay, rake and prow it in, the Case is clear;
> Or how should Cocks in equal Rows appear?
>
> Mary Collier, 'The Woman's Labour', lines 59–62

Whatever his blind-spots, however, and this is only one example of his inability to notice women's work, Duck's contribution to the representation of the eighteenth-century farmworker is a crucial one. At the end of the century, the comic representation of rural life developed by John Gay, James Thomson, Thomas Gainsborough and others may well have become a good deal more attractive to the workers in agriculture than the alternative we have already glanced at, the dignified, mild-mannered, sober and disciplined workforce represented in Stubbs' version of haymaking. 'The Thresher's Labour', however, took on that comic representation at every point, and repeatedly showed it up as at best wishful thinking on the behalf of the polite classes, at worst as a 'Cheat', an instance of how the exploited can imbibe the ideology of their exploiters.[10]

It was a lesson he came to stand as much in need of as Thomson himself. Duck's poetry attracted the attention of some well-connected friends, and in no time he found himself translated to London and a favourite of Queen Caroline. In one of his later poems he wrote about mowing once again, in a passage which shows him to have forgotten all that he had once tried to teach Thomson. He describes himself as on a trip back to his birthplace, Great Charlton in Wiltshire, when he comes across a scene of haymaking. He cannot wait to join in.

> Breakfast soon o'er, we trace the verdant Field,
> Where sharpening Scythes the lab'ring Mowers wield:
> Straight Emulation glows in ev'ry Vein;
> I long to try the curvous Blade again . . .   40
> So with Ambition burns my daring Breast;
> I snatch the Scythe, and with the Swains contest;
> Behind 'em close, I rush the sweeping Steel;
> The vanquish'd Mowers soon confess my Skill.   50
>   Not long at this laborious Sport I stay;
> But, with my friend, to *Charlton* take my Way . . .
>
> Stephen Duck, 'A Description of a Journey To Marlborough, Bath, Portsmouth, etc.' lines 37–40, 47–52

As Duck candidly acknowledges, he did not engage long in this futile competition, and it is perhaps not surprising therefore that he emerged the victor. The other mowers knew, no doubt, that mowing was neither 'laborious Sport' nor 'sportive Labour', but hard work, and that they would need to spare their strength in the morning if they were to get through the afternoon. Perhaps they had read and remembered 'The Thresher's Labour'; Duck had forgotten it.

Displacements and disappearances

I have argued that the representation of rural work as 'sportive Labour' was the inevitable result of the use of the comic mode in an attempt to produce a more credible, a more English image of the farmworker and of rural life in general. But as it became more and more possible to recognise the rustic clowns who appeared in painting and poetry as the inhabitants of a contemporary English, not an ancient Mediterranean landscape, so the comic image of the vulgar became less reassuring, more troublesome to the polite. It had the advantage that it could disguise labour as leisure and the exploitation of labour as the pursuit of a common interest, but in the process of doing so it necessarily produced an image of rural life which attributed to the rural worker a good deal more leisure than was good for them – or than was good for their employers. There was an increasing concentration on the importance of work-discipline as the century got older; the new discourse of political economy increasingly saw those employed in industry and agriculture in the character simply of producers; and anything which did not conform with that character was taken to subvert it. The image of a rollicking, amorous and drunken peasantry was certainly not good for work-discipline; and this image was conscientiously expelled from the representation of the rural worker in the poetry and painting of the last decades of the eighteenth century.

The more comic, and therefore the more apparently realistic the image of rural life became, the more leisure the farmworker appeared to enjoy, and the more subversive of good order that leisure seemed to be. The danger, however, which was attributed to the leisure of the rural poor, must be understood in relation also to the increasing problem that was believed to be posed by rural poverty in the late eighteenth century. Whether or not, as some eighteenth-century commentators believed and some modern historians have also argued,[11] the rural poor did indeed get poorer in the period from, say, the 1730s through to the 1780s, there was certainly a new awareness of the problem of rural poverty, of how to support the large workforce necessary at harvest-time but an embarrassment to their employers for much of the rest of the year. As the result of a wide range of economic developments, of which enclosure in its various forms is only the most famous, the workers in agriculture were increasingly becoming a landless proletariat, without the resources to support themselves when not in employment, and therefore more regularly dependent on the support of the parish. And the increasing sense of the poor farmworker as a problem, as a social, economic and political problem, was exacerbated by the fear that always attends the creation of a proletariat: a fear of the mass power of a working class with little to gain by good behaviour. This fear of the poor in general, as a class, whether rural or urban, is already beginning to be apparent in the decades before it was so much aggravated in the years after the French Revolution.

All these anxieties among the polite – a concern over work-discipline, over law and order, over poor-rates – exerted a pressure on the workers in agriculture to reconceive of their lives. It became particularly important to persuade the poor to identify themselves as the members, first and foremost, of their own little platoon, their own family unit, and not to think of themselves as members of a common class, with grievances in common and even with a common perception of possible remedies. To persuade the male farmworker to think of himself primarily or exclusively as the family breadwinner had two obvious advantages as far as the interests of the polite were concerned. It would encourage him to work harder, to secure the well-being of his family and to ensure that they were as little

Fig. 6.9 Thomas Gainsborough, *The Harvest Wagon*, 1767. Oil on canvas
120.7×144.8 cm. The Barber Institute of Fine Arts, Birmingham.

dependent as possible on the support of the parish; and it would encourage him
to conceive of his primary duties as domestic duties, directed to the betterment of
his family and not of his class.

There was no place for the comic in this more dutiful image of rural life; and we
can get an idea of how thoroughly it was expelled by comparing two paintings by
Gainsborough of the same subject, a wagon full of rural workers which has
stopped in a country lane to give a woman a lift. Both paintings have come to be
called *The Harvest Wagon*; the first was painted in 1767 (fig. 6.9), the second in
1784–85 (fig. 6.10). In the first, two clowns are struggling for possession of a bottle
of beer or cider; they are sharing the cart with two slightly dishevelled and
décolleté women, apparently their girlfriends, and with a third man who with little
care or ceremony is hauling another woman into the cart. Such a cheerfully comic
image may already have looked a little too vulgar by 1767, and the picture

Fig. 6.10 Thomas Gainsborough, *The Harvest Wagon, c.* 1784. Oil on canvas 121.9×149.9 cm. Art Gallery of Ontario, Toronto. Gift of Mr and Mrs Frank P. Wood.

remained unsold. The second version, however, was as successful as a painting could be; it was bought by the Prince of Wales himself. It was also much more in tune with the new attitudes to the representation of rural life. The brawling clowns have disappeared, and the nubile women have been provided with bonnets to keep their hair in place, and with babies to certify their matrimonial status; this painting is evidently intended for family viewing. The only remaining man is no clown but a proper gent, polygamous perhaps but with perfect manners; he is helping the standing woman into the cart with the greatest possible concern for her comfort.

The worker in agriculture appears as still more thoroughly subdued in a sequence of four paintings by Francis Wheatley, painted in 1799, and entitled *Four Times of Day (Rustic Hours)*. These paintings offer a transparently prescriptive image of rural life: the aim is no longer to show the poor as they are, but as

Fig. 6.11 Francis Wheatley, *Morning*, 1799. Oil on canvas 44.5×54.5 cm. Yale Center for British Art, Paul Mellon Collection.

they ought to be, industrious, sober, glumly cheerful. In the first painting, *Morning* (fig. 6.11), a father stands outside his cottage door, staring dutifully towards the middle distance, his place of work. He too is apparently polygamous; women in these pictures represent dependants as well as housewives, and so the more women a man is shown to be supporting, the more virtuous he is presumed to be. His womenfolk, demurely pretty, have come out to see him off; his children attempt vainly to detain him at home – 'Must you really go, papa?' In the next picture, *Noon* (fig. 6.12), the ages of the family have altered, but their virtue is as bright as ever, for rather than eat their lunch with the other harvesters who have presumably been reaping this field, our family sits solemnly apart, and identifies itself by its separation from the other members of the community. The third painting, *Evening* (fig. 6.13), shows the farmworker's wife (or one of them)

Fig. 6.12 Francis Wheatley, *Noon*, 1799. Oil on canvas 44.5×54.5 cm. Yale Center for British Art, Paul Mellon Collection.

working distractedly at her churn, while all her thoughts are for her husband, soon to return home after an exhausting day's labour; the children too are contributing their mite of labour to the family economy, and the other woman, whoever she is, has spent the afternoon washing, assisted by a third child of uncertain maternity. The sequence closes with *Night* (fig. 6.14); the wives are putting the weary children to bed, while their husband, thoroughly knocked up, has fallen asleep at the table, too tired to eat his frugal and well-earned crust. The painting invites our sympathy as well as our moral approbation, but it can invite the first only because it also invites the second. We feel sorry for the man, exhausted as he is, but if he had returned from work with energy to spare we would hardly believe that he had done his best for his wives and children.

These late paintings by Gainsborough and Wheatley are evidently images of

Fig. 6.13 Francis Wheatley, *Evening*, 1799. Oil on canvas 44.5×54.5 cm. Yale Center for British Art, Paul Mellon Collection.

the good poor, domesticated, sober, industrious. Except for *Evening*, however, they are not images of work, and none of them depict the work of the fields. In this they seem to me to be typical of the painting of rural life in the last decades of the century; and though it is certainly possible to find images of agricultural work from this period – we have already looked at one by Stubbs – there was very evidently a problem in representing arduous manual labour when it was no longer possible to deploy the resources of the comic mode. If labour could no longer be shown as happy, as sportive, how could it be shown? The image of wage-labourers, of a rural proletariat, selflessly and irremissively engaged in the back-breaking work of the fields was everywhere hinted at in paintings of farmworkers, but was very hard to represent, if the duty of the poor to labour

Fig. 6.14 Francis Wheatley, *Night*, 1799. Oil on canvas 44.5×54.5 cm. Yale Center for British Art, Paul Mellon Collection.

was successfully to be recommended to the polite and vulgar alike. That duty is usually represented, therefore, by its effects – a large family, a neat cottage – or as something which is about to be begun or has just been finished. Stubbs' solution, to represent agricultural labour as something between dancing and sleepwalking, is a response to the problem posed by the abandonment of the comic image of the poor, but it is not a typical response or one that was much imitated.

A similar problem afflicts the poetry, too, of the last decades of the century. Here for example are some passages from *The Favourite Village* (1800) by the popular poet of rural life the Rev. James Hurdis.[12] The first describes the hay harvest:

> My native vale, in loveliness array'd,
> Now let me paint thee, while the mower's scythe
> Thine herbage levels, harvest first conferr'd
> And least solicited, spontaneous gift,
> Abundance for the beast that toils for man.   315
> Thick swarms the field with tedders, tossing high
> And spreading thin upon the sunny sward
> The lock dishevell'd. Frequent is the maid
> That trails the rake, and he that builds the cock,
> Or, plunging deep his fork in every hill,   320
> Bears it aloft uplifted to the load.
> The team alternate to the peopled rick
> Moves in procession, soon reliev'd, and soon
> Alert returning to be fraught anew.

James Hurdis, *The Favourite Village*, Book 1, lines 311–24

Like the painting of Dixton Manor, this brief paragraph manages to include all the different operations involved in the hay harvest: mowing, tedding, raking the hay into piles, building the haycocks, loading the hay onto the wagon, carting it away to the rick, and returning to the meadow with the empty wagon. Like the painting of the hay harvest by Stubbs, however, it does this without any help from the comic muse: perhaps the only remnant of the comic is the phrase 'The lock dishevell'd', which in Thomson's account might have described the appearance of a young village lass, but in Hurdis' poem refers to the hay itself, spread out to dry on the ground. Obviously enough, Hurdis has got Thomson's description open on his desk, or well in the front of his mind, as he writes these lines. The opening line of Thomson's description, 'Now swarms the Village o'er the jovial Mead', has its (now no longer jovial) equivalent in Hurdis' 'Thick swarms the field with tedders'. But as the passage continues, the comic energy of Thomson's haymakers becomes a more and more distant memory, to be replaced by something altogether more orderly and disciplined. This is evident especially in the last three lines, describing the teams of horses and their wagons as they move 'in procession' from rick to meadow and back again: they work, rather as Stubbs' haymakers do, with an aesthetic discipline which seems to stand in for, to be the displaced representation of, the work-discipline which had come to be more and more insisted upon in the late eighteenth century.

In his description of ploughing, Hurdis exemplifies another solution to the problem of representing the wage-labourer: that is, to represent the work, its effects and circumstances, but to keep the worker out of sight:

> Now moves again, but with a sluggard's pace,
> Not well awake, the plough. The harness'd team
> Moves slowly forward, and not seldom stays,   215
> Impeded sore by congregated clods.
> The rooky tribe attend, and, perch'd at hand,

Watch the moist furrow with superior eye,
And brisk alight, upon the worm to prey,
Or sweeter grub unhous'd. Frequently there   220
Loiters, a grey-coat pensioner, the mew,
(His treasury the main left far behind,)
And shares the spoil terrene, with outstretch'd wing
The ploughman's clodded heal pursuing close,
And settling timorous. At length arrives   225
The hour of rest long look'd for, and the team
Of wearied steers, from the bright share releas'd,
Leave in the midst of the fresh field upturn'd
The plough recumbent, and with hurried pace
March cheerful homeward. Expedition clanks   230
The heavy chain which knits them pair to pair,
And oft the forward ox, impatient, drags
The lingerer behind, his brawny neck
Straining with pressure of the cumbrous yoke.

  James Hurdis, *The Favourite Village*, Book IV, lines 213–34

The whole operation of ploughing is here described with no reference at all to the
ploughman, except for the brief glimpse of his mud-covered heel in line 224. The
arduousness of the ploughman's task, as he guides and steadies the share through
this damp, heavy, clinging soil, is entirely displaced onto the oxen that pull the
plough. The 'hour of rest' is 'long look'd for' not by him but only by his 'team of
wearied steers'. When day is over, the oxen are uncoupled from the plough and it
is only they who experience the joy of release from labour. The plough is left
'recumbent' in the field, another image of relaxation displaced from the ploughman, who can be left invisible precisely because of this sequence of displacements.
  One final passage from Hurdis, this time his description of the corn harvest:

    Let Summer 'gin decline, yet pleasure still
  Shall with the poet dwell. Be the field brown:
  No longer now stand smilingly erect
  The bearded ear, or spike of nobler grain,
  But, sear alike, droop both, and hang the head,   5
  And stoop the shoulder, to their annual toil
  The keen hook calling and voracious scythe.
  How groans the soil with its incumbent load!
  Lo! in my native vale the reaper's hand
  Gathers the fruitful ear and binds the sheaf,   10
  Betimes industrious, nor its endless task
  Quits till the moon above the shadowy down
  Lifts her bright orb to light him to repose.
  Let morning dawn, and ev'ry village-team
  Comes forth to bear, or to the rick, or grange,   15
  The shocks of plenty in arrangement meet
  Along the bristly stubble-field dispos'd.

All hands are busy, and one common spring
Of lively int'rest actuates the scene.

James Hurdis, *The Favourite Village*, Book II, lines 1–19

As in the description of ploughing, a great deal is disclosed here about the arduousness of reapers' tasks, though they themselves remain almost invisible. Look for example at line 6, 'And stoop the shoulder, to their annual toil'; by itself, it reads like an account of the bending action of harvesters who are reaping with a hook, and so in a sense it is, though once again the arduousness of farmwork has been displaced, improbably enough this time, to the wheat and barley. It is they who 'droop … and hang the head'; it is they who 'stoop the shoulder', as a summons to the 'annual toil' of the harvest. The summons is directed not at the reapers but at their tools; this 'annual toil' is to be performed by 'the keen hook and voracious scythe', wielded, it turns out, by a single disembodied hand, which is all that is visible of the reapers themselves. The 'reaper's hand' is the autumn equivalent of the ploughman's heel: so anxious is this passage to keep the rest of the reaper's body out of sight that it is the hand, not the reaper, that is 'Betimes industrious' – out of bed early and hard at work – and it is the hand again that refuses to quit 'its endless task' before the moon has risen. At the end of the passage, this solitary hand is finally allowed to participate in the society of the village – it joins up with the other 'hands' busy with the harvest – but it is never permitted to rejoin the body from which it has been severed.

James Hurdis' friend William Cowper provides us with one more solution to the problem of representing the labour of the proletarianised farmworker, or rather of not representing it. In a passage from the first book of *The Task* (1785), Cowper describes a view in the countryside around the town of Olney in Buckinghamshire, his home when he was writing the poem.

How oft upon yon eminence, our pace
Has slacken'd to a pause, …
While admiration feeding at the eye,
And still unsated, dwelt upon the scene.
Thence with what pleasure have we just discern'd
The distant plough slow-moving, and beside   160
His lab'ring team that swerv'd not from the track,
The sturdy swain diminish'd to a boy!

William Cowper, *The Task*, Book I, 'The Sofa', lines 154–5, 157–62

What exactly is the pleasure involved in seeing the ploughman and his team? Is it the pleasure of making out a reassuringly familiar and almost invisible object in the far distance? Or is it the pleasure of only just being able to make out an object which is almost reassuringly invisible? It seems to be the second: that is, the pleasure in the passage seems to be focussed on a figure which is out of focus, the 'sturdy' ploughman reassuringly shorn of his strength, no more threatening, at this distance, than a child. Passages which offer a similar reassurance abound in the poetry of rural life in the period from the 1780s or so to about 1820. Here, for example, is Wordsworth in 1805, who has chosen to describe a fair in the Lake District from the security of the distant summit of Helvellyn:

> How little They, they and their doings seem
> Their herds and flocks about them, they themselves,
> And all that they can further or obstruct!
> Through utter weakness pitiably dear
> As tender infants are . . .
>
> William Wordsworth, *The Prelude* (1805), Book VIII, lines 50–54

The heart goes out to these tiny people just because they are tiny: because, seen from this distance, they appear so reassuringly powerless. They can 'further' nothing, they can 'obstruct' nothing. In a similar way, in the paintings of Constable, the farmworkers are often either invisible, their presence in the countryside to be inferred only from the effects of their labour, or else they are minute and distant, diminished into children, or into specks of white in the far background. It is by means like these that the fear of the political power of a working class in the making was both manifested and managed, in the painting as well as in the poetry of rural life.

NOTES

1   This chapter is a summary of a part of the argument of my book *The Dark Side of the Landscape: the Rural Poor in English Painting 1730–1840* (Cambridge 1980); it is offered here not as an original piece of work, though it does discuss some works of art and literature that I have not discussed before in print. As well as the other sources referred to below, the following works address issues similar to those addressed in this essay: John Barrell, 'The Golden Age of Labour', in Sue Clifford, Angela King, Richard Mabey (eds.) *Second Nature* (1984); John Barrell, 'The Private Comedy of Thomas Rowlandson', *Art History* 6 (4) (December 1983); Ann Bermingham, *Landscape and Ideology: The English Rustic Tradition, 1740–1860* (1987); Stephen Daniels, 'The implications of industry: Turner and Leeds', in *Turner Studies* 6 (1) (1986); Richard Feingold, *Nature and Society: Later Eighteenth-Century Uses of the Pastoral and Georgic* (Hassocks, Sussex 1978); Louis Hawes, *Presences of Nature: British Landscape 1780–1830* (New Haven 1982), especially chapter 5, 'Landscapes with laborers'; Ronald Paulson, *Literary Landscape: Turner and Constable* (New Haven and London 1982); Leslie Parris, *Landscape in Britain* (1973); Alex Potts and Neil McWilliam, 'The landscape of reaction: Richard Wilson and his critics', *History Workshop Journal* 16 (Autumn 1983); Michael Rosenthal, *Constable, The Painter and his Landscape* (New Haven and London 1983); Michael Rosenthal, 'Approaches to landscape painting', *Landscape Research* 9 (3) (Winter 1984); David Simpson, *Wordsworth's Historical Imagination* (1987); David Solkin, *Richard Wilson: The Landscape of Reaction* (1982); David Solkin, 'The battle of the books: or, the gentleman provok'd – different views on the history of British art', in

The Art Bulletin 67 (3) (September 1985); Donna Landry, *The Muses of Resistance. Laboring-Class Women's Poetry in Britain 1739–1796* (1990).

2 For pastoral and georgic in eighteenth-century poetry and literary theory, see J. E. Congleton, *Theories of Pastoral Poetry in England 1684–1798* (New York 1968) and John Chalker, *The English Georgic: A Study in the Development of a Form* (1969).

3 Any account of 'national identity' in Britain or England, especially in the eighteenth century after the Act of Union had pronounced England and Scotland to be one kingdom, quickly runs into the problem of where to use 'British' and where 'English'. On each occasion when I have to make a choice, I have done my best to use what seems to me the more appropriate of the two terms, but my choices are certainly open to be disputed.

4 For full accounts of what was at issue in eighteenth-century responses to *The Shepherd's Week*, see J. F. Congleton, *Theories of Pastoral Poetry*; William D. Ellis, Jnr, 'Thomas D'Urfey, the Pope-Philips Quarrel, and *The Shepherd's Week*', *Publications of the Modern Language Association* 74 (1959); and Adina Forsgren, *John Gay, Poet 'Of a Lower Order'* (Stockholm 1964).

5 I owe the point that Gainsborough's painting represents the meeting-point of enclosed arable land and common land to Julian Gardner: see Michael Rosenthal, *British Landscape Painting* (Oxford 1982), 32. Chapters 2, 3 and 4 of Rosenthal's book deal with issues similar to those discussed in this essay.

6 For an account of this painting, and for more reproductions of its detail, see John Harris, *The Artist and the Country House: A History of Country House and Garden View Painting in Britain 1540–1870* (1979) 248–9, fig. 291b, and colour plate XXIV.

7 All quotations from *The Seasons* are taken from the edition of James Sambrook, (Oxford, Clarendon Press 1981).

8 All quotations from Stephen Duck are taken from his *Poems on Several Occasions* (1736), reprinted in facsimile (Menston, Scolar Press 1973).

9 I owe this point to Donna Landry's essay, 'The resignation of Mary Collier: some problems in feminist literary history', in Felicity Nussbaum and Laura Brown (eds.), *The New 18th Century* (New York and London 1987). Quotations from Mary Collier are taken from a volume entitled *Stephen Duck, 'The Thresher's Labour', and Mary Collier, 'The Woman's Labour'*, eds E. P. Thompson and Mary Sugden, intro. E. P. Thompson (1989).

10 For more on how the comic pastoral was succeeded by a more solemn version of pastoral, and for the suggestion that the comic may have come to seem the preferable version to the rural poor in the decades around 1800, see Barrell, *The Dark Side of the Landscape*, 72–88. For Duck on the jollity of master to servant as a 'Cheat', see 'The Thresher's Labour', line 277, and Raymond Williams, *The Country and the City* (1975) 32, 87–90. Williams' book is of course the indispensable commentary on the poetry of rural life in this period.

11 For a recent endorsement of this view, see K. D. M. Snell, *Annals of the Labouring Poor: Social Change and Agrarian England 1660–1900* (Cambridge 1985) chapters 1, 3 and 4.

12 All quotations from James Hurdis are taken from *The Favourite Village, with an Additional Poem, (now first published) and a Tragedy* (1810).

Images of the rural in popular culture
1750–1990

STUART LAING

Introduction

Why images? Why not, in discussing rural life, go straight to the reality piercing through the deceptions and simplifications of inevitably distorting images? An affirmative answer might seem even more obviously required when discussing images drawn from *popular* culture where the imperatives of myth, fantasy and ideology will surely over-ride what, in serious art, might be presumed to be at least an authentic attempt at truth-telling.

Reality, however, is not so simple; the images we hold, individually and collectively, of any particular aspect of social life are themselves already part of that whole historical process requiring examination. What people think and feel about their lives and surroundings, how they *experience*, and orient themselves towards, the objective conditions of their existence – these are indispensable concerns within such an analysis. Such experience is, moreover, not a matter of direct and unmediated encounters between individuals and the material world, but rather of the construction of meanings through language and symbol, through the available stories and images circulating within their culture. Further, in the spheres of both individual action and collective social policy and endeavour, it will be the resulting perceptions, perspectives and ideas which (irrespective of whether they are 'correct' or not) decisively inform the way in which people attempt to make their own history. Whether considering the building of medieval village churches, eighteenth-century evictions and landscaping, the formation of nineteenth-century farm labourers' unions or the beginnings of the Council for the Preservation of Rural England, no account of rural change can be complete without an understanding of the ideas, hopes and beliefs informing the actions of those supporting (or, indeed, opposing) such changes.

The study of popular cultural images is only one aspect of this much broader terrain and one which generates its own particular questions and concerns. Such images are typically set in a quite specific communication context and constructed within particular media and genres containing their own technical requirements and formal conventions – a poem written to a known formula, a song sung to a particular local audience, a radio programme produced within a specific

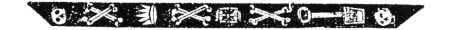

AN

ELEGY

Mr Gray WROTE IN A of Peterhouse

Country Church Yard.

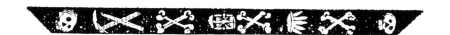

LONDON:

Printed for R. DODSLEY in *Pall-mall*;

And sold by M. COOPER in *Pater-noster-Row.* 1751.

[Price Six-pence.]

Fig. 7.1 Thomas Gray's 'Elegy'. The first edition, from a copy of 1751. Note the incorporation of *memento mori*. (Augustan Reprint Society, 31, 1951.)

institutional context. The images inscribed in such 'texts' are not spontaneous and free-floating; they are produced with a particular purpose. Equally, however, as they enter a whole culture and as they outlive their initial intentions, they may take on broader or different meanings. In particular, as regards the cultural products to be discussed here, they enter that general realm of the mythology of the rural which, especially since the early Victorian period, has become such a central part of the very idea of England and Englishness itself. In its contemporary form this is constituted as the belief that, 'somewhere . . . at the far end of the M4 or the A12 there are "real" country folk living in the midst of "real" English countryside in – that most elusive of all rustic Utopias – "real communities"'.[1] All three texts considered below (an eighteenth-century poem, a nineteenth-century song and a twentieth-century radio programme) have clear, but variable, connections with this pattern of belief and their comparative analysis demonstrates the significant continuities and the potential for alternative ways of seeing which have existed within popular cultural images of rural life since 1750.

Gray's 'Elegy': 1750

Gray's 'Elegy written in a Country Churchyard' is a poem whose origins suggest a social milieu quite opposed to anything usually implied by the term 'popular culture'. Its composition was begun by Gray sometime in the 1740s and completed in June 1750. Gray was then 34 and had settled for some years to the life of a scholar (with moderate, but sufficient, independent means) at Cambridge, often spending some months each year at his mother's house in the village of Stoke Poges in Buckinghamshire. The 'Elegy', although originally written for private circulation, created sufficient interest for Gray himself to sanction a public edition in 1751 when he learned of its imminent unauthorised publication in a magazine (fig. 7.1).

The poem itself draws heavily in its form and diction on classical and English literary precedent as well as on Gray's personal experience and philosophy; incorporated within its general meditation on the levelling effects of the grave on rich and poor alike is a distinctive image of English rural life, especially contained in the opening nine stanzas:

> The Curfew tolls the knell of parting day,
> The lowing herd winds slowly o'er the lea,
> The plowman homeward plods his weary way,
> And leaves the world to darkness and to me.
>
> Now fades the glimmering landscape on the sight,
> And all the air a solemn stillness holds,
> Save where the beetle wheels his droning flight,
> And drowsy tinklings lull the distant folds;

Save that from yonder ivy-mantled tow'r
The mopeing owl does to the moon complain
Of such, as wand'ring near her secret bow'r,
Molest her ancient solitary reign.

Beneath those rugged elms, that yew-tree's shade,
Where heaves the turf in many a mould'ring heap,
Each in his narrow cell for ever laid,
The rude Forefathers of the hamlet sleep.

The breezy call of incense-breathing Morn.
The swallow twitt'ring from the straw-built shed,
The cock's shrill clarion, or the echoing horn,
No more shall rouse them from their lowly bed.

For them no more the blazing hearth shall burn,
Or busy housewife ply her evening care:
No children run to lisp their sire's return,
Or climb his knees the envied kiss to share.

Oft did the harvest to their sickle yield,
Their furrow oft the stubborn glebe has broke;
How jocund did they drive their team afield!
How bow'd the woods beneath their sturdy stroke!

Let not Ambition mock their useful toil,
Their homely joys, and destiny obscure;
Nor grandeur hear with a disdainful smile,
The short and simple annals of the poor.

The boast of heraldry, the pomp of pow'r,
And all that beauty, all that wealth e'er gave,
Awaits alike th'inevitable hour.
The paths of glory lead but to the grave.

This version of village life, called into being from the gradually darkening
landscape by the voice of the meditating poet, has a number of distinctive
features. There is, firstly, an unproblematic integration of nature and agriculture;
the two become part of a single composition. Cattle, sheep ('drowsy tinklings'),
cockerels, owls and swallows are all equally placed within a world under
immediate human control, but one in which the pace of movement and the forms
of action are set by apparently natural regular rhythms (the slow winding,
plodding and fading of the opening or the more lively daily and yearly
agricultural round). It is above all a world from which the possibility of historical
development has been evacuated; the present 'plowman' and the 'lowing herd'
clearly belong to the same social moment as the past generations of his forebears.
The ploughing and harvesting (part of an annual cycle of repetition) suggest a
static community at the centre of which is a pure instance of the domestic division
of labour. The man returns to the home each day to the world of the 'housewife'

and children, from a joyous subjugation of nature to his own little kingdom of relaxation.

As the poem progresses the value of the villagers' lives ('useful toil') is measured against their lack of opportunity to enter the world of individual achievement, political ('some Cromwell guiltness') or intellectual ('some mute inglorious Milton'). Here the various conditions of poverty, rural isolation and low social status become conflated into a, not unattractive, single 'cool sequestr'd vale of life'. The poem as a whole, however, offers a point of identification not with the villagers themselves, but rather with the detached observer of the 'landscape', the melancholy poet who watches, meditates and judges, but does not participate and for whom (as one recent commentator rather sharply remarked), 'pensive country walks are the labour of the day rather than weary ploughing'.[2]

The poem's overall philosophical tone and perspective then rely heavily on this construction of an essentially timeless rural world of apparently self-sufficient agricultural producers locked in an unbroken cycle of daily routine, of ploughing and harvesting, of life and death. Such an image is powerful and attractive, but is worth contrasting with some of the broader social patterns emerging in the English countryside around 1750 – a date taken by Eric Hobsbawm in *Industry and Empire* as the starting point for his account of modern British economic history:

by 1750 the characteristic structure of English landownership was already discernible: a few thousand land-owners leasing out their land to some tens of thousands of tenant-farmers, who in turn operated it with the labour of some hundreds of thousands of farm-labourers, servants or dwarf-holders who hired themselves out for much of their time . . . And what is more, a good deal, or perhaps most of the industries and manufactures of Britain were rural, a typical worker being sometimes an artisan or small holder in his cottage increasingly specialising in the manufacture of some product – mainly cloth, hosiery, and a variety of metal goods – and thus by degrees turning from small peasant or craftsman into wage-labourer.[3]

A more detailed study of eighteenth-century social life and labour by Malcolmson also points to the importance of changing social relations within rural communities:

One sees, then, a long-term erosion of subsistence-oriented local economies in which use-rights played a vital role. And as these rights were lost, and the possibilities for a moderate degree of self-sufficiency (or 'independence') were steadily reduced, country people inescapably became more dependent for their livelihoods on wage-labour. Self-employment diminished in importance and money-wages from employers increasingly became virtually the sole determinant of a plebeian household's material sustenance.[4]

Gray's 'Elegy' was not of course offered as a direct account of contemporary rural life (as compared to such late Augustan poems as Goldsmith's 'The Deserted

Village' or Crabbe's 'The Village'); indeed its lack of concern for the detail of village society was precisely part of its appeal, especially during the nineteenth century when its vision of a rural life outside history and integrated with nature allowed it to outlast that mid eighteenth century vogue for poems of night and the grave which had helped to fuel its initial success. It was by then the very fact of the increasing pace of rural change and urban expansion which enhanced the attractiveness of this image of stasis and stable tranquillity.

Within a very few years of publication the 'Elegy' became established as among the most representative and memorable poems of its time; as Dr Johnson wrote in 1776 it 'abounds with images which find a mirror in every mind and with sentiments to which every bosom returns an echo.'[5] The 'Elegy' enabled Gray's reputation to survive the general reaction against much eighteenth-century poetry during the 'romantic' period of the early nineteenth century; 'it is the cornerstone of his glory', wrote Byron in 1821. Tennyson (in 1855) was reported to 'rather have written Gray's "Elegy" than all Wordsworth'[6] – echoing the widespread story of a century earlier that General Wolfe on the eve of storming Quebec in 1759 'would prefer being the author of that Poem to the glory of beating the French tomorrow'.[7] By 1882 Edmund Gosse, in his life of Gray, was terming it 'the typical piece of English verse, our poem of poems ... with a higher reputation in literature than any other English poem'.[8] Throughout this period the poem had wide circulation and became a fixed point of cultural reference. From the early 1750s it was printed in innumerable editions (many unauthorised) and its influence can be judged by the large number of imitations and parodies published – over 50 recorded by 1800 and a further 80 in the next century. Notably many of the parodies sought to re-apply the poem's mode and manner to an urban setting. The earliest known example was John Dunscombe's 'An evening contemplation in a college', which began 'The curfew tolls the knell of closing gates', to be followed by such examples as an elegy on the death of an opera (1765), 'the shrill bell rings the knell of curtain rise ...'. A century later such first lines were still being regularly composed – 'The muffin-bell proclaims the parting day' (*Punch*, 1856) and 'The clanging crow-bar rings the pile's decay' (urban renewal in Manchester, 1867).[9] The more straightforward influence of the 'Elegy' within the national culture was reflected in an article in the *Church of England Review* in 1837 which noted that Gray's work 'speaks from every marble slab, from every little tomb with its osier bands, from every straw-built cottage, and from every village church'.[10] Hardy's titling of *Far from the Madding Crowd* (1874) assumed that Gray's poem was common currency, while the place of the 'Elegy' within the growing formal education in the English literary heritage was confirmed by its inclusion in an 1881 'poetical reader suitable for the fourth standard of elementary schools ...'.[11] A year later it was included in Alfred H. Miles' *The Reciter*, 'A Selection of Popular Pieces for Reading or Recitation'.[12]

In 1912 the Everyman edition of Gray's work was published in which John Drinkwater's introduction rather implausibly attempted to praise Gray as, in effect, an early species of Georgian nature poet ('If Gray saw blue hills he called them blue not bluish'), but more significantly confirmed the almost unique status of the 'Elegy' as 'being one of the few excellent poems in the language that are really popular'. The poem 'was a chapter of simple things which ... have gripped a poet by their loveliness and poignancy'[13] and there can be little doubt that an intrinsic part of this appeal was its evocation of a timeless world of rural peace and simplicity available for contemplation and reflection.

London music-hall: the 1890s

At the time of the 'Elegy's' composition in 1750 England was predominantly a rural society. Even 50 years later nearly two-thirds of the population were still living in rural areas; however by the end of the nineteenth century much had changed. The 1901 census indicated that 77 per cent of the population were now living in urban districts and that only 12 per cent of males were employed in agricultural production, which itself contributed only about 8 per cent of national output. During the second half of the nineteenth century the rural population was in absolute decline against an overall increase between 1871 and 1901 from 31 million to 41 million. London especially was expanding, reaching nearly 5 million by the end of the century.[14]

Alongside this late Victorian phase of urbanisation and in tune with the improving ideas of 'rational recreation' came new attitudes to the countryside, which now came to be seen as a potential public amenity. At one social level the National Trust was founded in 1895; the same decade saw the beginnings of the cycling clubs and a further development in the pattern of mass leisure excursions out from the urban areas. Within towns and cities this was the period of the establishment of many public parks and recreation grounds, which in a number of cases were formed from the grounds of older manors or country houses swallowed up by urban expansion. On a smaller scale was the growth of the idea of the small private garden attached to the new urban or, more often, suburban dwellings in which the pleasures of the countryside and the taming of nature of the large country house gardens could be re-created in miniature with the cultivation of flowers, shrubs and neat lawns. According to one account of the rise of suburbia we should look to 'the suburban garden for the roots of the demand for suburban living'. Such gardens provided 'tangible evidence ... that the dream of being a townsman living in the country was something more than just an illusion'.[15] At the level of social policy Ebenezer Howard's influential *Garden Cities of Tomorrow* (1902) presented a vision of a new form of town planning and its accompanying way of life in which divisions between rural and

Fig. 7.2 The cover to the sheet music of 'If it wasn't for the 'ouses in between', by Gus Elen (from Martha Vicinus, *The Industrial Muse: a study of nineteenth century British working-class literature* (Croom Helm 1974), Plate 31).

urban were reconciled and a new integration occurred; in William Morris' *News From Nowhere* (1890) London itself has become transformed, by the twenty-first century, into such a place.

Such were the hopes and dreams of the planners and Utopian socialists, magnifying the ideals and desires reflected in the growth of the urban and suburban domestic garden. The view from the London working-class music-hall was, in contrast, often more pragmatic and rather less attuned to the perspective of 'rational recreation'. According to Gareth Stedman Jones this mode of popular entertainment had a number of distinctive characteristics in the period 1870–1900:

In working-class districts, where the multiplicity of occupations and the separation of home from workplace and the overcrowding and impermanence of apartments made any stable community life very difficult, the local hall with its blaze of light, sham opulence, its laughter and its chorus singing, fulfilled, if only in an anonymous way, a craving for solidarity in facing the daily problems of poverty and family life. Music hall stood for the small pleasures of working-class life – a glass of 'glorious English beer', a hearty meal of 'boiled beef and carrots', a day by the seaside, Derby Day and the excitements and tribulations of betting, a bank holiday spent on Hampstead Heath or in Epping Forest . . . Its attitude was 'a little bit of what you fancy does you good . . .[16]

One such song sung in these halls in the 1890s was 'If it Wasn't for the 'Ouses in Between', lyrics by Edgar Bateman, music by George Le Brunn and performed by Gus Elen (fig. 7.2). Elen was born in Pimlico in 1863 and among his earliest jobs were those of egg-packer, draper's assistant and programme seller. By 1882 he was operating as a pub entertainer on the south bank of the Thames, while in the summer he would join black-faced minstrel troupes on the beach at Margate and Ramsgate. In 1884 he began to appear in the London halls in a black-faced duo, but it was not until 1891 that he first performed his costermonger characterisation. This followed the success of the more famous Albert Chevalier in the same role. Typically the coster character would appear on stage, appropriately costumed, with his barrow or basket of fruit and vegetables, then pause to deliver his routine of songs or monologues. Two aspects of this figure are particularly worth noting. First the coster was a relatively free figure, out and about in the city streets; secondly with his fruit and vegetable produce he was in effect bringing the rural into the heart of the urban – a rather different way of mediating the two to that proposed by Ebenezer Howard. It was this latter aspect especially that Elen capitalised on in the performance of 'If it Wasn't for the 'Ouses in Between', which in its full version was sung as follows:

If you saw my little backyard, 'Wot a pretty spot!' you'd cry,
It's a picture on a sunny summer day:
Wiv the turnip tops and cabbages wot people doesn't buy
I makes it on a Sunday look all gay.

The neighbours finks I grow 'em and you'd fancy you're in Kent,
Or at Epsom if you gaze into the mews.
It's a wonder as the landlord doesn't want to raise the rent,
Because we've got such nobby distant views.

Oh it really is a wery pretty garden
And Chingford to the eastward could be seen;
Wiv a ladder and some glasses,
You could see to 'Ackney Marshes,
If it wasn't for the 'ouses in between.

We're as countrified as can be wiv a clothes prop for a tree,
The tub-stool makes a rustic little stile;
Ev'ry time the bloomin' clock strikes there's a cuckoo sings to me,
And I've painted up 'To Leather Lane a mile.'
Wiv tomatoes and wiv radishes wot adn't any sale,
The backyard makes a puffick mass o'bloom;
And I've made a little beehive wiv some beetles in a pail,
And a pitchfork wiv a handle of a broom.

Oh it really is a wery pretty garden,
And Rye 'ouse from the cock-loft could be seen:
Where the chickweed man undresses,
To bath 'mong the watercresses,
If it wasn't for the 'ouses in between.

There's the bunny shares 'is egg box wiv the cross-eyed cock and hen
Though they 'as got the pip and him the morf;
In a dog's 'ouse on the line-post there was pigeons nine or ten,
Till someone took a brick and knocked it orf.
The dustcart though it seldom comes, is just like 'arvest 'ome
And we mean to rig a dairy up some 'ow;
Put the donkey in the washouse wiv some imitation 'orns,
For we're teaching him to moo just like a cah.

Oh it really is a wery pretty garden,
And 'Endon to the Westward could be seen;
And by climbing to the chimbley,
You could see across to Wembley,
If it wasn't for the 'ouses in between.

Though the gas works isn't wilets, they improve the rural scene,
For mountains they would very nicely pass.
There's the mushrooms in the dust-hole with the cowcombers so green,
It only wants a bit of 'ot-'ouse glass.
I wears this milkman's nightshirt, and I sits outside all day,
Like the ploughboy cove what's mizzled o'er the Lea;
And when I goes indoor at night they dunno what I say,
'Cause my language gets as yokel as can be.

Oh it really is a wery pretty garden,
And soap works from the 'ouse tops could be seen;

If I got a rope and pulley,
I'd enjoy the breeze more fully,
If it wasn't for the 'ouses in between.[17]

Elen's song is structured by the opposition of a wide range of attributes and attitudes attached respectively to rural and urban life. The rural carries a number of diverse connotations. First, it is a specific, attractive, landscape – the 'rural scene' containing the appeal both of the post-Romantic untamed (the 'mountains'), and of the quaint and picturesque ('rustic little stile'). The rural scene is here essentially a spectacle which affords relaxation and leisure to the urban dwellers. Secondly, however, regular access to such delights is seen as a matter of class privilege – 'such nobby distant views'; this song's urban perspective is specifically that of the poor. More neutrally the countryside is seen as a place of working agriculture – cows, chickens, the harvest. Finally, in a way which echoes Gray's generally quite different perspective, there is a sense of the backwardness and lack of sophistication of the country dwellers – the 'milkman's nightshirt' and the 'yokel' language.

Urban life is very different. A picture of the overcrowding and barely controlled squalor of late Victorian London emerges – the 'little backyard' overlooked by neighbours, the dustcart, the gasworks, the soapworks and the sheer number of houses. At the same time there is a very strong identification with the particular way of life and with the very heart of London (the place names – Chingford, 'Endon and Rye 'ouse – can be used to pinpoint the precise area just north of the Thames in East London where the coster lives). Linked to this is a sense, despite the physical conditions, of the superiority of the urban perspective with its partly envious, partly satirical, imitation of rural life.

If the song simply described such oppositions as given then it would not be worthy of much analytical attention. Instead it offers two modes of mediation and commentary on the rural/urban dichotomy. In particular it plays continually with the idea of transforming the backyard into a garden – into, that is, not the rural scene itself, but rather its miniaturised and metaphorical equivalent. As early as 1855 two different observers (both employing a tone of upper-class superiority) noted the significance of this trend. 'The suburbs . . . are marvellously attached to gardening, and rejoice above all things, in a tree in a tub'[18] wrote J. F. Murray, while the Journal of the Royal Agricultural Society of England complained of the poor that 'You cannot find a place where they do not get a broken teapot in which to stuff, as soon as spring comes, some flower or something to give them an idea of the country.'[19] It is the pretensions of the urban and suburban gardeners (middle-class and working-class) and their 'idea of the country' as much as the rural dwellers themselves ('nobby' or otherwise) which form the target of the song – most notably in the re-cycling of discarded coster greengrocery to produce 'a puffick mass of bloom'.

A second and rather different kind of relationship between town and country is expressed by the double conditional of the chorus. The first conditional ('Wiv a ladder and some glasses' or 'If I got a rope and pulley') is essentially comic and ridiculous. The second then becomes in itself depressing and expressive of the claustrophobic character of working-class inner London as the city lies spread out on all sides. Even if you got to roof level you still wouldn't be able to see towards the edges of London; instead you would be faced with the immensity of the urban sprawl. In this final line of the chorus is embedded a clear desire for access to the open air and pleasures of the countryside for which no amount of playing at turning backyards into gardens can substitute. In Morris' *News From Nowhere* the narrator judges the transformation by seeing that 'The soap-works with their smoke-vomiting chimneys were gone; the engineer's works gone; the leadworks gone . . .'[20] Elen's song has no place for such fantasy; here the soapworks remain.

In the midst of this complexity is a line ('Like the ploughboy cove what's mizzled o'er the lea') testifying to the persistent influence of Gray's 'Elegy'; Elen in fact conflates the figures of the meditating poet and the returning plowman into an epitome of country life-style which the urban coster both emulates and parodies. Here, as elsewhere in its attitude to the rural, Elen's song proves to be a more multi-layered and self-aware text than Gray's poem, precisely because in also offering a perspective from outside the 'rural scene' it considers its own position of observation as part of the subject-matter, rather than as an objective and universal viewpoint. Inevitably, perhaps, the meanings of rural life looked rather different when viewed from the heart of the working-class districts of the biggest city in the world as against the peace and tranquillity of a country churchyard.

The Archers: 1950–90

Elen retired during the Great War (although he did make a few live appearances during the 1930s) and following his death in 1940 'If It Wasn't for the 'Ouses in Between' survived in the culture predominantly as a matter of memory. By then the rural population was barely one-sixth of the whole while in the urban areas cinema had displaced music hall as the major collective form of evening entertainment and increasingly radio was becoming the central medium for the transmission of contemporary song. By the late 1940s a wireless set had become a domestic necessity and radio was foremost in the formation of an increasingly singular national culture in a period when the BBC's role was still seen as including explicit propaganda to assist post-war reconstruction. To this end a meeting was held in Birmingham in June 1948 to discuss with farmers how best to use radio as a means for transmitting specialist information. Among the suggestions was to broadcast a 'farming Dick Barton', *Dick Barton* being a popular daily thriller serial. In May 1950 the resulting programme, *The Archers*, was allowed a trial week on the Midland Home Service and was then re-launched on the national Light Programme in January 1951.

The driving force behind the programme was Godfrey Baseley, then a producer of agricultural programmes, and his statement of intent, drafted in August 1950, shows that the original idea of a fictionalised farming information programme quickly became augmented by further thoughts on how to represent rural life. The main purpose was to:

... present an accurate picture of country life and in so doing draw portraits of typical country people and follow them at work and at play and to eavesdrop on the many problems of living that confront country folk in general ... The most important thing here is accuracy. To keep a good balance between the purely factual and the more entertaining aspects of country life and to keep in mind always that the programmes be directed to the general listener, i.e. the townsman, and through the entertainment develop an appreciation of the inexhaustible diversions to be found in the countryside.[21]

A mixture of intentions had now emerged, with a particular emphasis on constructing a positive image of 'country life' and the 'countryside' (it is these terms much more than 'rural' or 'village' that define the programme's sense of itself) for a predominantly urban audience (fig. 7.3). This was reinforced in the first national episode in 1951 when the announcer introduced 'an everyday story of country folk' (this mildly anachronistic term implying an element of timelessness) and then proclaimed the Archer family to be 'children of the soil and like most work-a-day folk they have their joys and troubles, their ups and downs'.[22] By April 1951 it had proved sufficiently successful to replace *Dick Barton* in a prime early evening slot and had increased its audience to 4 million. At this stage of the programme's development the policy intention was to aim for a content which was about 15 per cent instruction, 10 to 15 per cent 'natural history and folklore' and the remainder entertainment centering on the family of one of those small farmers who, according to Baseley, formed 'the hard core of the rural population'.[23] By the end of the first year the audience had reached 6 million and went on to peak at 20 million in 1955, just before the fast growth of television in the late 1950s caused a sharp reduction in all evening radio listening. *The Archers* however survived this potential crisis and in 1957 their 2,000th episode was marked by the BBC's publication of an edition of the *Borchester Echo* and *Doris Archer's Farm Cookery Book* (of which one critic remarked 'the recipes in this well-filled book have a country air about them, with a good homely fare and many farmhouse dishes').[24] By the late 1950s in fact *The Archers* had already come to embody certain traditional 'country' values and customs, many of which were regularly put to the test and challenged by the story-lines (youthful rebellion, new farming methods, incomers with new ideas), but which were generally vindicated and

Fig. 7.3 Members of *The Archers* cast on location in 1954. Left to right are Phil Archer (Norman Painting), Simon (Eddie Robinson), Mr Fairbrother (Leslie Bowman) and Dan Archer (Harry Oakes) (BBC Pebble Mill).

endorsed and remained the backbone and *raison d'être* of the programme (fig. 7.4).

Since then most debates about the programme's value (whether internal to the BBC or conducted in public) have turned on how or whether it should keep up with the times, with respect both to general social morality and habits (e.g. discussions of illegitimacy or divorce) and to the changing social structure of rural England. In the mid-Sixties one BBC regional information officer was asked to provide a critical assessment, part of which argued that the writing needed improving in terms of how it dealt with younger characters, but still concluded that 'Ambridge is a gentle relic of Old England, nostalgic, generous, corruptible, and (above all) valiant. In other words, the sort of British community that the rootless townsman would like to live in and can involve himself in vicariously.'[25] Shortly after, however, two of the programme's originators (Godfrey Baseley and Tony Shryane) produced an internal document, '*The Archers* as Radio Entertainment in the 1970s', which recognised that, 'No longer is it possible to think in terms of roses round the door and quaint old village pubs and "gaffers"

Chris Gittins   as Walter Gabriel   The Archers. *Yours Sincerely* *Chris Gittins*

Fig. 7.4 One of the all-time favourite characters from *The Archers*, Walter Gabriel (Chris Gittins) (BBC Pebble Mill).

sat on the bench outside. The whole status of village life has changed, particularly in the villages within an hour's journey by motorway from a big urban area ...' They described a new emergent social structure in which the small farmer was less important, as were village artisans and some village service occupations; they did nevertheless argue that 'listeners enjoy hearing various characters reminiscing about life in the village 20 or 30 years ago and this can be done quite naturally'.[26]

In fact the programme (like much else in Britain) entered a period of crisis in the early 1970s as two key members of the founding team departed (one through death, the other resignation) and, despite such marketing ploys as the BBC publication of *Doris Archer's Diary* in 1972 to mark the twenty-first anniversary (as well as a commercial firm's production of 'Doris Archer's Country Fudge'),[27] this sense of loss of direction persisted. Amidst the soul-searching it was recognised that the original informational role had now been almost entirely superseded by the entertainment function; equally however the programme did depend on the ability to persuade the listeners of its authenticity, in its depiction both of human relationships and of country and farming life. Each of the four main farms in *The Archers* had its own regularly up-dated economic model and an agricultural adviser attended the monthly script meetings to suggest story-lines and advise on detailed references to farming practices.

The underlying strength of *The Archers* however lay in the way it depicted and reinforced a particular image of the English rural way of life – an image which after the political and social turbulence of the 1970s was to come into its own once again in the heritage-conscious patriotic revivalist 1980s. When a new editor took over in 1979 he pre-figured this success with a summary of the programme's values:

In *The Archers* we show the changing of the seasons and reflect the tenor of rural life. We show a pleasant world, but not an unreal world ...

If, at times, we seem to show a complacent, rather entrenched middle-class society that enjoys itself, cares more about the harvest than world affairs, and refuses to agonise over the woes of the world or the terrors of the human condition, then that is what prosperous Midland villages are about. It is also what our listeners want to hear about.[28]

Such a perspective sees the programme as at the centre of the ideological construction of a certain form of Englishness:

The Archers has always been – though not always prepared to admit – the voice of the Shires, conservative, sensible and not particularly egalitarian. It has always radiated the belief that there is nowhere really in the world but England, and nowhere in England but a particular corner of Worcestershire and Warwickshire ...[29]

It was this combination of rural peace and English identity that led one writer to remark at the time of the Falklands war in 1982 that the way in which the way of life of the Falklanders was being depicted made it seem as though 'the Nazis had taken over the Archers'.[30] When Liz Rigbey then producer of *On Your Farm* became editor in 1986 she saw 'farming content as the bedrock of the programme. Listeners may not be interested in agricultural detail, but out of this detail arises story-lines which everyone can understand.' Her instructions to writers were 'to give urban listeners access to 15 minutes of countryside'.[31] While she hoped to introduce 'some of the changes I've seen in rural communities ... I fear too much of the truth would prove painful to our listeners'.[32]

Throughout the various attempts to strike a balance between entertainment and realism, tradition and innovation lies a common assumption that *The Archers'* importance is that it will be generally regarded by its listeners as a definitive statement about the essential nature of village or 'country' life. The programme, of course, contains more elements than that; it is an especially successful example of the continuous serial format (sometimes loosely referred to as 'soap opera'), a form which poses particular problems for the cultural analyst. Unlike the 128 lines of the 'Elegy' or the four verses of Elen's song the full text of *The Archers* (from 1950–90) would run non-stop for three and a half months. An exhaustive discussion of the hundreds of story-lines, the history of the Archer family or the particular variations of the genre within the programme are beyond the scope of this essay. Rather it may be possible to look for the underlying assumptions about English rural life which are embedded in the programme at a deep level. Such are distilled especially in the occasional BBC books which purport to present the reality and history of Ambridge which provides the scene on which the dramas and narratives are played out.

A particularly illuminating example is *Ambridge – an English Village Through The Ages* (1981), a book supposedly based on an oral history project and a landscape survey carried out by various of the programme's characters. The format includes genuine photographs of nineteenth- and early twentieth-century village and farming life and is composed as a pastiche of local history writing (with etymologies of the programme's place-names and facsimiles of medieval manuscripts in which Ambridge and Borchester are mentioned). The opening words also show a wish fully to authenticate Ambridge as part of what we all know as the English countryside:

Borsetshire is justly famed as the 'pastoral county', a land of quiet hills, slow-moving rivers and small villages . . . This is the country Stanley Baldwin must have had in mind when he wrote of, 'the sounds of England, the tinkle of the hammer on the anvil in the country smithy, the corncrake on a dewy morning, the sound of the scythe against the whetstone, and the sight of the plough team coming over the brow of the hill, the sight that has been seen in England since England was a land'.[33]

In such a formulation Ambridge is placed both within specific English history and within that timeless sphere inhabited also by the village of the 'Elegy' (a sphere of observed sights and sounds rather than participation). *The Archers* itself (as a radio programme) is shown to have a curious and paradoxical relationship to this construction of the rural; the opening pages of *Ambridge – an English Village* lament the decline of the 'folk memory' caused by the advance of literacy, travel, television and *radio*, which have caused the need for this 'captur[ing] on tape the last breath of country life as it has existed for a thousand years'. It is then *The Archers* (as a cultural project in preserving and broadcasting the vestiges and values of 'country life') which is offered as a substitute for that which (in this vulgarised mass society thesis) its very medium of radio has helped to destroy; it is perhaps worth noting in passing that the appeal of that other most successful British 'soap opera' *Coronation Street* is often structured in the very same way.

Breathtakingly *Ambridge – an English Village Through the Ages* also claims that 'for a thousand years' (between the Saxon period and 1850) 'the life of a cottager in Ambridge hardly changed', and a record of a typical 'Ambridge Year' is re-constructed from Plough Monday through 'flea-sweeping' in March to beating the bounds, to the Christmas Hunt. This notion of the annual cycle is echoed in another book *The Ambridge Years* (1984) in which 'Dan Archer' re-tells the story of his 84 years in Ambridge through reminiscences about each month in turn. The pattern of social change, the events of Dan's life, the agricultural year and the seasonal cycle all become part of the same narrative. While many other continuous serials on British television and radio have come and gone, *The Archers* is if anything gaining in strength by virtue of its longevity; precisely because it is based on notions of family inheritance, tradition and the deep structure of 'timeless' country folk, it derives further plausibility from the fact that it has now become part of that very tradition which it was set up to depict.

In conclusion: as countrified as can be

At one level there is very little in common between the formal elegy, the comic music-hall song and the 40-year-old radio serial. In medium, genre and intended audience they differ widely. All however take the 'country', the 'rural scene' as a space demanding interpretation for a predominantly urban audience and each interpretation makes sense in terms of the particular *kind* of urban audience addressed (or which has since taken it up). Gray offers universal and timeless truths authenticated through the values and way of life of the villagers. Elen sees the attractions of being 'countrified', the fake solution of the back-garden, but also the realities of urban living which cannot be wished away. *The Archers*, in a society in which less than 3 per cent of the workforce are in agricultural employment, uses a plausibly realistic background of farming and contemporary rural life both to balance its 'human interest' story-lines and to authenticate its deep structure – the creation of the archetypal English village with unshakeably deep roots in English history and countryside.

Through these quite different intentions some features of a single image-complex of ruralism remain, as does one particular figure – that of the 'plowman' or ploughboy. From the fourteenth century on (Langland's *Piers Plowman*) through innumerable sixteenth and seventeenth century lyric poems, to the 'Elegy' and to many popular songs of the nineteenth century ('The Ploughboy and the Cockney', 'The Pretty Ploughboy'), the image persists as a powerfully charged definition of the rural life connoting variously hard work, strength, simplicity and naivety. Ploughing, by horse or by tractor, remains a central symbol of that supposed direct relationship between man and nature around which the appeal of the country life to the urban dweller so often centres; it also remains a fundamental reality in any arable farm's working life. As so often in popular culture 'image' and 'reality' are parts of a single social and cultural process.

NOTES

1 H. Newby, *Green and Pleasant Land?* (1979) 14.
2 J. Steele, 'Thomas Gray and the Season for Triumph', in J. Downey and B. Jones (eds.), *Fearful Joy* (Montreal 1974) 212.
3 E. J. Hobsbawm, *Industry and Empire* (1969) 29.
4 R. W. Malcolmson, *Life and Labour in England 1700–1780* (1981) 144.
5 S. Johnson, *The Lives of the Poets* (1776).
6 A. Macdonald, 'Gray and his critics: patterns of response in the eighteenth and nineteenth centuries' in Downey and Jones (eds.), *Fearful Joy* (Montreal 1974) 191.
7 E. Gosse, *Gray* (1889) 145.
8 *Ibid.*, 97.
9 All cited in N. Sutherland, *A Bibliography of Thomas Gray* (New Haven 1917).
10 Macdonald, 'Gray and his critics', 187.
11 Sutherland, *A Bibliography of Thomas Gray*, 90.
12 A. H. Miles, *The Library of Elocution* (1882).
13 J. Drinkwater, (ed.), *The Poems of Thomas Gray* (1912) vii–xiii.
14 G. E. Mingay, 'Introduction: rural England in the industrial age', in G. E. Mingay (ed.), *The Victorian Countryside* I (1981) 3.
15 F. M. L. Thompson, 'Introduction: the rise of suburbia', in F. M. L. Thompson (ed.), *The Rise of Suburbia* (Leicester 1982) 15.
16 G. Stedman Jones, 'Working-class culture and working-class politics in London, 1870–1900: notes on the remaking of a working class', in B. Waites, T. Bennett and G. Martin, (eds.), *Popular Culture: Past and Present* (1982) 108.
17 A shorter version of the song was recorded by Elen and is available on the LP 'You Have Made a Nice Old Mess of it', Topic 12T396 (1979).
18 D. A. Reeder, *Suburbanity and the Victorian City* (Leicester 1980) 3.
19 Mingay, 'Introduction', in *The Victorian Countryside*, I, 9.
20 W. Morris, *News from Nowhere* (1890) 7.
21 W. Smethurst, *The Archers: the First Thirty Years* (1980) 18.
22 *Ibid.*, 20.
23 *Ibid.*, 18.
24 G. Berryman, *The Life and Death of Doris Archer* (1981) 98–9.
25 Smethurst, *The Archers*, 95.
26 *Ibid.*, 133–4.
27 Berryman, *The Life and Death of Doris Archer*, 155.
28 Smethurst, *The Archers*, 151.
29 *Ibid.*, 198–9.
30 A. Barnett, *Iron Britannia* (1982) 101.
31 *The Sunday Telegraph*, 16 November 1986, 14.
32 *The Listener*, 22 May 1986, 20.
33 J. Aldridge and J. Tregorran, *Ambridge – An English Village Through The Ages* (1981) 1.

JOHN LOWERSON

Although some attempts have been made, a *mystical geography* cannot really be mapped yet it is an essential description of how many English people view the rural world. The phrase was used by Terence Ranger in a study of western missionary activities in Zimbabwe where he demonstrated the adaptation of externally introduced theological structures and liturgical practices to indigenous beliefs and the way in which this produced specific regional and local foci for tribal custom.[1] This chapter examines the concept in an English context and demonstrates some aspects of the complexity, continuity and modification of values which are often ascribed to the countryside by a society frequently portrayed as urban, secularised and agnostic if not downright atheistic. It deals with the interplay of ideas of 'holy space' and people, the patterns of institutional religion, the invention or rediscovery of 'mystical geometry' and literary treatments both in 'high' and 'popular' culture. It is impossible to examine these entirely discretely or at great length here but they represent major influences on the ways in which the English regard their physical and social landscapes.

An ecclesiastical framework

There is a very important sense in which England as a whole is regarded as a holy place. This is not 'Holy Earth' in a Dostoievskian mode but we must acknowledge that the sense of a special separateness has percolated it in ways far beyond its exploitation by patriotic politics, since at least the sixteenth century. The idea of a *hortus clausus* (a walled garden, symbolic of the virginal Queen Elizabeth I and her protected nation) is best expressed in Shakespeare's 'Scepter'd Isle' speech, reiterated by Churchill but more obviously shown recently in a slim volume in which the landscape photographer Fay Godwin illustrated the stanzas with evocative pictures.[2] In keeping with what has become the norm since the Romantic movement this is almost invariably depicted as rural. It is, in fact, older. There was a substantial expression of it amongst seventeenth-century Anglicans such as Izaak Walton and Thomas Traherne; another, Henry Vaughan, wrote:

Fresh *fields* and *woods*. The Earth's fair *face*,
God's *foot-stool*, and mans *dwelling-place*.
I ask not why the first *Believer*
Did love to be a Country liver?[3]

Despite the best efforts of nineteenth-century economic liberals the idea of a major industrial city as fitting the mould has seemed a stark contradiction in terms. Yet the articulation of the idea is rarely fully developed; it depends rather on a gnomic shorthand, key sentences, remembered lines from poetry, implied rather than wholly expressed, the 'English heaven' of Rupert Brooke's notorious patriotic poem, 'The Soldier', which implied that, if foreigners had heavens, they would be distinctly inferior.[4]

A good example of this can be found in a collection of essays published at the end of the Second World War called *Countryside Character*, illustrated *inter alia* by the late Peter Scott. The introduction begins by referring to 'unchanging' nature and continues, 'Spiritual strength is deeply rooted in every corner of this island', before claiming that basic to rural life is an inevitable appreciation of God.[5] Yet, even after the victory of the war and the saving of the *hortus clausus* from a foreign threat, it now needed protection and maintenance in the face of an increasingly hostile urban society. The reiteration of these supposedly fundamental values is usually portrayed in tension with the demands of the latter. Almost inseparable from this is the assertion rather than testing of the assumptions; they are taken for granted as part of the common heritage of all right-thinking Englishmen: 'There is much simple and sincere patriotism in the countryside and I think this is at least partly due to the fact that this land, England, is so much more visible and tangible in the country than it is in the towns.'[6] Some 40 years ago, with no sense of irony or of likely contradiction, an ecclesiastical biographer could make the claim that, 'In the countryside God seems nearer.'[7]

We shall return to some further discussion of that but it is necessary here to reflect on how this has been worked out institutionally. It needs to be remembered that in Christian terms this is the most significant, predominantly historical, experience. Since the Reformation it has been largely dominated by Anglicanism. The reasons for this should be obvious; in legal terms, as the 'state church', the Church of England is the pastoral authority for some 16,000 parishes. In reality this has had to be modified somewhat since the seventeenth century by denominational and regional considerations. Despite fluctuating official bans for some centuries, indigenous Roman Catholicism remained strong in parts of northwest Lancashire and areas of aristocratic protection such as Arundel in Sussex. The older Dissent, Baptists and Independents, flourished in parts of the Midlands – one thinks of Bunyan's Bedfordshire and Northamptonshire – despite sporadic persecution.[8] It was also singularly fissiparous in those many parts of the Sussex Weald where gentry influence was minimal. In the later eighteenth century, Methodism developed its particular hold on the West Country and East Anglia. Despite a universal nominal Anglican presence, the local patterns of worship and spirituality were singularly varied and distinctive in a way which has drawn down a great deal of historical enquiry.[9]

The picture in the later twentieth century is, however, much modified. The general decline in regular churchgoing, from over half to around a tenth of the population since the mid nineteenth century, has affected most Nonconformists even more than the Established Church. It is commonly held that England now has more Muslims than Methodists, although this is a predominantly urban picture. Whilst the Free Churches have withdrawn wholesale from many rural areas, or at least conducted a strategic retreat to chapels kept open in market towns, the Church of England has been obliged to maintain its presence, at least nominally. It has had to do this whilst facing a major decline in its ordained manpower, an estimated drop since 1914 of some 50 per cent to around 11,000. This has occurred paradoxically during a period of heightened expectations of the priesthood. Since the 1950s the communion service in its various guises, which can only be celebrated by a duly ordained priest, has come to be central to almost all Anglican worship, as distinct from the non-sacramental matins that was the previous norm and which could be led by a deacon or a licensed lay person.

This has been exacerbated by a view of the availability of 'our vicar' and of levels of personal attention to rural parishioners that grew out of models provided by the exceptional seventeenth-century Wiltshire incumbent, George Herbert, developed and made much more widely available in the nineteenth century.[10] They were fostered by the very theologically disparate Evangelical and Oxford Movements which demanded high levels of personal holiness and a systematic pastoral oversight by dedicated village clergymen whose *doyens* were John Keble and Charles Kingsley, both Hampshire incumbents; their overt theological differences were subsumed by their common assumptions about the relationships of clergy and their flocks. What emerged was an expectation that a 'gentleman in every parish' would lead his people to heaven by personal example, charity and exhortation. In many ways it produced a 'golden age' of clerical provision that the First World War ended: to 'holy place' was added 'holy person' in a form which even the most active of the many dynamic late Victorian urban clergy could never really expect to achieve.[11] At the close of the twentieth century the Church is having to adapt professionally to a very changed picture, trying to keep churches open for tiny congregations by grouping benefices together to be served by one paid incumbent who may or may not be helped by 'lay readers' or by retired and non-stipendiary clergy (fig. 8.1). More recently some of the more sparsely populated and predominantly rural dioceses, such as Lincoln and Gloucester, have taken to training and ordaining 'local ministers' chosen from the

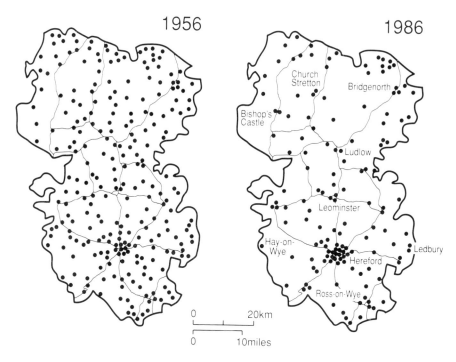

Fig. 8.1 The decline in clergy provision has been strongest in deeply rural areas. This survey of the diocese of Hereford indicates the pattern clearly (adapted from R. Lewis and A. Talbot-Ponsonby (eds), *The People, the Land and the Church*, Hereford Diocesan Board of Finance 1987, p. 190).

affected parishes to cope with manpower shortages. There has been considerable discussion as to whether the parochial model with its attendant, even if shared, incumbent is appropriate for late twentieth-century rural conditions but there is a powerful lay, as well as clerical, reluctance to move away from the essentially localised structure with its strong overtones of personal as well as spatial holiness. It has now been recognised centrally that parish boundaries are key elements in local spiritual maps.[12] It is but one example of the ways in which the Church of England, although numerically marginal, retains some cultural dominance.

Folk religion

Set against actual institutional decline in the countryside there has to be considered the nature and place of 'folk' religion, often known also as 'implicit' or 'common' belief. This incorporates singularly disparate elements, sometimes noticeably at odds with the relatively rational theological teachings of the ecclesiastical establishment. Because of its nature its extent is not easily measured and there have been few attempts at investigating it by comparison with the sort of work done overseas by Ranger and other anthropologists. Yet it is broadly assumed to exist and with a strong rural base. The author of a recent study of inner-city religious practice could make the following claim with little proof but no sense of insufficiency: 'Cutting across . . . regional variations are the contrasts between urban and rural life and a tendency for religion (traditionally observed) to persist more strongly in rural communities; a tendency that may be equally true for common religion.'[13] In this sense, the symbiosis between the official and the common is clear.

In terms of the Church establishment, folk religion hovers most noticeably around the 'hatching, matching and despatching' of the rites of passage. Funerals are particularly important. These are seen as expressions of the community's interaction rather than just the preserve of the Church's committed membership – 'communal' rather than 'associational' – distinguishing the village Anglican church from the eclectic suburban one. This is brilliantly illustrated in Susan Hill's semi-fictional *In the Springtime of the Year*.[14] And it is essentially syncretistic in its beliefs. It is often at odds with received rational theology but there is no sense of the irrational or illogical amongst those who hold it. It arises out of a singularly complex combination of older pagan (literally 'of the earth') forms and expectations, superstitions, local customs and rights, mingled with parts of Scriptural teaching. Traditionally these have been expressed in the language of the Authorised Version and the Book of Common Prayer but there is adequate scattered evidence for assuming that it is readily able to accommodate the less-rounded language of newer liturgical forms as well as the jargon of technology. Later Victorian and early twentieth-century observers tended to assume that this belief structure and language of a 'secret people' would disappear as industrialisation and urbanisation took hold but it has proved singularly resilient and adaptive to newer modes of expression.[15]

In the mid 1980s an incumbent in rural Sussex buried a local farmer in the isolated graveyard attached to the rarely used medieval church at the edge of his parish – worship normally took place in the Victorian church in the shifted centre of population. After the burial (itself more likely to occur rurally than the 'cleaner' disposal by cremation favoured by the vast majority of townspeople) the widow, a strict Nonconformist of fundamentalist Biblical views, expressed her gratitude by saying that at least she knew that her husand had been buried amongst his friends and relatives so that they could have happy parties in the churchyard when everyone in the village was asleep. She saw no incongruity between the statement and the teachings which had just been expressed in the words of commital.[16]

Many country clergy have had similar experiences which surface only occasionally in chats with colleagues or in published memoirs. Their ancedotal nature is central to the experience because their telling reinforces the patterns, just as it does amongst the people themselves. By comparison with oral accounts there have been comparatively few studies by recent scholars but such as have appeared have pointed to the continued extent of the phenomenon. Despite Keith Thomas' attempt to prove that magic went into terminal decline after the English Reformation recent work suggests considerable continuity.[17] In his study of nineteenth-century north Lindsey, Lincolnshire, James Obelkevich essayed bravely to reconstruct evidence of folk beliefs' resisting the sort of clerical interventionism outlined briefly above.[18] Subsequently we have seen David Clark's stimulating investigation of the interplay between acquired Methodist forms of belief and work-related superstitions in the North Yorkshire fishing village of Staithes. There the older forms of avoiding ill-fortune were expressed through identifying omens: if a woman appeared when men were on the way to the boats, then fishing was called off lest there be disaster. Similarly, a whole range of alternative language had been developed to prevent direct reference to pigs, mention of which would bring misfortune. Instead the word 'grecian' was used.[19] On the Isle of Portland, with its extensive stone quarrying, rabbits were held to be portents of evil – in fact they were, since their extensive burrows could lead to the unexpected collapse of faces on which men were working – so they were never mentioned by name but referred to instead as 'underground mutton'.[20] In the technology of the new farming, 'agribusiness', it is clear that the anthropomorphising of such equipment as combine harvesters and computers is continuing this tradition.

Yet this is less often seen as an alternative to Christianity than as a reinforcement of it. One might reflect that this could be seen as an exercise in false confidence building by rural clergy depressed at their apparently declining role but it is more likely to reflect the inescapable and adaptive interplay between official and local religious practices. In a very perceptive study of country religion in the early 1960s an Anglican bishop wrote:

The typical countryman, living as close to the soil as he does, is bound to have a streak of earthiness in him, of paganism in the real sense of that word. Unlike the townsman whose daily life is concerned with ledgers or machines, over which apparently he has complete control, the countryman is in daily contact with forces which he can partially tame but never wholly dominate. Superstition was part of his make up.[21]

Recent attempts to suggest that this represents the survival of language rather than belief are less than convincing.[22]

Apart from its role in marking life's crisis points, folk religion shows itself most clearly in its links with the ritual calendar, when it expresses the annual rhythms of the local community. The most popular demonstration of this is the Incarnation, at Christmas, celebrated with Midnight Mass. By comparison Easter, which has even greater doctrinal symbolism, is more thinly observed although it has acquired all the paraphernalia of Spring festivities, with new bonnets, egg-rolling and so on. The incorporation of such items like this on the Christian fringe grew very largely out of a perception by many Victorian rural clergy that they risked losing their flocks altogether if they did not meet people where they were. By far the best example of this, and one which has continued to grow in popularity, with attendance often exceeding the official ritual points of Christmas and Easter, is the Harvest Festival. Since it was virtually created in the 1840s it has become highly formalised. Churches are dressed in ways which reflect the preoccupations of a farming past, with centrepieces of specially made harvest loaves and sheaves of corn which have to be separately gathered and preserved since modern harvesting just cannot produce them. And there are the invariable favourite hymns, derived from Psalm 65. To that the twentieth century has added another, grimmer, celebration, that of Remembrance Day. With the rare exception of the 'fortunate villages' which lost no-one in the First World War or the Second this has become highly ordered, centred on war memorial and church and resistant to change.[23] One of the easiest ways in which a rural incumbent can lose popularity is to substitute new hymns for those traditionally used. Less powerfully the church has also involved itself in regionally distinctive expressions of folk belief such as welldressing in Derbyshire, plough services in East Anglia and blessing boats in small ports.[24]

All this allows for the identification of the Church of England with rural life in a total sense, despite low actual attendances. The fuller implications of this were noted clearly by the religious correspondent of *The Times* in 1988:

It is Englishness and Anglicanism as one concept, and it is a creed which does not require its members to go anywhere near a church as such, for the whole nation is felt to be hallowed ground, and at the same time one vast charitable society for the benefit of its members.[25]

This was certainly not just the 'Englishness' imposed on the national culture by the rural romanticism of urban dreamers from the Edwardian South East.[26] The writer was using it to illustrate the inherited communal view of much English religious practice by contrast with the emphasis on the individual and instrumental associations in Conservatism under Mrs Thatcher. Such inherited assumptions do make much of the rural world a stony ground for aggressive 'church growth' evangelism which is often based on suburban models of the 'gathered' nature of religious affiliation.[27] It has become a particular problem since the later 1960s because of the expansion of many villages by 'incomer' populations and there is a sociology of religious tension yet fully to be investigated in terms of the pressures being brought to bear on parish churches. This formed a significant part of the recent Church of England report *Faith in the Countryside*, although that proved rather bland by comparison with its urban surveys.[28] Its best public airing has been through the medium of *The Archers*, whose 'everyday story of country folk' has included encounters with clergy more urban-minded than the village expected.

Yet even that programme has been used to reassert the traditional assumptions of the essential godliness of country people. The church porch on a Sunday morning is a frequently used place of encounter for the leading characters and it offered a singular *reductio ad absurdum* when the BBC's most popular religious television programme, *Songs of Praise*, was broadcast using Archer characters as if they were real people. Its producer was reported as saying, 'They represent something ... older: a staunch community and a religious faith, rooted in the English countryside.'[29]

Such a loose formulation normally enjoys a rather sharper focus in the physical fact of the local parish church. Since the liturgical and often romantic reordering of churchbuildings by so many of the reforming Victorian clergy there has emerged a much more overt sense of attachment to the building as such. It may have existed before, particularly during the later Middle Ages, but it has never been so clearly articulated in popular terms as implying a collective sense of holy place which goes far outside the individual community where the church is located. Between the destruction of decoration common during the Reformation and the relatively recent reintroduction of spiritual symbolism (crucifixes and so on) the most obvious iconographic function of rural churches was as repositories for the artistically and verbally florid memorials of the higher social orders. The claim that 'Here Lyeth the Body of the Truly Pious and most ingenious Young Lady' to be found on one Sussex tomb is modest indeed by the standards of her class.[30] The contribution of the twentieth century in particular has been to extend the idea of the country parish church through art, literature and popular media as an icon in itself; it is not always clear, however, whether it is the building as Christian symbol or as the focus of a broader and extremely diffuse rural mysticism which is being venerated. The dilemma is well, if with unconscious irony, illustrated by the introduction to an exhibition of countryside paintings done in the early 1940s: 'The church, as physical and spiritual focus of village life, served as a symbol of settled existence, an emblem of peace and continuity and a repository of nationalist sentiment. The church's role transcended [*sic*] religion.'[31]

Aesthetic considerations apart it is usually the role of the fabric as a holy sponge which attracts attention. In the words of T. S. Eliot it is a place 'where prayer has been valid'.[32] In *The Magic Apple Tree* Susan Hill encapsulated this view most elegantly:

imprinted on to the fabric of the church itself, into the stone of the walls and the brass of the rails and the stained glass of the windows, being absorbed into the ancient building as everything before it has been so absorbed, every hymn and anthem and voluntary, every blessing and vow, every petitionary prayer, every praise in the morning and thanksgiving at evening, every bidding of welcome to a child and of farewell to a soul.[33]

This despite the innumerable local histories of bitter personal conflicts in churches. The greatest populariser of this nostalgia was the late Sir John Betjeman, whose best-selling poetry, guidebooks and television programmes coincided with growing car ownership to make country churches accessible to far more people than the enthusiastic amateur antiquaries who had patronised them before.[34] The paradox is that this occurred at the time, the 1960s, when declining attendance figures and rural population shifts were making the survival of many buildings increasingly questionable. Popular affirmation of churches as tourist attractions was being set against the concerns of many ecclesiastical authorities over 'redundant plant'. This new interest combined with a local defensiveness in many rural areas, in which non-churchgoers were often as vocal as the regulars to protect what they saw as the essential focus of village life. Betjeman himself summed it up in his 'Verses turned in aid of a Public Subscription':

> And must that plaintive bell in vain
> Plead loud along the dripping lane?
> And must the building fall?
> Not while we love the Church and live
> And of our charity will give
> Our much, our more, our all.[35]

It was a view, the encapsulation of past and present place, that could be shared by professed non-believers such as the rural writer, Fraser Harrison, just as strongly as by believers: 'The church moves me too ... because it unifies the village and its landscape in a single, reciprocal creation.'[36] It made for the survival of many buildings which had little architectural merit but which were seen as a keystone in the romanticised composition of a balanced, organic and non-urban landscape. There is a steady trickle of new books on the English parish church, almost invariably rural; one of the odder features of some recent ones is that they were written by actors who have made considerable film and television careers out of portraying amiable English eccentrics. They seem to share with Betjeman the advantage that the holy fool can be treated as an almost infallible guide to the really serious matters of life.[37]

These books use photography considerably, with a strong emphasis on the idealised location of the church as the compositional centre of layouts, tower or spire dominating surrounding buildings or fieldscapes. This emerges from a tradition of almost routine but iconographically powerful English rural painting and engraving which grew largely out of the late Victorian rediscovery of England's threatened folk and spiritual rural roots. Between the wars of this century it found major expression on the covers of guidebooks, works such as Batsford's 'English Heritage' series and in the illustrations provided by landscape artists such as the Norfolk-centered Claughton Pellew for the *Radio Times* (fig. 8.2) and the *Countryman*.[38] It still continues strongly in the pictures to be found

Fig. 8.2 The idealized English Christmas. The Norfolk landscape painter Claughton Pellew designed this cover for the Christmas edition of the *Radio Times* in 1930. At a time of mounting economic crisis it was the old England's sense of wonder that was recalled.

in annual calendars, in television advertisements pretending to purvey wholesome products and even in the background to a television weather forecasting slot current on the BBC at the time of writing, where a stream curves gently between trees and meadows towards a church spire; that for a vast majority of viewers who live in conurbations.

To return to Fraser Harrison: 'The church's salient position on the skyline marries the community with its countryside, while pointing to transcendent aspirations.'[39] A similar but more poignant value has often been attached to the country's several hundred surviving monastic ruins whose lack of recent use makes them slightly more mysterious. By comparison, although there has been a recent growth of interest in Dissenting chapels they contribute largely only to the mental maps of their particular adherents.[40]

Pagan revivals

Mystical geography is not exclusively Christian. The later twentieth century has seen a much more widespread appearance of views of the spiritual significance of landscape in which the Christian presence may be treated as either a relatively recent addition or even a barrier to discovering the essential mystical significance of the English countryside. There is in this some of the popular religion already discussed but it also has a powerful input from pseudo-scientific and literary sources which have exploited recent commercial opportunities to the full. Some of this may be grouped loosely under the generic title of 'New Age' beliefs but there are strong elements of individual syncretism or of hazy local groups. Because of the very nature of the landscape features which are involved it has a much more powerful regional focus than spatially diffused Christianity – the most obvious location is in 'old Wessex', an area that may owe rather more to the loose mappings of Thomas Hardy than it does to the political or spiritual realities of the Anglo-Saxon kingdom.

Underpinning the mystical attachment to landscape has been a paradoxical linkage with post-Enlightenment science and an assumption that certain energy patterns can be identified with a precision that owes more to Newtonian geometric order than it does to recent explorations of chaos and relativity in astrophysics. Its origins lie in the work of archaeology's eighteenth-century founding father, William Stukeley, who combined systematic fieldwork with attempts to find a mystical and patriotic explanation for the artefacts he examined.[41] It was furthered by the later Victorian interplay between archaeology and anthropology. The excavation of Cranborne Chase, on the Dorset–Wiltshire borders, by General Pitt-Rivers and the diggings at Maiden Castle, the giant hill-fort outside Dorchester, were matched by antiquarian enthusiasts elsewhere, made available in a welter of national and local journals and in imaginative writing and illustrations such as the leading Arts and Crafts Movement designer, Heywood Sumner, provided for Wessex.[42] To the varied reflections of large numbers of rural clergy were added the imaginings of creative writers, best seen in Hardy's creepy story, 'A Tryst at an Ancient Earthwork'.[43]

Scientific archaeology eventually diverged sharply from its more verbose hangers-on but the latter have continued to develop tangential answers to questions which the nature of archaeological evidence and technical interpretation often leaves open. The most successful of these has been the development of 'mystical geometry' or 'geomantics', the attempt to relate 'earth currents' to prehistoric sites, such as Stonehenge or the nearby Silbury Hill. By far the best known of these systems of explanation is that produced in the 1920s by Alfred Watkins when, in his *Old Straight Track*, he posited the existence of long series of 'ley lines' linking scattered points in the countryside, such as church steeples, barrows and sacred trees, together.[44] Roman roads, green lanes and the straight paths imposed by Parliamentary enclosure were all held to demonstrate the validity of his theories. Watkins was a flour-miller with antiquarian enthusiasms and he was careful to limit his claims to discernible evidence, but his concern with 'a flood of ancestral memory' allowed others to build a considerable mystical superstructure on his early suggestions.[45] Conventional science and historical geography have sedulously avoided lending credence to Watkins' claims but this has not stopped, it has probably even encouraged, a steady growth in the popularity of geomantics. The availability of bicycles, charabancs and private cars led in the 1930s to the emergence of a Straight Track Postal Portfolio Club whose members made regular expeditions along Watkins' suggested paths. It went out of existence in 1948 but has been succeeded by a host of individual enthusiasm and by a flow of printed works attempting to spread both the message and the regional identification of the lines.[46]

The focus of all this attention, despite its nominal linking with Anglo-Saxon Wessex and the imagined chivalric kingdom of the Romano-British King Arthur, has been in the pre-Roman and essentially prehistoric world of the Celts and the preceding early kingdoms. This has allowed for extremely imaginative reconstructions of the ritual use of sites such as Stonehenge without the encumbrances of testable written evidence. There, that remarkable sub-Romantic invention, the Druidic movement, has been augmented by the more aggressively emotional Travellers, a loose mixture of post-1960s sub-cultures.[47] On to their beliefs has been welded a mixture of early Christian legends, particularly those dealing with the Holy Grail (variously the chalice used by Christ at the Last Supper or the cup which collected his blood spilled at the Crucifixion) and of theophanies, the personal appearances of Christ or such suitable figures as the Blessed Virgin Mary. Percolating through it all has been a sort of English Gnosticism, the belief that the universe can be explained and power achieved over part of it by the discovery of ancient mysteries, the discernment of essential symbols and the employment of previously hidden rituals.

The result is a remarkably flexible meld of beliefs with strong associations of place. The former Anglican bishop of Southwark, Mervyn Stockwood, told in his autobiography, *Chanctonbury Ring*, how he rarely ever made a major decision in his life without walking and meditating around the prehistoric Sussex earthwork of that name, a favoured place for local nature mystics and white witches.[48] Similar influences can be seen in the work of some of the leading twentieth-century English painters and plastic artists. In both his photographs and paintings Paul Nash drew on prehistoric chalkland features, megaliths and mysterious figures such as the White Horse.[49] More recently the sculptress Elizabeth Frink, who lives in Dorset, has seen ley lines as a true rendering of purpose in Nature, a means of expressing mystical links and balance in the landscape.[50] The flow of line, particularly in the Wessex Downland, and the presence of figures outlined on hillsides, such as the Cerne Abbas Giant or the Long Man of Wilmington, are repeated and explored in a tradition of English art which moves beyond the representational. The landscape in this is ascribed a being in itself rather as Hardy created Egdon Heath as the entity of spiritual power in *The Return of the Native*.

Surrounding and exploiting these there has grown up a minor publishing industry which has found a strong outlet in two related late twentieth-century movements; the outdoor walking boom whose roots lie in the 1930s and the Green groups which flowered in the 1980s. The opening up of long distance footpaths based largely on prehistoric trade and pilgrimage routes such as the Ridgeway and a concern for saving green lanes has spawned a range of pocketable guidebooks in which matter-of-fact information is combined with an emphasis on using the mystical elements of the routes to generate self-discovery and spiritual renewal. A recent walker's guide to old paths in East Anglia reminds its users that, '. . . in following known ley lines, or in searching out new patterns, you will find that you have become as aware of yourself as you are of the places through which you walk'.[51]

Whilst such a statement might appear unexceptionable to anyone given to outdoor pursuits it must be set in the context of wider cultural movements which are often neo-pagan in emphasis. The growth of interest in the occult (the possession of mysterious knowledge and power) was readily observable in the often quite considerable sections of related volumes which appeared in many mainstream bookshops in the 1980s. Witchcraft groups in places like the Sussex Weald claim to be rediscovering the ancient ways of basic religion. There are considerable tensions between black and white magic; the former attracts bad publicity and police concern because of its links with child abuse, the latter often exploits the media to project an image of being attuned to the forces latent in an

Fig. 8.3 Glastonbury Tor. The ruined church of St Michael dominates a natural mound encircled by ridges which have offered decades of attraction for discerners of mystical puzzles.

essentially benevolent landscape. One such group recently stood on some ancient Kent stones to incant against the building of a Channel Tunnel rail-link through the local fields; far from being an isolated or eccentric incident it was supported by hundreds of villagers involved in the protest.[52]

These movements have developed managerial and capital networks which are far from using prehistoric methods to manage their concerns. Electronically based desktop publishing and stock management are linked with the handicraft production of potions and ancient symbols for sophisticated marketing outlets. They are based in places which usually appeal to the whole range of syncretism, with Pagan/Celtic/Christian overlaps. Since the 1960s the key centre has been Glastonbury, the spiritual centre of the ancient kingdom of Avalon (fig. 8.3). There Arthurianism, the veneration of the Virgin Mary, Christian pilgrimages and hippy rock festivals mingle and Geoffrey Ashe and other writers have contributed a steady flow of claims that the entire local area is marked with the easily discernible lines of a mystical geometry. These are based on the identification of the 'Glastonbury Zodiac' in 1929 by a young Grail artist, Kathryn Maltwood, and have been tied into an attempt to revive 'England's Jerusalem', which has little to do with the Blake poem since Sir Hubert Parry's musical setting annexed that to more nationalistic mainstream middle-class Nature mysticism.[53] More recently, the organisational focus of this mystical alternative has tended to shift to Totnes in Devon, which has a less readily perceived spiritual past. What was a hippy hangover has been translated into quite crisp settlement and business terms with alternative schools, adult education seminars, publishing, earth shoe factories and shops selling mystic symbols and powerful crystals. Much of this is underpinned with subcontracting and by-employment in local cottages which has done a great deal to revive declining rural economies.[54] On a wider scale it has become part of the new folklore of feminism, which includes courses on 'Magic, Mystery and Suspenders; Art for Women' and 'natural products' retailing, claiming witchcraft antecedents for modern treatments for pre-menstrual tension.[55]

Mystical tourism has also become a minor industry. One aspect of it makes an interesting contrast with Glastonbury and Totnes: the earlier spiritual centre, Walsingham in Norfolk, where the medieval pattern of Marian pilgrimages was revived between the two world wars by an aggressive Anglican vicar, Father Hope Patten.[56] There, tea shops mingle with those selling religious tracts and kitsch souvenirs not too far removed except in mode of production from their medieval counterparts (fig. 8.4). As with Glastonbury and Totnes parking charges and overnight accommodation provide a steady income for locals during the pilgrimage seasons. For those who wish to follow the correct routes, discovering landscape as well as self, there is a substantial number of guide books comparable to those used in European touring. One such, *The Traveller's Guide to Sacred England*, bears on its cover the familiar profile of Salisbury Cathedral but its essential message is that almost any major pilgrimage centre has roots which go back far beyond the Christian period. Of the sites it recommends by far the greatest concentration is clustered in the Wessex area and almost all are accorded Megalithic origins. As with most other works of its type it catalogues the most obvious places but it also points to the continued importance of much lesser

Fig. 8.4 The Norfolk village of Walsingham was the site of an early medieval epiphany of the Blessed Virgin Mary. It became a major pilgrimage centre until the Reformation. Since the 1890s it has been revived and reconstructed as the closest thing England has to Lourdes.

places in local belief structures.[57] Just outside Penzance in Cornwall, deep in fields and hedges, is the Holy Well of Madron, going back at least to the days of Celtic Christianity (fig. 8.5). Although the Reformation theoretically swept away such devotions it remained in surreptitious use. When Methodism spread in the area prayer meetings were held there, as they were also in local prehistoric village sites such as Chysauster. The visitor who penetrates the muddy paths and tangled thickets which surround it will still find crosses made of twigs bearing torn rags, the remnants of the prayer messages left at the shrine. It is unclear which deity is being addressed.

For all these movements Nature is often both the location of God or Gods and divine in itself; in the language of professional theology it is both panentheistic and pantheistic. Kenneth Grahame preferred it as pagan. Apart from essays so entitled, he gave it a symbolic place in *Wind in the Willows*, where Pan appears to bless rural innocence: 'This is the place of my song-dream, the place the music played to me', whispered the Rat, as if in a trance. 'Here, in this holy place, here if anywhere surely we shall find Him.'[58] The idea of 'secret places' in Nature where the receptive can encounter both the sense of the distant past and the transcendent is expressed equally strongly by Rudyard Kipling in *Puck of Pook's Hill* and in *Rewards and Fairies*.[59] These works are supposedly children's books – their

Fig. 8.5 The Holy well of Madron, Cornwall. Surrounded by thickets and a ruined chapel this natural spring has attracted worshippers since the days of Celtic Christianity. Crosses fashioned roughly from twigs are adorned with rags or papers with prayers on them.

continued popularity suggests that, for middle-class children at least, there has been an early implanting of nature mysticism for some decades.

Literary contributions

The confusion of identified values we have discussed has also been singularly reinforced in the last hundred years or so by literature produced more specifically for adults. The Romantic movement spawned an idyllic vision of an organically spiritual landscape which still reverberates in poetry. The earlier twentieth-century Sussex parson, Andrew Young, incorporated his people and parish into epic verse.[60] More recently C. H. Sisson's poems reached a level of seriousness which is less popular than that we have already noted in Betjeman.[61] This vein of writing touches darker levels in some of the work of Ted Hughes but its most complete expression has been in the Celtic influences to be seen in the Anglo-Welsh priest–poet, R. S. Thomas, writing on the Lleyn Peninsula, over-looking Bardsey, the Island of Saints.[62]

Within the bounds of 'high culture' fiction the key figure in persuading a wide

Fig. 8.6 A Derbyshire well-dressing. Water's vital contribution to human settlement has allowed natural springs to be invested with sacred properties for millennia. The survival of such practices has remained strongest where Christianity has given overt support to such practices whilst trying to annexe them to itself.

readership that the countryside was the abode of spiritual forces was Thomas Hardy who lost his Christian beliefs at a relatively early age. A happy and productive world of rural religion had gone for him – paradoxically the book that established him publicly, *Under the Greenwood Tree*, celebrated simple religious faith. His later works repeatedly assumed the mystical, and usually malevolent, role of place in fostering tragedy. We have noticed the anthropomorphising of Egdon Heath – in *The Woodlanders* it is forest and trees that house ill omens, in *The Mayor of Casterbridge* an ancient amphitheatre with its memories of shed blood promises future sadness. They spoke of much more than literary devices and the artifice of plot construction.

In these terms, Hardy's literary heir was John Cowper Powys. The latter's *Glastonbury Romance* of 1933 centres on the *genius loci* and its reiteration of the Grail legend. He returned to this theme when he wrote, in the preface to the 1953 edition, 'The Grail is older than Christianity as it is older than Glastonbury Tor.'[63] His work grew out of a self-accepted syncretistic deism: 'What I aimed at when I wrote this book . . . was to convey a jumbled-up and squeezed together epitome of life's various dimensions.'[64] Powys has probably been less widely read than Hardy, undeservedly, but he met nonetheless the need of many urban readers to find an historical *locus* against which to measure unpalatable change. Both Hardy and Powys rejected orthodox Christianity but were deeply informed by a sense of the mysterious, occasionally even the numinous, and the importance of the transcendental expressed in place. One of Powys' brothers, Theodore, produced a lesser but remarkable allegory of the visit of God to an English village in *Mr. Weston's Good Wine*.[65] Since the Second World War it has been Iris Murdoch, exploring the possibilities of a personal God, who has carried on this tradition. It is less place-specific than that of the earliest writers but in both *The Bell* and in *The Message to The Planet* she has set her complicated networks of personal relationships in areas suffused with dense spiritual pressures: the latter exploits the presence of a group of New Age travellers, the Stone People, to explore the religious force of the central characters.[66] The televising of Kingsley Amis' *The Green Man*, with its theme of a revived past malevolence, took the concerns to a much wider audience than his readership.[67]

This approach represents a literary peak that is important but far removed from reinforcing beliefs in terms of a popular culture. It looms over an iceberg of populist writing which is strongest in dealing with ghosts, spiritual possession and mystery. It has donnish origins, rooted in the Edwardian antiquarianism of E. F. Benson and M. R. James.[68] Between the Wars Mary Webb, most notably in *Precious Bane*, continued to foster it. Even the remarkably funny piece of debunking, Stella Gibbons' *Cold Comfort Farm*, reinforced the mode she sought to destroy.[69]

The later twentieth century has produced a huge quantity of pulp fiction whose principal outlets are the chain bookstores and the book racks of supermarkets.

The most substantial in form and content are also those most firmly hyped by the publishers. Leading the field is James Herbert who explores themes of diabolical and basic elemental earth forces locked in permanent cosmic conflict, fought out at focal points in the English landscape. In *The Shrine* the thinly disguised West Sussex village of Henfield becomes the battle ground around a demonically simulated vision of the Virgin Mary; in *The Magic Cottage* a small part of the New Forest serves as the mouth of Hell. Good invariably triumphs but the reader is left to assume that this is only a temporary victory in a battle which will break out elsewhere in the countryside.[70]

Herbert's work is thoroughly constructed and quite well grounded in the various theologies he explores. Below him, cheaper and more rapidly produced, lies a vast pool. Two examples must suffice. In *The Quick and the Dead* Judy Gardner built a story round the return of Tudor witchcraft in a weekend cottage; it was originally serialised in that extremely respectable women's magazine, *Good Housekeeping*.[71] The most prolific contributor to this *genre* has probably been Guy N. Smith who had 20 short novels in print at the time of writing. They included *Bats Out of Hell* and *The Sucking Pit*. The plot structures are crude, the characters stereotypes, but they are firmly located in a tautly described rural England. This is not particularly surprising since Smith is also the highly competent author of a string of other works such as *Ferrets and Ferreting for the Amateur Gamekeeper*, produces books on smallholding and contributes regularly on shooting and wildlife matters to the *Shooting Times*.[72] It is difficult to trace the wholesale impact of such writing yet it obviously feeds a popular sense of an eternal cosmic battle between good and ill that is being fought out in an essentially rural English context. For that to happen there has to be a fairly general assumption that the countryside is full of places with permanent spiritual characteristics, what some clergy dealing with psychic matters call 'place memory'.[73]

This whole stream of production, as well as the patterns discussed earlier, give the lie to claims that modern society is basically rationalist, scientific and unbelieving. Whatever other uses may be made of the English countryside by the urban majority it is still widely regarded as an area where 'place memory' determines much of daily life, either benevolently or through conflict. With rare exceptions it is difficult to ascertain how far rural people themselves share or absorb these views; it might be expected that some local adaptation takes place because of the major role of the mass media in continuing to propagate them. The maps which are available for tracing this *mystical geography* often have little more modern cartographic relevance than those earlier efforts which were marked, 'Here be Dragons'. It is unlikely tht *mystical* will replace *physical, social* or *historical* geography in terms of the systematic analyses favoured by academic disciplines but it cannot be ignored as a significant element in forming modern English urban expectations of what the countryside is really for.

NOTES

Some of the references are to recent television and radio broadcasts. It is an important indication of the role played by predominantly urban media that the reiteration and reporting of some of the issues I have discussed are more likely to appear there than in print.

1   T. Ranger, 'Taking hold of the land', *Past and Present* 117 (1987) 158ff. Professor Ranger developed the theme from ideas current in earlier African anthropology – see A. Shorter, 'System, ritual and history: an examination of the work of Victor Turner' in T. Ranger and I. N. Kimambo (eds), *The Historical Study of African Religion* (1972) 144 and 147. I am grateful to him for this information.
2   Fay Godwin, *This Scepter'd Isle* (1989).
3   Henry Vaughan, 'Retirement' in L. C. Martin (ed.), *Henry Vaughan: Poetry and Selected Prose* (Oxford 1963) 436; Thomas Traherne, *Centuries* (1960) and Izaak Walton, *The Compleat Angler* (many editions). See Ronald Blythe, *Divine Landscapes* (1986). On Traherne, see G. Dowell *Enjoying the World* (1990).
4   R. Brooke, 'The Soldier', *The Collected Poems* (1918) 7.
5   R. Harman (ed.), *Countryside Character* (1946) 8.
6   P. Mullen, *Rural Rites* (1984) 107.
7   S. C. Carpenter, *Winnington – Ingram* (1949) 349.
8   Blythe, *Divine Landscapes*.
9   R. Currie, A. Gilbert and J. H. Horsley, *Churches and Churchgoers, Patterns of Church Growth in the British Isles Since 1700* (Oxford 1977) and D. M. Thompson, 'The churches and society in nineteenth-century England: a rural perspective', in G. J. Cuming and D. Baker (eds), *Popular Belief and Practice* (1972) 267ff.
10 G. Herbert, *The Country Parson* (1956 edn).
11 See O. Chadwick, *The Victorian Church*, 2 vols (1966 and 1970), especially volume II, chapter 4; A. Russell, *The Clerical Profession* (1980) and *The Country Parish* (1986); A. T. Hart, *The Country Priest in English History* (1959). The issues were also discussed in *Lord of the Land*, BBC 2 Television, 3 July 1990, which profiled the mediatory roles of a Lincolnshire vicar holding a multiple benefice.
12 R. Lewis and A. Talbot-Ponsonby (eds.) *The People, the Land and the Church* (Hereford Diocesan Board of Finance 1987); Russell, *Country Parish*; the shift towards a central response is represented in *Faith in the Countryside* (Worthing 1990), the report of the Archbishops' Commission on Rural Areas. Its considerable implications will take some years to put into practice.
13 G. Ahern and G. Davie, *Inner City God* (1987) 50; N. Silversides, *Folk Religion: Friend or Foe?* (Nottingham 1986); R. Towler and A. Chamberlain, 'Common Religion', *Sociological Yearbook of Religion in Britain* 6 (1973) 1–28.
14 S. Hill, *In the Springtime of the Year* (1974).
15 E. W. Martin, *The Secret People* (1955).
16 Personal communication to the author.
17 K. Thomas, *Religion and the Decline of Magic* (1971).
18 J. Obelkevich, *Religion and Rural Society, 1825–1875* (Oxford 1976).
19 D. Clark, *Between Pulpit and Pew* (Cambridge 1982).
20 *Kaleidoscope*, BBC Radio 4, 5 October 1989.

21 F. West, *The Country Parish, Today and Tomorrow* (1964) 6.

22 A. Wilkinson, *The Church of England and the First World War* (1975) 294ff.

23 See I. Opie and M. Tatem, *A Dictionary of Superstitions* (Oxford 1989) x–xi.

24 M. Baker, *Folklore and Customs of Rural England* (1974).

25 C. Longley, 'When the State takes on the mantle of Christianity', *The Times*, 8 February 1988.

26 See A. Howkins, 'The discovery of rural England' in R. Colls and P. Dodds (eds.), *Englishness: politics and culture 1880–1920* (1986) 62ff.

27 See J. Richardson (ed.), *Ten Rural Churches* (1988); L. J. Francis, *Rural Anglicanism. A Future for Young Christians?* (1985); C. Edmondson, *Strategies for Rural Evangelism* (Nottingham 1989); Rural Theology Association, *The Rural Church Towards 2000* (Northants 1989).

28 Archbishops' Commission on Rural Areas, *Faith in the Countryside*.

29 Reported in *The Radio Times*, 13–19 February 1988, 17. For more on *The Archers* as media image of the English countryside see chapter 7 by Stuart Laing in this volume.

30 Words on the tomb of Sybilla Stapley in St Mary the Virgin, Ringmer, East Sussex. See also C. Rawding, 'The iconography of churches: a case study of landownership and power in nineteenth-century Lincolnshire', *Journal of Historical Geography* 16 (2) (1990) 157ff.

31 Placard at 'Recording Britain', Victoria and Albert Museum, London, Summer 1990.

32 T. S. Eliot, 'Little Gidding', *Four Quartets* (1951) 51.

33 S. Hill, *The Magic Apple Tree* (1983) 87.

34 See, for example, J. Betjeman, *Collins Guide to Parish Churches of England and Wales* (1980).

35 J. Betjeman, *Collected Poems* (1958) 174.

36 F. Harrison, *The Living Landscape* (1986) 61.

37 D. Sinden, *The English Country Church* (1988); R. Briers, *English Country Churches* (1989).

38 T. Wilcox and A. Causey, *Claughton Pellew, 1890–1966* (Hove 1990).

39 Harrison, *Landscape*, 62.

40 See J. Hibbs, *The Country Chapel* (Newton Abbot 1988).

41 *Chronicle*, BBC 2 Television, 20 December 1989 and S. Piggott, *William Stukeley* (1950).

42 H. Sumner, *The Ancient Earthworks of Cranborne Chase* (1913).

43 T. Hardy, 'A tryst at an ancient earthwork', *Stories and Poems* (1970) 71ff.

44 A. Watkins, *The Old Straight Track* (1925).

45 P. Devereux and I. Thomson, *The Ley-Hunter's Companion* (1979) 10–11; W. Bloom and N. Pogacnik, *Ley Lines and Ecology* (1985).

46 Devereux and Thomson, *The Ley-Hunter's Companion*.

47 *Sunday Times*, 2 April 1989, B18.

48 M. Stockwood, *Chanctonbury Ring* (1982) 98.

49 P. Nash, *Fertile Image* (1975); C. Colvin, J. Drew and A. Noble, *Paul Nash Places* (1989); R. Cardinal, *The Landscape Vision of Paul Nash* (1989).

50 Discussed in an interview with Peter Levi, *Faith, Art and Vision*, Channel 4 Television, 19 July 1989.

51 S. Toulson, *East Anglia, Walking the Ancient Tracks* (1988) 17.

52 Reported in *Notes in the Margin*, BBC 2 Television, 1 February 1990.

53 J. Michell, *Traveller's Guide to Sacred England* (1989) 141.

54 C. Bennett, 'Visions in the land of milk and honey', *The Sunday Correspondent*, 17 September 1989.

55 The course was offered by the Women's Branch, Brighton WEA, in autumn 1990. The advertisements, from the firm 'Heath and Heather', appeared in *The Guardian* through the summer of 1990.

56 C. Stephenson, *Walsingham Way* (1970).

57 Michell, *Traveller's Guide*.

58 K. Grahame, *The Wind in the Willows* (1908, 1987 edn) 115 and 'The Rural Pan', *Pagan Papers* (1898) 65ff.

59 R. Kipling, *Puck of Pook's Hill* (1906) and *Rewards and Fairies* (1908) – for a discussion of the place of these, see M. Wiener, *English Culture and the Decline of the Industrial Spirit, 1850–1980* (Cambridge 1981) 57.

60 E. Lowbury and A. Young, *Andrew Young: The Poetical Works* (1985).

61 See C. H. Sisson, 'Burrington Combe', *Exactions* (Manchester 1980).

62 R. S. Thomas, *Later Poems* (1984) and *The Echoes Return Slow* (1988).

63 J. C. Powys, *A Glastonbury Romance* (1933, 1953).

64 *Ibid.*

65 T. F. Powys, *Mr. Weston's Good Wine* (1927).

66 I. Murdoch, *The Bell* (1958) and *The Message to the Planet* (1989).

67 K. Amis, *The Green Man* (1969), televised by the BBC in autumn 1990.

68 M. R. James, *The Collected Ghost Stories* (1931).

69 M. Webb, *Precious Bane* (1924); S. Gibbons, *Cold Comfort Farm* (1932).

70 J. Herbert, *The Shrine* (1984), *The Magic Cottage* (1986).

71 J. Gardner, *The Quick and the Dead* (1981).

72 See *The British Library Catalogue of Printed Books*, 'Guy N. Smith'.

73 See M. Perry, *Deliverance* (1987), chapter 4.

The rural/urban fringe as battleground 9

PETER AMBROSE

This chapter grows partly out of an ongoing research project based at the University of Sussex Centre for Urban and Regional Research, and funded by the Economic and Social Research Council and the Swedish National Building Research Institute.[1] The project takes as study areas the county of Berkshire, nine communes north of Stockholm in the 'E4 corridor' to Uppsala, and the metropolitan area of Toulouse in south-west France. These areas were chosen because they are all experiencing very rapid employment growth and restructuring. The growth includes a disproportionately large number of jobs in 'new technology' manufacturing, in research and development activities, and in financial and other producer services. There are two important points about growth in these employment groups. First, incomes tend to be higher than average because there is a high managerial and technical component in the occupational structure and second, growth in these sectors often has the effect of drawing new employees into the area rather than simply re-employing people from existing industries.

The main aim of the study is to see how well the housing provision systems adjust to this sudden surge of growth in employment and in housing demand. This adjustment, or lack of it, has implications not only for the larger urban centres but also for the many rural communities within commuting range of these centres. Within the larger towns themselves, building land is in short supply. It is often land that has been built over before, and for that reason is often not attractive to housebuilders because of possible complications when digging foundations or possible pollution from previous industrial use. In addition such sites may have a potentially higher value if developed for commercial uses. For these reasons the growth pressures frequently spill over into the adjacent rural areas on the rural/urban fringe. The effects may be felt up to 30 to 40 miles away if transport systems allow. In all three case study areas there are fast modern motorways which permit ever longer-range commuting and this is typical of many other similar areas. The employment growth effects are therefore being felt by an increasing number of rural communities.

The general expectation was that since housing supply is inelastic in the short term – it is difficult rapidly to produce hundreds or thousands of extra houses –

there may well be 'bottlenecks' in housing supply. These bottlenecks tend to manifest themselves as steep rises in house prices and rents. This produces extra financial pressures on people who already live in the areas, especially if they are not involved in the new higher paid industries. Another effect is that existing employers in the area, especially employers who are not themselves in the rapid growth new technology and financial services sectors, begin to experience recruitment problems centred partly around the high local cost of housing for potential employees. This might especially apply to public sector employers such as education or social service departments. It is also likely, although difficult to demonstrate, that potential employers who would otherwise have located in the area are discouraged from doing so because they are aware of the high local housing costs. Finally it is reasonable to expect that the wage costs of employers operating in the area will be increased in two ways as a result of high housing costs. First they will feed through into higher wage claims and settlements and second it may be necessary to offer relocation packages of various sorts to attract labour, especially executives and other key workers.

In the light of this hypothesised set of effects it is instructive to compare the housing supply responses of the three different housing systems, the British, Swedish and French. From existing knowledge the British system of land development can be characterised as somewhat less regulated than that in France while the Swedish system, with its long-established tradition of public intervention, is rather more regulated than both. This in turn produces a range of policy responses with Britain at one extreme, with a very high proportion of speculative housing built for sale, and the E4 corridor at the other. In the latter area the more careful regulation of the promotion of housing, the phased land-release mechanisms and the cheap loans to builders under the State Housing Loan system enable considerable public leverage to be exerted over the development process. The key finding of the work so far[2] is that house and land-price inflation in these 'boom' areas has been far more severe in the British case than in the two others.

These considerations set the scene for the rest of this chapter which concentrates on the pressures on rural communities just outside the urban fringes. Given the structure of the land-use planning system in Britain, this focusses attention especially on the Green Belt areas around major cities and conurbations. The Green Belt policy was part of the 1946–47 era of planning legislation.[3] It was enacted under the Labour government of the day as a response to the 'ribbon development' pattern of the inter-war years which produced linear forms of development along the arterial roads. This had the effect of linking up neighbouring towns and despoiling disproportionate areas of countryside. The effects were exacerbated by the surface extension of the underground lines around London which went right out into the rural fringes in the neighbouring counties and produced immense development pressures in an area up to 15 miles out from the centre of London.[4]

A Green Belt consists of land that is designated for special protection in the Structure Plans of the county planning authorities surrounding the city. In the case of a mono-centered city such as London, this land forms a continuous belt around the built up area. Sometimes, as in the case of the West Yorkshire conurbation, the protected area consists of the remaining rural interstices between the network of urban areas. The main intention here is to prevent the towns coagulating into an urban mass. Within the designated areas there is a general presumption against urbanisation and development applications have additional planning hurdles to surmount. The aims of Green Belt policy are therefore to prevent outward sprawl from the existing built up area and to allow urban residents to have some contact with the countryside – although the extent to which Green Belt land does actually provide areas where you can walk your dog and so on has been seriously questioned over the years. Green Belt policy has the further purpose of protecting valuable farmland, especially Grades 1 and 2 land. It is likely that high-intensity farming will be taking place in these areas because of the proximity to urban markets.

The overall effect of a Green Belt is to exert an 'artificial' constraint on the tendency of large urban areas to get larger by peripheral expansion. This is especially the case in those parts of the country where the economy is booming and new investment is seeking to come in and create more jobs. This often has a 'multiplier' effect and stimulates more jobs in the service industries such as retailing, education and health administration. The development constraint arising from this restraint policy displaces pressures from the urban fringe to two other areas. There will be additional pressures *inside* the built up area where there may be land for redevelopment right near the core of the city itself (in the former dockland areas in London or Cardiff or Leith for example). In these inner parts of the city there may also be additional pressures to convert or 'gentrify' housing where lower income people are currently living. Because of the attractiveness of their architecture or proximity to the city centre they may be converted into very desirable areas for housing upper income people.[5] The other areas to feel extra pressures are those just *beyond* the Green Belt. This general pattern of constraint on peripheral expansion has been a structural feature since the Second World War and, at least in the case of London, only a small percentage of the designated area has been lost to urbanisation.

One other feature of the British planning system should be noted. Regional or sub-regional planning is very poorly developed. There are no authorities which have any statutory power to condition events or to promote strategic solutions at any scale larger than the county. Also, since the attack on the metropolitan authorities in 1986, there are no adequate agencies to integrate the planning of the conurbations and cities with that of the rural areas and communities to which they are functionally related. In the eyes of many critics land-use planning has beome an increasingly *ad hoc* process without any strong strategic element. This tendency does not reflect the preferences of professional planners but rather the free-market ideologies adopted by successive governments during the 1980s.

It is precisely those rural communities within commuting range of large and expanding urban areas which form the setting for the processes to be discussed in the rest of this chapter. Strictly speaking these communities are neither economically nor socially 'rural' any more.[6] They are often characterised by expensively converted farm cottages and manor houses, sometimes complete with swimming pools, from which men and women with decidedly 'urban' jobs set forth every morning in the Volvo estate to drive to the nearest station. An overview of all this can be obtained while stacked up around Heathrow waiting to land. The settlements in these areas have been termed 'discontinuous suburbs'.[7] That is to say they are settlements which appear 'freestanding' but which are functionally simply a suburb of the metropolis. They just happen to be separated from the metropolis itself by a thin swathe of green fields and farming.

The farming carried on around these settlements is often intensive and, as we will see in a moment, the owners of the land and the nature of the farming has changed very dramatically indeed over this century and especially in the years since the Second World War. It has become increasingly energy intensive and much more heavily dependent on chemical fertilisers and pest controls. The activity has also, partly as a consequence, become much more capital intensive. Machinery has increasingly replaced labour in virtually all branches of the industry. So while evidently there is agricultural activity there are very few farm workers. Despite this falling demand for agricultural labour it is often difficult to attract enough young workers into the industry. In fact in some ways the industry is not so much in a state of change as a state of crisis.[8]

One difficulty is that the housing costs which have to be faced in these villages cannot comfortably be paid by people on an agricultural wage. Most villages of this kind have their small group of perhaps six to 12 council houses – characteristically placed a little way off centre from the historic core of the village. Often these were built in the decade or so after the last war in recognition that if farming was to remain a low-wage industry then workers would need low-rent housing. In the period since 1979, local authorities have been under increasing government pressure to sell off this housing under the Right to Buy policy and to increase rents towards 'market levels'. The provision of lower-cost or lower-rent housing for the residual number of people who are still necessary to work the land is an important issue which has only recently received the attention it deserves.[9] Initiatives to provide such housing often have broad support not only from housebuilders[10] but also from employers who naturally wish to continue to pay the low wages traditional in rural areas.

The developers, and especially the house builders, have a very strong interest in these areas. If they can find land to build executive housing within easy commuting range of the rapidly growing employment centres, then they have a very ready market for their product. In the market conditions of the 1980s it was usually executive housing that had the most reliable sales. In the course of one interview with a director of a major housebuilding firm it was asserted that at least up to 1988, when property values began to level out, they could sell £300,000 houses as fast as they could build them – especially around old-established market towns 20 or so miles out from London. While this rosy outlook has been undermined towards the end of the 1980s by factors such as the stock market recession and high mortgage interest rates, and the 1990s may bring competition from overseas construction interests, the areas in and around the Green Belts remain the most promising hunting grounds for the housebuilding industry. The main problem from the house-hunter's point of view lies in the builders' collective lack of interest in providing lower-price housing. The reasons for this should become clearer in a moment.

The extent to which the housebuilders are successful in getting significant supplies of land to build on in these areas, 'busting the green belt' as it is often called, depends on a number of factors.[11] These include the rate of employment growth within commuting range and thus the need perceived by the local authority planners, and central government, for the planning system to release more land for development. It depends also on the strength of the conservation interests in the rural areas, towns and villages, and partly also on the presence or absence of available building land within the nearby conurbation itself. Finally it depends upon the degree of enthusiasm for protecting the Green Belt on the part of those structure planning authorities responsible for it. This factor, and various of the others, will ultimately be influenced by central government in the shape of the Department of the Environment. In recent years the Department's view has swayed from heavily pro-conservation to heavily pro-development, depending partly on the Secretary of State in office.

During the 1980s this issue of development on the urban/rural fringe has been perceived by the House Builders' Federation as 'a bloody battle'. This rather lurid formulation is not entirely out of place. Very powerful interests, and immense sums of money, are involved. The issue is all about who has the greatest power to condition what is going to happen, in other words how much development is going to take place. A battle, of course, requires protagonists. This is a complicated battle because instead of the usual two protagonists there are in this case at least six discernible interest groups lining up and doing battle.[12] The rest of this chapter is devoted to a consideration of each of the six in turn.

Old landed interests

The first of these, although decreasingly important now, are the old landed interests. These are the historic group of landowners, often titled, who up to the early years of the twentieth century held land as their prime form of wealth whether for its farming or minerals value. For them land was also a source of political interest and prestige, something which gave them a seat in the House of Lords in many cases. It also established their dominance in the local social hierarchy in relation to the many workers they were employing on their estates. Elements of this hierarchy, and the habits of deference that go with it, are still evident. For example even in the 1970s in a quite large 'commuter' village in Sussex, it was still almost impossible to persuade some farm workers to put up a Labour poster even though they clearly supported the party's cause.

Over the past one hundred years this landed group have suffered a number of reverses.[13] These began in the 1870s when the great agricultural depression affected the profits from land (unless these were based on minerals) and they followed on through the 1890s and into the early years of the twentieth century. At this time there were a number of moves by the Liberal party to impose new taxation on rural land. At least four separate taxes were proposed in the 1910 budget that affected the profitability and inheritance value of land. These measures, and the political climate leading up to them, led to considerable disinvestment by the historic land-owning interests. This continued from that time right through to the early and mid 1930s. In the latter part of this period the era of mass speculative housing development for owner-occupancy began to produce the estates which are still with us and which largely characterise the outer fringes of most of our cities.[14] They were built on land which at the time had decreasing agricultural value but certainly an increasing value for sale to housebuilders.

These historic landed interests then are the first identifiable protagonists in the six-sided battle. In relative terms they have lost significance economically, and probably socially in most places. Their concerns are often with issues such as access to the countryside[15] although it would be unfair to say that that was their only interest in the urban fringe issue. They have been overtaken in significance by the second group who approach the management of agricultural areas on the urban fringe in a much more instrumental way. These are what might be termed 'new agricultural interests'.

New agricultural interests

The transformation in support for British agriculture had its origins in the Second World War when self-sufficiency in food became a key strategic aim. This placed a tremendous premium on agricultural activities. Since the war there has

Fig. 9.1 A form of land use becoming ever more common in Green Belt areas – not a stately home, but the group management centre in northern Sussex of one of the world's largest multinationals.

been a massive broadening of the array of support structures for agriculture, encapsulated now in the Common Agricultural Policy of the EC. These changes have led new sets of interests to look at land, especially land close to urban markets, primarily as a promising arena for investment (fig. 9.1). These interests are therefore more narrowly 'instrumental' in their approach and they are driven by the imperative to maximise long- and medium-term returns on investment. Such a requirement calls for rational investment strategies, good management practices, a close look at the changing cost-effectiveness of crop patterns and farming technologies and above all a close eye on changes in the CAP. It also calls for a more co-ordinated political strategy towards decision makers, whether in Whitehall or Brussels. Increasingly also it has implied more energy-intensive methods of farming, even on Grade 3 land, and massive increases in borrowing in order to finance these various changes.[16]

One consequence has been that the indebtedness of the British farming industry to the City has increased by a factor of something like 12 in real terms since 1947. Unfortunately the interest rate has been used increasingly by monetarist governments of the 1980s as the main mechanism for regulating the economy and this has seriously affected the finances of many farming enterprises. As the interest rate has fluctuated widely, responding to factors which have little to do with the performance of the farming industry (such as balance of payments difficulties), so it has become increasingly difficult to make the books balance. It has also complicated the task of devising a forward investment strategy at the level of the individual enterprise because future interest costs cannot be assessed. Thus the general effect of high and fluctuating interest rates has been to de-stabilise agricultural financial strategies.

It has even been argued that without massive price support systems, there would actually be no point in farming in Britain. It has been pointed out that in 1980/81 the subsidy input to support British farming totalled £1.928 million.[17] In the same year the net income for British farmers was £1.162 million. The conclusion drawn is that the total net income available from farming as an activity would be highly negative without the level of subsidy deriving principally from the Common Agricultural Policy. This subsidy is a support for farm *revenues*. But since the value of any piece of land reflects the net revenue derivable from it, multiplied by some appropriate factor, the support has in fact immensely increased the *capital values* of the land – and will continue to do so as long as there are expectations that the revenue support will continue.

The factor to be applied to equate revenues with capital value depends directly on the rate of interest. If, say, a 5 per cent return can be obtained from some other activity with equivalent risk to farming, then the capital value of land will be 20 times the net annual revenues (thus giving a competitive 5 per cent return on the capital value). But if 20 per cent can be obtained elsewhere in the investment market, the land value will fall to only five times the net annual revenues (thus bringing the financial yield to the new competitive level of 20 per cent). In other words, capital value varies inversely with the interest rate. When one is high the other is low. Whether land values go up or down really doesn't matter (unless of course you happen to own some). The essence of the argument is that, as a matter of policy, rapid changes in the rate of interest have occurred over the last decade or so. This, in turn, has produced rapid changes in current valuations. Thus agricultural interests are now operating in a quite different commercial environment from the older, more stable days of farming before the late 1960s. In those days the interest rate could be expected to remain relatively constant and future trends in the value of agricultural land were that much more predictable.

The collective agricultural interest is articulated formally by the National Farmers' Union, which sees itself as the guardian of the 'National Farm' and sometimes by bodies such as the Council for the Protection of Rural England.[18] The Union argues strongly against urban fringe development, asserting, for example, that every ten acres lost to housing development around rural communities results in the effective loss of 20 acres of farmland. They believe that apart from the land actually taken for development, the new population in the area, with their dogs, children and so on, tends to reduce the productive capability of the land around the new housing. There is therefore a strong NFU case against expansion into the urban fringes.[19] This does not normally prevent individual farmers queuing up to sell parcels of land here and there for the very good reason that the capital value of land takes an enormous jump once it has been zoned for housing development.

As an example, in South East England good quality agricultural land might be valued at £1,500–£2,000 per acre in 1990. But land zoned for housing development in and around the Green Belt, and even further out than that, may be worth between £0.5 million and £1 million or more if available for housing development. This value 'falls out of' a calculation by the housebuilder, normally made before the bid for the land is made, about the number of houses that can be built on the site, their construction cost and what they can be expected to sell for.[20] The enormous values therefore reflect the high prices obtainable for new housing in these areas – itself partly a product of the volume of house purchase credit available to potential buyers bolstered by the tax concessions available to purchasers. This increase in land value by a factor of possibly several hundred occurs at the point when legal consent is given by the planning authority for the land to be converted from agricultural to housing use. That decision may, of course, be anticipated and speculative trading may occur in advance of re-zoning. Clearly value increments of this order of magnitude can powerfully reduce the charm of farming and provide a powerful incentive for individual farmers to sell.

Housebuilders

This brings us to the third main group participating in the battle – the housebuilders themselves. In the context of most modern industries of comparable size and significance, the housebuilding industry is rather a strange one.[21] Compared, for example, to the motor vehicles industry it has not achieved high degrees of technological development and in some ways is still using methods that go back thousands of years. People can still be seen on modern building sites going up ladders carrying buckets. The ownership pattern, too, has remained highly fragmented. In Britain something like 20 housebuilders account for perhaps 50 per cent of housing output. But the remainder is produced by tens of thousands of businesses of all sizes down to one-person operations. Most of the big ones now tend to be part of multi-purpose conglomerates or groups of companies, for example the Trafalgar House group, within which separate housebuilding divisions or companies operate on a partly independent basis.

Two large and powerful groups of capitalist entrepreneurs therefore come into conflict with each other in the urban/rural fringe. There are first the big capital agricultural and financial interests who own large areas of the land on which housing development may well be permitted at some future date. They are currently farming it as efficiently as possible but they no doubt also have an eye to

Fig. 9.2 Part of a newly-built speculative estate in central Berkshire. The density seems very high for 'up market' housing and this has the effect of pushing up land values in the 'scramble for land' (photograph by James Barlow).

the future potential development value realisable on the land. Secondly there are the big capital housebuilders who need to acquire landbanks for their current and projected future building programmes. As a sub-plot, these big builders are in competition with the many medium and small-sized builders who also need land and very often do not have the resources to search systematically for it or to hold it for future needs. These various interests are in conflict over the share of profits to be derived from the process of converting land from one use (agriculture) to another (housing). That conflict is therefore about the price at which development land changes hands. The higher the price, the more the farming and landowning interests are gaining; the lower that price the more the housebuilder interests are gaining. The eventual house purchaser unfortunately does not gain much at all except a considerable long-term debt (fig. 9.2).

The demand for the product, new housing, is relatively secure in the areas we are discussing, primarily as a result of the success of the local economies. But here recent decades have shown that caution has to be exercised. Local economies need not only to be buoyant – they need also to be diversified and to have good long-term prospects. A housing boom such as that which occurred in the Aberdeen area, narrowly based on non-renewable mineral resources, is less likely to attract the interest of large-scale nationally based housebuilders. Construction interests will therefore try to take a longer-term view. They will be attracted to the highly diversified areas of employment growth where if one branch of industry fails to develop as expected there is the chance that another may.

These so called 'hot spots' are also the areas where foreign entrepreneurs may well be interested in investing. For example a Japanese company may want to set up a plant which will market products to North Europe as a whole, rather than just to Britain. Unless there are compelling reasons otherwise, it will probably look to the more successful areas in the South East rather than to an older industrial region. During the 1980s, under neo-liberal economic policies, patterns of regional development have become more uneven. Generally speaking richer areas have become richer and poorer areas poorer.[22] The unevenness has been if anything accentuated by the pattern of large scale infrastructural initiatives, both private and public. These include, for example, the M25, the Channel Tunnel and the proposed rail link from the tunnel to London. All these factors have tended to work together and feed off one another in sharpening the differences between the 'have' and the 'have not' regions and in conferring more growth pressures on attractive rural/urban fringe areas.

Although not attracted by short-term 'boom-bust' local economies, housebuilders do not have the same kind of very long-term interests in an area as do the developers of commercial schemes such as retail and leisure centres and offices. The housebuilder, by the nature of his operation, is rapidly in and out of the development process. He buys land, perhaps holding it for a few years before developing. He then builds a product upon it and sells the house plus site. He is therefore not left with the kind of long-term risk that a commercial developer faces when developing a shopping centre on a 99-year lease with a medium- or long-term pay-back period of perhaps 20 or 30 years. Once the purchase loan has been taken out and the house purchased it is the buyer and the mortgage lender who bear these risks. More realistically it is the purchaser because the lender can always foreclose and recoup most or all of the loan by selling the property.

The housebuilders' strategy in urban fringe and rural areas follows a logical chain of argument. First he needs to sell more of the product to increase both profits and market share. But in the late 1980s and early 1990s the recession and the high interest rates are cutting deep at the capacity of first-time and other purchasers to pay the kind of price the housebuilder is looking for. Therefore, to extend the market, the price of the product must if possible be reduced in real terms. But at this point the housebuilder runs up against a number of constraints. For example it is next to impossible to reduce the materials input costs, since many of the main materials suppliers operate as cartels. There is also a limit below which the housebuilder cannot reduce labour costs without major investment in the kinds of new technology which would increase labour productivity. But it has been some time since the housebuilding industry had the confidence about future prospects to think along these lines.

It follows that two of the major cost elements, materials and labour, are difficult to reduce in the short term. This places cost-cutting attention on the third main input – land. If the prices paid for land could be substantially reduced this would help reduce total costs. It is the much-publicised view of the House Builders' Federation that if the planning system would release a few thousand more acres every year, especially in areas under heavy growth pressures, then the scramble for land would be reduced and this in turn would sharply reduce the prices that housebuilders have to pay for it.[23] The HBF go on to argue that this would result in substantially lower house prices. There must be some doubt about the latter part of this argument. It is difficult to believe, if a housebuilder suddenly got land at one-quarter of the price he had previously paid, that he would sell houses commensurately cheaper. This would be to deny the effect that the volume of purchase credit has on house prices. It does however follow that the general strategy of the housebuilding industry is to seek to get considerably more land released by the planning system so as to ease the land-search problem and reduce one important cost factor. One means of developing this strategy is to carry out studies in collaboration with planning authorities to assess the land-supply situation.[24]

Conservation interests

The fourth set of interests are those concerned with conservation. They are a very diverse coalition with different degrees of 'greenness'.[25] There are, for example, what one might call the genuine 'core' of conservationists, those interested in the rural heritage, the beauty of the landscape, the wildlife, the preservation of hedges, and so on. They take the view that we should pass on the countryside to coming generations in much the same condition that we inherited it – or if possible better. There is another group in the conservation coalition, probably much smaller, who have an interest in preserving the old hierarchy of social relations based on position in the agricultural system of production and the various skills and crafts necessary to support it. Their interest is often in preserving 'country ways of life'. They are probably of little significance politically except perhaps in areas rather more remote than those we are dealing with here.

There is a third group of conservationists who are far more significant. These are the 'pull-up-the-ladder' group of recent arrivals – the 'born again conservationists' or NIMBYs ('not in my back yard'). The group has come to these 'rural areas' primarily to enjoy leafy seclusion. The last thing they want is another group of arrivals. In other words they are rigidly opposed to any more housebuilding if it will spoil their view or possibly have an adverse effect on property values. They may well be in favour of more development in the general vicinity, perhaps a motorway giving better access to centres of employment, but they will often use their considerable expertise to organise resistance to development in, or within sight of, their particular village.

This coalition of conservation interests is represented by a number of organisations, for example the Country Landowners' Association which is an old-established group representing a relatively narrow range of interests. Perhaps more notable in the context of modern planning battles has been the Council for the Protection of Rural England. The Council employs expert research staff and has a very broad-based vision that is by no means confined to the old preservationist ideals of the CPRE when the P in its title stood for Preservation. In fact, during the 1980s CPRE has made common cause with organisations such as Shelter who want to see more housing developed on 'brownfield' sites near city centres, particularly low-rent housing for lower-income people. In recent years CPRE has been a trenchant critic of the neo-liberal free-for-all mentality which has emerged as the dominant government approach to the events in the urban fringe battlefield and they have produced or sponsored a number of rigorously argued reports.[26]

Central government

This brings us to the fifth set of interests, those of the central state. From 1979 to 1990 these were embodied in the three successive Thatcher administrations. These governments have had a consistent ideological position: a predisposition towards neo-liberal views, and 'free market' solutions. These political, some would say ideological, positions carry with them an inherent unease about any form of 'planning'. State regulation in this sphere, as in all others, has been regarded as a burden on the 'enterprise economy'. The economic aim has been above all else to get the inflation rate down, to keep it down, and to get the economy out of recession by increasing productivity and output. These aims have regional and sub-regional implications. Government policy has been very much to reward 'successful' regions, for example by increased infrastructural investment, and not to spend money on incentives to attract new industry to those less-successful parts of the country, the parts where old traditional industries are in decline. By its pattern of support, or rather non-support, for public transport it has shown that it has very little interest in the more isolated rural areas.

The cumulative effect of these policies has been to make the pattern of development more uneven, to encourage more new investment to gravitate towards the 'hotspot' boom regions. This exacerbates the pressures on the housing supply arrangements in these areas, particularly since much of the new industry prefers 'greenfield' sites, and fuels the demands for more development land to be released. In areas such as Berkshire it is overwhelmingly speculatively built owner-occupied housing that has been built.[27] In fact by 1989 such housing represented 91 per cent of completions in the county. Rented housing, by contrast, has become far more difficult to find. This has led to a considerable debate in housing circles. The argument has frequently been made that the administrations during the 1980s have had their own politically inspired interests in extending home-ownership rather than supporting the provision of rented housing. It has been argued since the 1920s that the more indebted the society and the more it is tied in to property ownership, the more politically stable and conservative it will be. This is the frequently heard 'stake in the system' argument.

Comparative study shows this to be a particularly British political obsession. In other European countries there is no automatic or presumed relationship between property ownership and any particular set of political beliefs, intentions or actions. In the Swedish case study area, parts of the E4 'corridor' leading north from Stockholm, there has in fact been a sharp decline in the provision of speculative housing for sale over the period of rapid employment growth since 1980. Britain alone appears to have this carefully fostered attitude about the virtues of property ownership and 'standing on one's own two feet'. This is, of course, a fraudulent claim. Owner–occupiers, while actually in the mortgage-paying stage, are receiving far more subsidy than any other category of housing user.[28] They are very successfully, if unwittingly standing on other people's feet.

The overall effect of these policy stances has been that the speculative builder, who Aneurin Bevan once described as 'by nature not a plannable instrument', has been given what is sometimes termed 'all assistance short of actual help' to provide the housing necessary to underpin the growth in areas such as rural Berkshire. The 'assistance' has been indirect and has often taken the form of central government revisions upward of the volume of land released in local and structure plans. 'Help' would mean actual supply side subsidies in the form of a flow of land to constructors at sub-market prices and/or construction loans at sub-market cost (both these form an important part of the Swedish housing supply arrangements). Ironically the adherence to traditional and ill-thought-out housing support policies has produced a number of problems for the British governments of the 1980s.

The free-for-all which has been encouraged in the greenfield areas has provided quite heavy Tory backbench unease, and even resistance. Something like 90 or so Tory MPs represent constituencies in these rural/urban fringe areas. Most of their voters prefer conservationist policies rather than a less regulated approach to development. This backlash from Conservative voters and MPs has been difficult for the Department of the Environment to handle. This was particularly so when an accident-prone Secretary of State, Nicholas Ridley, scored a spectacular own goal by criticising NIMBYs who held up development while trying personally to stop building which was spoiling the view from his own house. He has subsequently moved on and out.

There is a further contradiction. The very free-market economic strategy which the government espouses, one deriving directly from neo-classical economics, demands good mobility of labour. It demands that the 'hotspot' areas are not inhibited in their growth by difficulties in the recruitment of managers, techno-crats, and skilled manual staff. But the effects of housing policy in the Berkshire case have been a rapid rate of house price and land price inflation – greater by far than the rates observed in the Toulouse and Stockholm growth areas. The reasons are discussed elsewhere[29] and cannot be explored here. So the sharp regional differences in house price inflation that have occurred in the 1980s, and perhaps more important the shortage of rented housing, have in many people's judgement reduced the potential for labour mobility. They have made it more difficult to move from low to high housing cost areas, and they have also inhibited the propensity of people in high housing cost areas to move out to lower cost areas for fear that they would never be able to afford to move back.

There is a consequent problem for the government. Since housing costs are an important element in the price index by which inflation is measured, the rapid growth in personal housing costs in the rural/urban fringe areas is contributing significantly to the official rate of inflation and working through in the form of increased wage demands and costly housing relocation packages. This in turn is working to undermine the government's main economic priority. These prob-lems of rapidly inflating housing costs are difficult to solve in the short term except perhaps (if one accepts the argument of the housebuilders) by a significant increase in the amount of land released by the planning system for development. But that goes precisely against the conservation interests of a large number of Tory MPs whose voters would be highly displeased. In any case one would still be left with a lack of regulation on the amount of house purchase credit available and the effects this must be having on prices and thus the general inflation index.

The planning interest

The sixth interest is the planning interest. By this is meant the interests of the professional planners and planning committees who prepare the statutory structure and local plans in the context of which the development process proceeds. The ideal scenario for any trained professional planner is to achieve a balanced pattern of development in any given area – a harmonious match between the increase in jobs and properly phased increases in housing provision, educational and social service facilities, and physical infrastructure such as road capacity, water and sewage services and so on. Over recent decades this search for

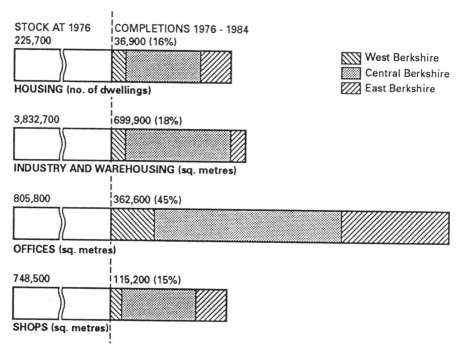

STOCK AT 1976   COMPLETIONS 1976 - 1984
225,700   36,900 (16%)

West Berkshire
Central Berkshire
East Berkshire

HOUSING (no. of dwellings)

3,832,700   699,900 (18%)

INDUSTRY AND WAREHOUSING (sq. metres)

805,800   362,600 (45%)

OFFICES (sq. metres)

748,500   115,200 (15%)

SHOPS (sq. metres)

Fig. 9.3 An extract from the *Review of Berkshire's Structure Plan*, 1986, discussing the nature of the growth in the County in the early 1980s. Note how the rate of growth of office space has outstripped that of other uses.

balanced development has led some rural planning authorities to select out 'key villages' for development. These are villages which already have a certain 'critical mass' in terms of population and existing facilities. The logic here is that expensive investment in physical and social infrastructure should be directed towards villages with a reasonable chance of future success rather than towards smaller settlements with a more doubtful long-term future.

Whether such policies are pursued or not, and there are certainly arguments against the strategy, it is contrary to the land-use planner's instincts and training suddenly to release hundreds of acres of land for housing development if there is no thought-through strategy for the concurrent provision of these complementary facilities. This is however precisely what has happened in a number of cases in the 1980s.[30] Structure plans prepared locally have been forwarded to the Department of the Environment for ministerial approval. There have then been over-riding additions to the amount of land to be released for development without, in the view of the local planning authority, adequate consideration of the implications for health or education services which may already be starved of funds and overstretched (fig. 9.3).

What of the future?

Given a continuance of governments ideologically uncomfortable with the notion of 'planning', as has been the case in the 1980s, there is a danger that the pattern of development in high growth rural/urban fringe areas may become highly unbalanced. So as far as one can see there will be a continuing need for what has been termed 'the planning interest' as one factor affecting events in the battlefield. Most people, and certainly many media commentators, seem to believe that it is 'the planners' who are responsible for all the adverse effects of runaway growth in the rural communities within commuting distance of rapidly expanding towns. This view does great injustice to planners and reflects a very partial understanding of the full range of forces that are at work here. At least equal power – and probably a much greater share as a result of the policies of the 1980s – lies with one or other, or a combination, of the other five interest groups we have considered. Maybe one aim for the 1990s should be to seek a more balanced relationship between the private and public sector forces at work in these areas.

The battle that is taking place on the rural/urban fringes in high growth employment regions of the country is partly about profits, partly about politics, and partly about a general concern for the countryside. Organisations and people representing all those interests are involved in it. It takes a different form in different areas. Around Edinburgh, which has rapid growth in financial service activities, a very strong conservation lobby, and a large amount of derelict former mining and dock land, there is a particular slant to the issue with the Scottish Office attempting to divert development towards 'brownfield' old urban sites while the builders continue to seek their preferred greenfield sites.[31]

Around London during the 1980s there have been various attempts by consortia of housebuilders to bust the Green Belt on a very large scale with plans to develop so-called 'new towns'. These have been presented as a continuation of the post Second World War 'new town' concept. But critics claim that there is very little in common between the two ideas. The post-1946 New Towns aimed to be socially balanced communities with a mix of employment and social facilities to meet residents' needs so that the town was, as far as possible, 'freestanding'. The consortia house builders' aims are rather different. They feel that if they can get land released in very large amounts to build instant towns for up to 20,000 people all within about 25 to 30 miles of London, this will solve the housing supply difficulties at a stroke. Critics argue that such developments are unlikely to include a full range of employment and social facilities but will instead be speculative owner-occupied estates on a very large scale. This is certainly what they look like at present and many people have been relieved that so far successive Secretaries of State have turned down such proposals as those for massive new residential development at Foxley Wood in northern Hampshire.

Fig. 9.4 The 'Brownfield' solution to housing pressures. Some of the 13,000-plus houses built in London's dockland redevelopment since 1981 – very few of them affordable by the original residents of the area.

So it remains to be seen how this conflict affecting rural communities outside the urban fringes will work out as the 1990s proceed, and how rural areas will be restructured.[32] In the long term, given the strictly limited amount of land available in these islands, it could be argued that the only rational way to proceed is to re-use large amounts of derelict land available *within* the existing built-up areas rather than to claim yet more rural land for development. Once new land is built over it is difficult to see how it would ever revert to rural use. Part of the answer must therefore be to re-use 'windfall' areas like London's docklands – but emphatically not to allow an unplanned free-market bonanza such as we have seen in that area in the 1980s and which, even now, may well be carrying the seeds of its own destruction (fig. 9.4).[33] The issue of where and how development should take place in the 1990s, whether in relation to rural or urban areas, is far too important to be left to the forces that have tended to be dominant in the 1980s.

NOTES

1   J. Barlow, P. Ambrose and S. Duncan, 'Housing provision in high growth regions. A comparative study of four European sub-regions', *Scandinavian Housing and Planning Research* 5(1) (1988) 33–7.

2   J. Barlow, 'Owner-occupier housing supply and the planning framework in the "boom" regions. Examples from Britain, France and Sweden', *Planning Practice and Research* 5(2) (1990) 4–11.

3   M. Elson, *Green Belts, Conflict and Mediation in the Urban Fringe* (1986)

4   A. Jackson, *Semi-detached London: Suburban Development, Life and Transport, 1900–1939* (1973)

5   N. Smith and P. Williams, *Gentrification of the City* (1986)

6   P. Ambrose, *The Quiet Revolution* (1974)

7   J. Connell, 'The metropolitan village; spatial and social processes in discontinuous suburbs' in J. Johnson (ed.), *Suburban Growth: Geographical Processes at the Edge of the Western City* (1974)

8   G. Cox, 'The farm crisis in Britain' in D. Goodman and M. Redclift (eds.) *The International Farm Crisis* (Basingstoke 1989)

9   P. Cloke, *Rural Planning: Policy into Action?* (1987)

10 D. Clark, *Affordable Homes in the Countryside: A Role for Private Builders* (Action with Communities in Rural England, and the Home Builders' Federation 1988)

11 J. Short, S. Fleming and S. Witt, *Housebuilding, Planning and Community Action: The Production and Negotiation of the Built Environment* (1986)

12 P. Ambrose, *Whatever Happened to Planning?* (1986)

13 D. Cannadine, *Lords and Landlords: The Aristocracy and the Towns 1774–1967* (Leicester 1980) and *The Decline and Fall of the British Aristocracy* (Yale 1990)

14 J. Rose, *The Dynamics of Urban Property Development* (1985)

15 Country Landowners Association, *Agreeing on Access: Landowners and the Countryside* (CLA 1983)

16 T. Marsden, 'The role of banking capital in the British agro-food complex' in T. Marsden and J. Little (eds.), *Political, Social and Economic Perspectives on the International Food System* (1990)

17 R. Body, *Agriculture, the Triumph and the Shame* (1982)

18 D. Baldock and D. Conder, *Removing Land from Agriculture: the Implications for Farming and the Environment* (Council for the Protection of Rural England 1987)

19 P. Lowe, G. Cox, M. MacEwan, T. O'Riordan and M. Winter, *Countryside Conflicts: the Politics of Farming, Forestry and Conservation* (Aldershot 1986)

20 R. Goodchild and R. Munton, *Development and the Landowner: An Analysis of the British Experience* (1985)

21 M. Ball, *Rebuilding Construction: Economic Change in the British Construction Industry* (1988)

22 D. Massey and J. Allen, *Uneven Redevelopment* (1988)

23 House Builders Federation, *Homes, Jobs, Land: The Eternal Triangle* (HBF 1985)

24 West Sussex County Council, *Housing Land Supply in West Sussex at 1st July 1986* (WSCC 1987)

25 P. Lowe and A. Flynn, 'Environmental politics and policy in the 1980s' in J. Mohan (ed.), *The Political Geography of Contemporary Britain* (Basingstoke 1989)

26 L. Gould, *Conserving the Countryside: Costing It Out*, (Council for the Protection of Rural England 1989); Council for the Protection of Rural England, *A Place in the Country* (CPRE 1990)
27 J. Barlow, *Who Plans Berkshire? Land Supply, House Price Inflation and Housing Developers* (University of Sussex Urban and Regional Studies Working Paper 72, 1990)
28 C. Oldman, *Who Says There's No Housing Problem?* (Shelter 1990)
29 Barlow, 'Owner-occupier housing supply . . .'
30 Ambrose, *Whatever Happened to Planning?*
31 Dartington Institute, *Countryside Around Towns in Scotland. A Review of Change 1976–85* (Countryside Commission for Scotland 1987)
32 P. Lowe, T. Marsden and R. Munton, *The Social and Economic Restructuring of Rural Britain: A Position Statement* (Economic and Social Research Council 1990)
33 Ambrose, *Whatever Happened to Planning?*

Image and analysis: new directions in 10
community studies

SUSAN WRIGHT

Images of rural communities are found not only in poetry and art, music hall, radio programmes and advertising, as discussed elsewhere in this book. They are also promulgated by academics. In this chapter I will examine the images which are embedded in the academic study of rural communities.

All purveyors of culture, whether they be the editor of *The Archers*, a rural vicar, or academics, including anthropologists who are the focus here, use prevalent cultural images in their work. What anthropologists try to do, however, is to stand back and examine conceptualisations of society, including their own. We try to do this when we study contemporary everyday life. Even so, these analyses revolve around imagery which is so prevalent and taken for granted, that it goes unnoticed at the time. With the benefit of hindsight, we can look critically at academic studies undertaken by previous generations and discern their implicit conceptualisation of society.

In this chapter I will examine the earliest rural community studies by anthropologists in order to uncover their implicit ideas about what a rural community is and how it is organised. These were not exposed clearly in the criticisms of community studies which were made in the 1970s, but they raise issues which may contribute to the current resurgence of attempts to find a way to analyse and write about rural communities.

Early rural community studies

Work began on rural community studies just before the Second World War and they burgeoned as a genre soon afterwards. The studies were made by a researcher living in a particular rural area for a year or more. Participant observation was the main method of study, along with questionnaire surveys, use of the census, and other statistical and historical material.

The earliest studies were made at a time when an idea had popular appeal in Britain that the raw detail of everyday life could be experienced, described and collated so that, cumulatively, a picture of the variety of 'life in Britain' would emerge.[1] Now it is realised that it is not possible simply to describe society; any description orders facts explicitly or implicitly according to the author's idea of how society is organised. The early community studies are not just about rural society at the time of the research, they are also about the way anthropologists at that time thought social relations were structured.

It is possible to find common ideas and images about rural communities implicit in the earliest community studies even though they were ostensibly very different from each other. Before and after the Second World War community studies were being made in Europe, the United States and the Third World, and the early rural community studies in Britain came from five separate initiatives.

The first European rural community study was initiated in 1931 by Lloyd Warner of Harvard University. It was made in Ireland. Previously, in the 1920s, Lloyd Warner had led a team of 30 researchers in an investigation of the social organisation of a New England town which was given the pseudonym, Yankee City.[2] He became involved in another large Harvard project to study Ireland in a similar way. He made an initial survey in 1931 and set up two of his Yankee City protégés in a two-year field study. Then the war intervened and the project grew no larger.

The resulting book by Arensberg and Kimball is still a major influence on rural studies.[3] It is an account of two townlands in County Clare, consisting of scattered family farms, a couple of small hamlets and a nearby market town. Arensberg and Kimball describe in elegant detail the daily work on the family farms; the annual round; the transitions in the life cycle; and the succession of generations. They analyse the social organisation of the family and community as a system bound up with the economy of the small farm. They see every element of the social organisation as fulfilling a function and solving a problem which has to be overcome if the society is to run smoothly as an integrated whole. The result is an image of self-sustaining rural harmony. I will examine this image in more detail below.

The second initiative in community studies started in Wales. It was entirely separate from the first one, and was set up before Arensberg and Kimball had finished writing up their monograph. In 1939 the professors of anthropology and geography at Aberystwyth University encouraged an extramural tutor, Alwyn Rees, to make a study of the parish in mid-Wales to which he was posted.[4]

This was another area of scattered family farms (fig. 10.1). Rees studied the farmhouse, kinship, neighbours and politics. He argued that the traditional social life of the Welsh with their emphasis on kinship, neighbourliness, hospitality and lack of hierarchies was being corrupted by the latest in a long line of cultural and economic invasions by the English bringing urban standards. This opposition of rural and urban is found in other community studies and again I will return to it below.

In this Welsh initiative, as in the American one, the aim was to have many studies, capturing different settings of Welsh life. This was delayed by the war,

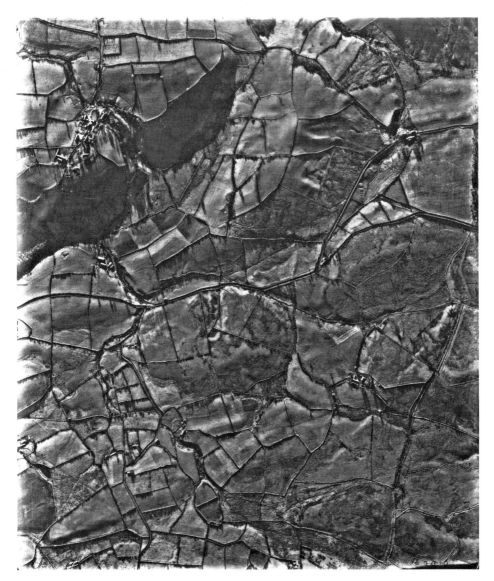

Fig. 10.1 Llanfihangel-Yng-Ngwynfa. A late 1940s aerial photograph shows the parish at the time that Alwyn Rees was working there. Note the scattered pattern of family farms in this part of Mid Wales so characteristic of the upland locations being studied at this time (© Crown copyright/MOD reproduced with the permission of the Controller of HMSO).

but in the 1950s Rees' postgraduates at Aberystwyth made several short studies.[5] One of these students, W. M. Williams, who was also influenced by Arensberg and Kimball's Irish study, in 1949–51 went to Cumbria to study Gosforth.[6] This was another upland area of family farming but included a village as well. It was next door to the building site of a now famous nuclear power station. In 1959 Williams went to study change in another area of upland family farming in Devon, called by a pseudonym, Ashworthy.[7]

The third initiative was in Scotland. Between 1947 and 1951, Littlejohn made an ethnography in his vacations from Edinburgh University. His location was a parish he called Westrigg in the Cheviots on the Scottish Borders.[8] The parish had no village but had a geographical centre with a post office, school, smithy and public hall. He studied a very different kind of farming to the family farms which were the focus of previous community studies. There were 14 dispersed sheep farms with workers' cottages. The farms varied from 400 to over 6,000 acres. All but one employed labour (up to 11 employees). Only one could be considered a family farm. Like Williams he was concerned to analyse change, but unlike Williams he saw change in the parish as the development of class relations and of distinctive class cultures.

The fourth initiative started when Ronald Frankenberg, a student at Manchester University, did not follow the traditions of his department by studying local politics in a village in Africa or some other colonial setting. Instead he went to an area on the Welsh border, not far from where Rees had stayed. However, the society he studied from 1953–54 was very different. Instead of Rees' upland family farms, he chose a village which had been built round a slate mine. The mine had closed and the men commuted daily out of the village for work. Frankenberg and his wife remained with the women of the village during the day, and he made a study of the local politics of men and women in the carnival, the football club and the parish council.[9]

A few years later, an anthropologist from the London School of Economics chose her fieldwork location in a very different way from any of her male contemporaries. Isabel Emmett went to North Wales as the wife of a resident of an area near Blaenau Ffestiniog. Between 1958 and 1962 she studied the dispersed farms and four small settlements in an area of declining slate quarrying, near another atomic power station.[10]

These five groups of studies arose from separate initiatives. They did not aim to collect coherent comparable sets of data. They were interested in different issues and focussed on different aspects of society. Connections between them arise from ideas and images about rural communities that pervade academic analyses of the time about how social relations are organised.

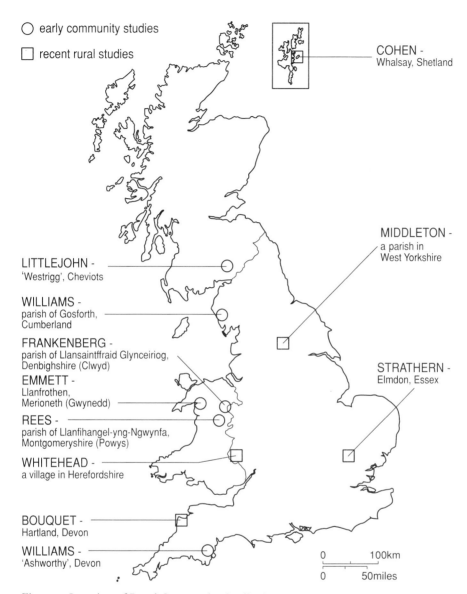

early community studies

recent rural studies

COHEN -
Whalsay, Shetland

MIDDLETON -
a parish in
West Yorkshire

LITTLEJOHN -
'Westrigg', Cheviots

WILLIAMS -
parish of Gosforth,
Cumberland

FRANKENBERG -
parish of Llansaintffraid Glynceiriog,
Denbighshire (Clwyd)

EMMETT -
Llanfrothen,
Merioneth (Gwynedd)

REES -
parish of Llanfihangel-yng-Ngwynfa,
Montgomeryshire (Powys)

WHITEHEAD -
a village in Herefordshire

STRATHERN -
Elmdon, Essex

BOUQUET -
Hartland, Devon

WILLIAMS -
'Ashworthy', Devon

0   100km

0   50miles

Fig. 10.2 Location of Rural Community Studies in Great Britain.

Common themes in the early community studies

The first theme that connects these five separate initiatives is the kind of location sought for study. Figure 10.2 shows these studies were as far flung as possible from urban centres. They were in upland areas where people spoke strong local dialects of minority languages: they were isolated and 'truly rural'. Maps of other countries in Europe[11] reveal a similar concentration of studies at this time in peripheral areas, inaccessible in upland location and local language. The Alps did quite well, but the Saami in northern Scandinavia best fitted the bill.

I have strayed a long way over the English boundary drawn round this book, but the choice of location of these early community studies tells us much about how 'rural' was conceived at that time. 'True' rurality was located in peripheral areas of Europe which had a separate identity, language and way of life. It was an 'unchanged' vestige of what was perceived as an 'earlier' existence, soon to be wiped out by the influence of distant urban centres.

Imagery of change, especially modernisation, is the second theme common to the studies. Ideas of modernisation were prevalent at the time. Some academic studies were explicitly about modernisation. In others, the widespread influence of these ideas can be found as an implicit theme. Modernisation was conceived as change from a simple society to a complex society. It was seen as a change creeping out of the urban centres and spreading over the countryside. Modernisation was seen to have two aspects, economic and social, and I will outline them in turn.

Economic modernisation hinged on the idea of progress from simple to complex technology and to a diversified economy. Within Britain, and within the world as a whole, it was common to think of individual villages and societies on a graded scale from simple to complex according to their technology and economy. At the top of the scale were urban centres of capitalism, exemplified by the image of a factory in a city. In stages down the scale were towns, villages and hamlets, with un-nucleated family farms in the countryside at the other extreme.[12] A curious effect of this notion was to place British rural communities, as vestiges of a previous existence and as distant from the urban centres, on the edge of the capitalist economy. This is an amazing notion when the place of food production and food processing in the postwar capitalist economy is considered, let alone when it is recollected that two of the community studies mentioned in passing that nuclear power stations were nearby.

Rees exemplifies the idea that rural communities were located on the edge of the capitalist economy. At the beginning of the book he tells how the farmers were tenants of a large landed estate, working at a loss each year until the end of the war. After the war, the landlord sold his estate to the tenants, and the 1947 Agriculture Act made their pastoral production profitable. This very 'factual' account of their transition from exploited tenants to solvent own-account farmers can be contrasted with the end of the book where, in expostulating against the spread of urban values through modernisation, Rees refers to the same changes as 'the conversion of a way of life into a means of production'.[13] He is suggesting that the farming community is becoming part of the national capitalist economy – as if it were not before.

The second aspect of modernisation was social. Here social organisation is conceived as changing from simple to complex. Simple society, so called, is where people interact with each other in several ways at once: your butcher who is your cousin is also your local councillor, and you cannot argue with one of his roles without arguing with all of them. The opposite is construed as a complex society, where roles are differentiated. Not only are your butcher, your cousin and your councillor different people, but you only know that aspect of each of these persons. The person in this setting is conceived as fragmented. For example, Rees talks of the postwar modernisation of the countryside as causing 'the initial stages of social atomization' characteristic of urban societies where people are lacking in 'social wholeness'.[14] He concludes the book:

The failure of the urban world to give its inhabitants status and significance in a functioning society, and their consequent disintegration into formless masses of rootless nonentities, should make us humble in planning a new life for the countryside.[15]

Rees was not alone in constructing the rural community as a simple society threatened by modernisation and the supposedly deleterious effects of urbanisation – the fragmentation of the person and the community.

The 'march of modernisation' model reached its apogee in a volume by Frankenberg in 1966.[16] This was a compilation of existing rural and urban community studies ordered in terms of increasing economic complexity and social differentiation. At one end of the scale was the Truly Rural defined as a marginal part of the capitalist economy, 'in relative isolation from the mainstream of agricultural and industrial development', where we 'can study community as a whole' and 'as a more or less self-contained and self-sufficient system'.[17]

The book progresses from 'simple' and 'traditional' to 'complex' and 'modern'. After several examples of the Truly Rural the book passes through Village in the Country, and Small Towns to Bethnal Green, and ends with the new Urban Housing Estates. It was written in a tone of celebration at the achievement of a systematic picture of British society built up from detailed accounts of everyday life in different 'types' of community. The book sold well and went into several reprints as a Pelican paperback. But not long after it was produced there was a wave of criticism of community studies. These criticisms were directed at community studies in the United States, Europe and the Third World as well as Britain. For a while, criticising community studies was a major academic industry.

Criticisms of community studies

I will consider three major criticisms of the early studies which arise from the imagery of community which underlay the analyses. The representation of community in the studies was ahistorical; it relied on a model of functional equilibrium; and it could not cope with change.

There is a tendency for the studies not to be rooted historically. The exception is Littlejohn's study of the Scottish borders. He traced the administrative and landowning history of the area to show how the parish used to be an important arena of power. With the formation of the county council, and with the effects of postwar legislation, the parish was no longer important. People's horizons were not bounded by it, and they belonged to regional unions and voluntary associations which were class-based.

Several studies refer to postwar changes in land ownership, especially where tenants of estates became own-account farmers. But, as in Rees' study, the tendency is to lose sight of detailed processes of historical change and to write more abstractly of modernisation and rely on its images of transition from 'simple' to 'complex' society. Rarely is there more than a glimmer of the extensive postwar legislation, the 1947 Agriculture Act with its system of support for farmers' incomes, the new planning system, the Education Act, and establishment of the National Health Service. Where these major changes in the state are mentioned, as in Rees, they are expressed as part of the deleterious creeping urbanisation and modernisation which disrupts what Frankenberg (above) referred to as self-sufficient and self-contained rural communities.

The idea of communities being self-sufficient and self-contained introduces the second criticism of the early studies. They treated communities as isolated units existing in 'functional equilibrium'. This means that every feature of the society is considered to exist because it fulfills a function or overcomes a problem necessary for the society to continue. Every feature is also thought to intermesh with every other feature of the society so that the whole is in an equilibrium of harmony and balance.

These ideas were made explicit by Arensberg and Kimball and by Williams, but they were also a theme in the other studies, apart from Littlejohn's. For example, Arensberg and Kimball describe the system of impartible inheritance as tied in with the late age of marriage. This in turn is connected to transitions in the role of the ageing parents and the means of dispersing the non-inheriting kin as the next generation takes on more of the farm work. Every feature of the organisation of the family and community has its own function for the maintenance of the farm economy, and all the functions integrate to form a stable and enduring social and economic system in well-balanced equilibrium. The result is an image of rural harmony in a self-contained and self-regulating system.

Not in Arensberg and Kimball's hands, but at its extreme, this notion of a self-contained community existing in self-regulating equilibrium extended into an assumption that a community was a self-contained arena of power. The studies considered stratification within the community but, as Bell and Newby point out,[18] rarely did British community studies connect the local distribution of power to the political system in the county or the country. Analyses were based on an image of community as a free floating unit not located in the political economy of the state.

The third criticism is that the image of community as an isolated unit which exists as a functionally integrated system in equilibrium has difficulty accommodating change. Any disruption is treated as a temporary hiccough which is soon overcome and a healthy equilibrium restored. Arensberg and Kimball suggested that the peasant society of County Clare was so functionally integrated that it carried on regardless of what was happening elsewhere:

> The forces operative within that structure are of such a nature as to allow the society of which they are a part to continue to function in essentially similar fashion through the welter of economic, political and other events which have impinged upon the human beings who have successively filled the structure.[19]

Their image of unchanging peasant society is seriously questioned by later work. Connell showed that the family system described as traditional and unchanging by Arensberg and Kimball was a recent development.[20] It had come about a hundred years before when the Famine and exorbitant landlordism had made unviable a previous system of partible inheritance and early marriage.

Williams, the most explicit British exponent of this functionalist approach tries to accommodate change. The community in his first study,[21] a Cumbrian village near the nuclear power station, he treats as an integrated and unchanging whole. In his second study, in Devon,[22] he tries to introduce the possibility of social change into this model of community. He does this through the idea of 'dynamic equilibrium'. He sees change as coming in two ways, from stimuli external to the community, and from actions, like a conflict, which is local to the community. He argues that especially in the latter case, where an event upsets the harmony of all the intermeshed aspects of the society, particular functions are gradually re-jigged, and in time the social structure attains a new equilibrium.

Williams' idea of dynamic equilibrium still treats community as a self-contained and bounded unit, not located in the wider economy and politics of the state. This remained a problem with community studies: how to conceptualise the local in relation to the state, and in a way that accommodates change.

This problem was not solved at the time of the onslaught of criticisms about community studies. Rather than trying to understand processes of social transformation, the emphasis in the late 1960s and 1970s was on classifying and defining community. The key example in this regard was Hillery's 94 definitions of community.[23] Exponents of community studies tried to make 'community' into a secure analytical concept, on a par with the way 'family' was considered at that time. When these attempts were deemed to have failed,[24] for ten years very few people made community studies, and fewer still dared to publish.

At the same time as community studies were receiving such criticism, rural studies started to be undertaken on areas larger than communities. The impetus for this came from the reorganisation of local government in 1974, the new structure planning process, and the deprivation debate.[25] Rural problems began to be researched on a larger scale for which district or county policies could be devised. Gradually however, planning studies again began to ask what particular problems looked like from the perspective of village communities. Even though 'community' had faced dissolution as an analytical concept, this did not make community go away. It remained an important aspect of life in the countryside. In the resurgence of local studies in the 1980s, many conceptual and analytical problems from the early community studies still had to be resolved.

New approaches to community studies

The starting point in a search for new directions is perhaps to ask in what sense those earlier studies were community studies. I have suggested that they put a boundary around everything in a village or a group of farms and called it 'community'. On closer examination, that may not be quite accurate. In the studies, 'community' is an arena of social activity between on the one hand, the household, and on the other, the state.

Household organisation is mentioned in all the studies, but in none is it fully examined. Littlejohn refers to the distinctive domestic cultures of each class and he exemplifies this through a vivid vignette of the different ways tea is taken.[26] He describes the greater distance between husband and wife in working-class households than in middle-class ones. But he does not discuss the division of labour and of authority in the farm households, let alone in the working-class households – he just says that it 'is the same in this community as in the rest of the nation'.[27]

Where community shades into state, Littlejohn gives more information. He describes how the parish is no longer the locus of kinship, economic relations, or union organisation: all span a wider area. The focus of his study is public activity in the locality, which is informed by considerations emanating on one side from the household and on the other from the state.

Rees concentrates on a similar public space. On households, he gives plentiful ground plans of houses, but leaves tantalising gaps in his account of how the space is used during the family life cycle. He describes the farm work but never explains how it is organised. There are two paragraphs on the woman of the household.[28] They say there is a division of labour between the sexes and the activities of the woman are confined largely to the house and farm yard. In addition to her household duties, she raises poultry and makes butter. She markets these products herself, and on the proceeds she runs the house and clothes herself and the children. Her budget is independent of her husband and Rees says she is secretive about this. This is perhaps not surprising, as Rees seems not to have asked equivalent questions of the men, about their side of farm production and what they spend the proceeds on.

On relations between the community and the state, Rees' monograph keeps the political context of anglicisation and state policy in view, but this serves to define the public space he is interested in. The community life of these scattered family farms takes place when visitors gather by the hearth of a family's living room. Then what had been private space is transformed into a public, community arena.[29] He considers this community, which is situationally created out of the living room in each house, to be threatened by encroaching English and urban standards which equate community with a nucleated settlement crowned by a public hall.[30]

Frankenberg defines most clearly this space which shades off on either side into the household and into the institutions of the state. He describes the buses leaving the village in the morning, going past the closed slate quarry and taking the men to employment in new factories which some authority – he does not give details – has deemed should not be in the village. The people he meets are in the public arena, on the football pitch, in the village hall, at committee meetings and at social occasions. He describes climbing a hill and looking sadly down on the rows of houses in the housing estate and wondering what went on inside them.[31] Frankenberg's community lay between the slate roofs of the houses and the slate spoil of the quarry on the edge of the village.

In each of the studies there is a social arena, and usually a physical space too, which is taken to be the community. It is the *locus* of public social organisation, situated between the front doors where the private space of households starts, and the edge of the village or parish where 'community' becomes 'state'.

I suggest that the first new direction in community studies is a re-examination of the boundaries around the community arena. This involves studying the organisation of households, which can be done now that the 1970s and 1980s have brought an awareness of gender issues. It also entails locating the rural area in the political economy of the state. This will enable community to be reconceptualised for analytical purposes. It still leaves the question of how the idea of community is used by the people themselves. This is the second new direction in community studies, and it will be important to emphasise that 'community' is an idea, not a social or geographical entity.

Gender issues in community studies

In the early community studies there is an occasional glimpse of women as well as men in the public arena of community. Frankenberg, in his brilliant analysis of local politics, finds women and men at odds over their aims for the football team. The women are not on the committee but they raise the money and do the washing to reproduce the team. When they withdraw their support, Frankenberg follows them into the formation of a carnival committee. This move by the women causes village identity to be no longer propounded through the men of the football team, but through a carnival queen.

Other studies reveal more antagonism between the genders. Rees calmly talks of a male youth group which terrorises women who do not conform to their idea of proper conduct. In one case they gathered round a woman's house, threw dead rodents through the window and stuffed a chicken down the chimney. Rees assures us that it was not as anti-social as it may seem because a majority of the community secretly approved the young men's actions. He passes it off as boisterous horseplay![32]

Sexual antagonism was interpreted differently once feminism began to influence anthropology in the 1970s. Whitehead studied sexual antagonism in Herefordshire and interpreted it as a means through which men controlled women in the household and in public spaces.[33] In fieldwork in a village in Yorkshire, Middleton encountered patrolling behaviour by a young male group similar to that described by Rees.[34] She shows that there are systematic constraints on women's use of space in the household, the village, and beyond the village, with an undertone of violence.

Such studies broke with the assumption of earlier ones that family and community are sites of consensus, mutual interest and harmony. An early contribution to this debate came from Frankenberg who, in a reassessment ten years after *Communities in Britain*, called for household-based studies of gender relations of production and family ideology in order to understand the perpetuation of asymmetries of power between men and women.[35] Households in particular came to be seen as complex units with inequalities by generation and by gender in terms of control over property, control of the means of production, of disposable income, and the labour of other family members. Studies were made to see how these inequalities were maintained, especially through the subordination of women in marriage by economic dependence and violence.[36] In Britain these studies concentrated mainly on inequalities between men and women over domestic budgeting and income allocation.[37]

In British rural studies, these feminist research interests which focussed on gender relations in the household, have come together with the work of those advancing the restructuring thesis.[38] This argued that as capital was reorganised internationally, in rural as in urban localities in Britain, new patterns of employment developed alongside a restructuring of patterns of social reproduction and political struggle. The household was seen as the site in which individuals experienced the intersection of all the different aspects of restructuring.

It was also recognised that in different areas, people were experiencing restructuring differently, and more importantly, were responding differently to it. This led to a rethinking of the ways relations between households could be analysed in order to understand how distinctive local patterns of social inter-action and struggle emerge. No longer could the characteristics of the formal economy (defined variously as production, in capitalist enterprises, outside the home) be taken to explain local class politics. Nor could the old analytical divides between social and spatial sites of production, consumption and reproduction be sustained. Urry suggested we have to look at social relations within and between households to discern how class relations, local state practices and gender relations come together in distinctive forms in different localities.[39]

These inter-household relations have been called 'local culture', 'everyday experience', even 'community'. Urry suggested a reworking of the term 'civil society', as a space separate from the economy and the state.[40] This term would cover the diverse realm of local political, ideological and cultural practices through which personal and collective identities are constructed.

There is always a lag between the proposal of new theoretical ideas and testing them out empirically.[41] However, Bouquet's work, whilst deriving more from the feminist than the restructuring debate, contributes to both.[42] Her starting point is gender relations of production in farm households in the parish of Hartland in north west Devon. She says she is analysing social relations within and between farm households and she resists the use of community as an autonomous system; she is examining how, in the farm household, local, regional and global forces intersect. I will present her analysis in a slightly re-worked form, to suggest how the study of gender relations provides a way of connecting changes within households, the community arena and the state.

Bouquet traces changes in the sexual division of labour in the farm household from the early nineteenth century to the 1980s. The sexual division of labour has gone through three phases. First, in the early nineteenth century, both men and women were equally engaged in agriculture throughout the year. This was when the ox was both the energy source and the source of milk, and the plough and the dairy were linked. Bouquet says men's and women's work were connected through the breeding cycle of the ox. Although this was a more equal sexual division of labour than she describes for later periods, I think she does not make enough of the sexual asymmetries which nevertheless existed. This can be represented through the scythe and the sickle in agriculture: men used heavier, more efficient tools whilst women had weaker, less productive ones. Aspects of the economy besides agriculture, and especially women's domestic work, are not mentioned. With these caveats, this early period was one of equal sexual relations of production.

The second period Bouquet identifies was in the mid nineteenth century when there was a separation between the specialisation of men's and women's agricultural work. The plough and the dairy became separate. The horse was introduced and men concentrated on mixed agriculture. Women specialised in dairy production and marketing after the 1865 cattle plague in London created a market and the building of a railway made retailing milk from Devon to London possible. Women controlled the processing of milk products. They were in charge of the labour, they controlled the income, and they ran their house on the proceeds.

In the third phase men took over all work outside the farm house and women specialised indoors, catering for tourists. As so often happens, men took over women's occupations when these became mechanised. After 1933, marketing was done through the Milk Marketing Boards and processing of milk products was done in butter and cream factories (for example the Torrington factory opened in 1930). Dairying itself became mechanised in the 1940s when electricity supplies enabled milking machines to be introduced. Men took over the dairying and marketing. Women were reduced to faces on the packets of the new factory produced 'farmhouse' butter. At the same time, the decline in agricultural servants meant that more space became available in the farm house. Women developed a new specialisation as they took in paying visitors.

This classification of three periods is based on the intersecting of changes in the sexual division of labour with changes in the energy sources and in the farm economy. They in turn derived from changes in the national economy and state policy. Bouquet provides a model which connects different configurations in gender relations of production in the family farm to changes in state policy.

She also shows how, as resources and their distribution in the household changed, interrelations between households were transformed. In this way she connects changes in the sexual division of production to changes in what others have called the community (although it does not encompass all the aspects of Urry's civil society). This can be traced through the same three phases.

In the first phase, the age of the ox in the early nineteenth century, in the context of uncertain tenancies and levels of production restricted by the available energy sources, farm families devised a system of devolving the land intact to one heir. Other sons entered a profession, emigrated or became agricultural servants. In the life cycle of a farm family, the resources of land and labour were rarely matched. At any time, some households had land but not enough labour; others had insufficient land and had to sell labour. The result was the establishment of servant-giving and servant-taking relations between households across the locality.

In the middle phase, the age of the horse and the cow, this system was transformed. Instead of households finding themselves at different times servant-givers and servant-takers, a fairly permanent differentiation was established between those families which owned farms and other families which sold agricultural labour.

In the third phase, when men did all the farm work and women's domain was inside the house, relations between households in the locality became organised differently by men and women. Bouquet associates changed relations between men with the effects of the policies of the Ministry of Agriculture, Fisheries and Food. In the 1950s MAFF guaranteed farmers' incomes as long as they invested in machinery and displaced agricultural labour. For the first time, a system of family farming was established, with the farm family providing all the male agricultural labour. Relations between households in the locality which had been based on buying and selling agricultural labour, were severed. The process of individuating farmers increased with the treadmill effect of MAFF's policies. Farmers who borrowed hard to buy equipment had to expand continually to meet their higher costs.[43] To do this they worked increasingly longer hours themselves. Each farm bought its own equipment and was self reliant for labour. In a crisis, like a heavy snow fall, farmers still needed each other. Otherwise, the effect of MAFF's policies was to individuate farmers: households were no longer linked by servant-taking and servant-giving between farms, or by farms employing a labouring class.

Women in this period specialised in catering for tourists. They controlled the income that accrued and used it to invest in improvements to the house. They also used their income to invest in facilities in the village that were important for tourism. Bouquet gives examples of women supporting the village shop and raising the money to give the village band a new uniform. Beyond an immediate interest in tourism, women also responded to the under-provision of state services in rural areas. They raised funds for equipment for the local health services and for a voluntarily organised hospital transport system. Bouquet gives little detail about these activities, but it is clear that the effect of government cuts on rural services was to increase links between farm women who invested time and money in 'the community' (fig. 10.3).

Bouquet's study shows that whereas the effect of one set of government policies was to reduce inter-household links between men, the effect of government cuts in rural services was to increase links between farms and with villagers through women.

Bouquet's analysis is strong where the earlier community studies were weak. She provides a way forward which overcomes the two problems in earlier studies of first, treating community as isolated from household and from state, and second, of not being able to accommodate change. By focussing on gender relations she shows how the sexual division of labour in the farm economy is linked to the organisation of relations between households in the locality, and to state policies. She shows how historically these interlinkages between household,

Fig. 10.3 A group marketing venture 1990. How Devon 'farmers' wives' choose to represent their farms. Note the absence of human agency in the representations: external nature, internal scenes, but no people!

'community' and state have gone through a sequence of transformations. She does not cover the latest transformation, the restructuring of rural areas such as north west Devon, and the aspects included in the study of relations between households would have to be increased to test that thesis.

Symbols of community

These new analyses presumably contain a new academic imagery representing the way anthropologists and other social scientists implicitly conceptualise relations between people in society. We are still too close to them in time to be able to stand back and discern this imagery. What is evident at this stage is that these new analyses do not consider the images people themselves use about their community.

The earlier studies revolved around a word in popular usage and tried to examine it as a sociological and geographical phenomenon: they tried to put a boundary around the people and place called 'community' and study its content. I mentioned above that the critics of the 1960s and 1970s dissolved community as a watertight sociological category, and studies since then have shied away from the word. But people still use the word in their everyday lives. The result is that new analyses of the kind I have discussed so far have tended not to examine how the people they are studying image their own society.

Bouquet is a case in point. In her book, her material analysis of social relations within households and between households is not connected to the way people talk about these things themselves. We do not catch the sound of their voices. A later article begins to make this connection.[44] It starts with an analysis of the organisation of the farm household and then shows that the farm family does not mean the same thing to all its members. Differences between men and women are expressed in their uses of space in the house, where they draw boundaries differently and use contrasting symbols.

This article points in the new direction community studies in my view should take. The next stage would be to link an analysis of relations not only within households but also between households to the symbolism through which the men and women involved express their different perceptions of those relations. This symbolism includes not only family and the use of space within the house, but also their images of locality, rurality and community.

While no study yet combines that kind of analysis of social relations with the imagery the people use, there has been a second area of work setting out new directions in the study of community as a symbol. Strathern's study of Elmdon in north west Essex examines how kinship provides an idiom for expressing the meanings that different people have for the village.[45] The material was collected in the 1960s, a time when middle-class incomers, not least from Cambridge

Fig. 10.4 Elmdon, north-west Essex, Strathern's setting for *Kinship at the Core*. The apparently clearly bounded space of the nucleated village belies the complexity of the processes by which people create symbols of community and belonging.

University, were moving into the village. At the same time, the working class of the village were suffering the effects of rising house prices and of cut-backs in agricultural employment (fig. 10.4).

In this setting, Strathern finds a strong idea that there are some 'real' Elmdon villagers as distinct from other villagers. The identity of other villagers in the community revolves around their relationship with the 'real' Elmdoners. These 'real' Elmdoners are four families whose names are associated with the old prestigious working-class agricultural occupations. Around this 'core', there are layers of newcomers who came before the First World War, between the wars, and especially the commuters, weekend cottagers, and retired people who started moving in during the 1950s.

Strathern searches for the substance of the 'real' Elmdoners' core position. It becomes clear that their high position in the agricultural hierarchy has disappeared with changes in the industry. They own no land, no houses, and have no assets apart from their labour. They do not play a visible leadership role in the village. Their 'property' is symbolic. It is a proprietorial claim to identification with the village, its jobs and its accommodation.

If the 'real' Elmdoners own no material assets, how do they hold such power in the village that incomers relate to the village through them? The answer lies in villagers' notions of community. Incomers see 'community' as all the people in the village joining in an activity. They think of the whole village as a community with the 'real' Elmdoners as its special representatives and the holders of tradition. The incomers' characterise their own role as inheriting the old paternalist landowners' responsibility for providing welfare and putting on special occasions. They feel they have a responsibility to provide leadership in the village, this place where events should be organised by and for all residents. In other words, they need the 'real' Elmdoners to join in for the community to be working successfully.

On the other hand, 'real' Elmdoners see community as constituting different interest groups. They themselves claim village assets, the local jobs, houses and traditions, but proclaim themselves powerless in relation to the other interest groups. Their only power is to boycott newcomers' activities with which they disagree – a stance which disturbs the middle-class notion of community.

Unfortunately there is a gap in the field material between the 1960s and a later study in the 1970s which is reported in an epilogue to the book. During the intervening period there is no information on the ways changes in the meaning of 'village', 'newcomer', 'villager', 'real Elmdon' and 'community' were negotiated. By 1977 'real Elmdon' has no currency. There is a shrunken number of 'villagers', the only term now used in opposition to newcomers. The latter, with their committee culture, dominate the village, and it seems that 'villagers' have lost the power even to boycott.

The material from Elmdon in the 1960s catches one form that images of community can take. The word conjures up different ideas of how local society should be organised. These contrasting ideas are negotiated between different groups, either in a continuing contest over opposed meanings for the same symbol, or, as seems the case in Elmdon, until one becomes dominant.

It is this kind of material that Cohen uses to develop a more theorised interpretation of the ways people use community in everyday speech. He argues for an interpretation of the use of community as a symbol.[46] Cohen characterises symbols as simultaneously expressing similarity and difference. They are also, importantly, ambiguous. They do not simply stand for something, they allow each individual to draw on their own idiosyncratic experience to supply part of their meaning. The meanings ascribed by different individuals to the same symbol will be in some respects shared and in others different. Symbols embrace the different meanings people give them without exposing those differences.

To exemplify this, Cohen refers to the symbol of nuclear disarmament.[47] In a demonstration when this symbol is displayed, sympathisers can all associate themselves with it, and have a sense of belonging. However, if they debated among themselves what kind of disarmament they wanted and how it should be achieved, they would all disagree. A parallel example would be half a dozen villagers looking at their village church. They might all see in its shape and setting a symbol of their village, but if asked to explain what meaning the church had in the village, they might all argue with each other. The form of the symbol can be shared by a group, but its content varies with each member's unique orientation to it.

Most symbols do not have a visual expression, but are ideas. They are conceptual, even if they have a material dimension. Unlike the earlier community studies, community is not treated as a place with a structure of institutions capable of objective definition and description, and through which everyone is supposed to be integrated into consensual ways of thinking and behaving. Cohen is trying to capture members' experience of community. He suggests that as a symbol, community has forms which are held in common (ways of behaving, even uses of words) but whose content, the meaning members give to those forms, may vary greatly. A symbol does not integrate; it aggregates a variety without imposing uniformity. Symbols are:

ideal media through which people can speak a 'common language', behave in apparently similar ways, participate in the 'same' rituals, pray to the 'same' gods, wear similar clothes, and so forth, without subordinating themselves to a tyranny of orthodoxy.[48]

Community as a symbol is created through the everyday lives of its members. It encompasses this variety without exposing discord, by common forms which express apparent coherence at the boundary of the group. These are not physical boundaries, but boundaries around categories which arise situationally between sets of people within a locality, or between the people of a locality against other localities or the state.

Cohen criticises the earlier idea of the march of modernisation out of the towns and across the countryside, which was to change so-called simple societies into complex ones. He says that this model implies people are vessels that can be emptied and new ideas poured in. It treats people as passive recipients of culture, not as participants in the active creation of culture. Looking back on the changes that were going on when the early community studies were being written, he says the policies and programmes which were designed to reduce difference have had the opposite effect. They have been met with an aggressive rebuilding of boundaries on symbolic foundations.

This rebuilding of symbols of community in the face of modernisation has been done in many different ways. An image which had a traditional form, especially one threatened with redundancy by new changes, is imparted with new meaning. Alternatively, an image which derives from an alien form, especially from the agent which threatens, is fundamentally reconstituted with indigenous meaning. It is then turned to face the outside agent which is confounded by the simultaneous familiarity and strangeness of an image it generated but no longer understands. Villages and localities have produced a public face of community by coalescing internal variety into a simple image to mark their symbolic boundary and stand against the intrusions of business, local government or the state.

Conclusion

If Bouquet's work provides a new approach to analysing transitions in the social relations within households and between households in the political economy of the state, then Cohen's work restates community not as a sociographic reality but as a symbol, a politicised assertion of boundary in a continuous restatement of belonging. The challenge is to bring these two new directions in community studies together into an analysis of social relations which shows how the men and women concerned express their different perceptions of their relations through their contrasting meanings for common symbols of family, community and state.

NOTES

1 See for example Mass Observation's objectives, C. Madge and T. Harrisson, *Mass Observation* (1937).
2 C. Bell and H. Newby, *Community Studies* (1971) 101–2.
3 C. Arensberg and S. Kimball, *Family and Community in Ireland* (Cambridge, Mass. 1940).
4 A. Rees, *Life in a Welsh Countryside* (Cardiff 1950).
5 E. Davies and A. Rees (eds.), *Welsh Rural Communities* (Cardiff 1960).
6 W. M. Williams, *The Sociology of an English Village: Gosforth* (1956).
7 W. M. Williams, *A West Country Village: Ashworthy. Family, Kinship and Land* (1963).
8 J. Littlejohn, *Westrigg. The Sociology of a Cheviot Parish* (1963).

9   R. Frankenberg, *Village on the Border. A Social Study of Religion, Politics and Football in a North Wales Community* (1957).

10 I. Emmett, *A North Wales Village: a Social Anthropological Study* (1964).

11 See J-L. Durand-Drouhin and L-M. Szwengrub (eds.), *Rural Community Studies in Europe* (Oxford 1981).

12 For a fuller discussion of this point, see S. Wright, 'Development theory and community development practice' in H. Buller and S. Wright (eds.), *Rural Development: Problems and Practices* (Aldershot 1990).

13 Rees, *Life in a Welsh Countryside*, 167.

14 *Ibid.*, 168.

15 *Ibid.*, 170.

16 R. Frankenberg, *Communities in Britain* (1966).

17 *Ibid.*, 45.

18 Bell and Newby, *Community Studies*, 220.

19 Arensberg and Kimball, *Family and Community in Ireland*, 150.

20 K. H. Connell, 'Peasant marriage in Ireland: its structure and development since the Famine' *Economic History Review* 14 (1961–62) 502–23.

21 Williams, *The Sociology of an English Village*.

22 Williams, *A West Country Village*.

23 G. A. Hillery, 'Definitions of community: areas of agreement', *Rural Sociology* 20 (1955) 111–23.

24 M. Stacey, 'The myth of community studies', *British Journal of Sociology* 20 (1969) 134–47.

25 B. McLaughlin, 'The rural deprivation debate: retrospect and prospect' in P. Lowe, T. Bradley and S. Wright (eds.), *Deprivation and Welfare in Rural Areas* (Norwich 1986) 43–54.

26 Littlejohn, *Westrigg*, 127–9.

27 *Ibid.*, 122.

28 Rees, *Life in a Welsh Countryside*, 62–3.

29 *Ibid.*, 43.

30 *Ibid.*, 163.

31 Frankenberg, *Communities in Britain*, 16.

32 Rees, *Life in a Welsh Countryside*, 83.

33 A. Whitehead, 'Sexual antagonism in Herefordshire' in D. Barker and S. Allen (eds.), *Dependence and Exploitation in Work and Marriage* (1976) 169–203.

34 A. Middleton, 'Marking boundaries: men's space and women's space in a Yorkshire village' in P. Lowe., T. Bradley and S. Wright (eds.), *Deprivation and Welfare in Rural Areas* (Norwich 1986) 121–34.

35 R. Frankenberg, 'In the production of their lives, men(?) . . . sex and gender in British community studies' in D. Barker and S. Allen (eds.), *Sexual Divisions in Society: Process and Change* (1976) 25–51.

36 See for example K. Young, C. Walkowitz and R. McCullagh (eds.), *Of Marriage and the Market* (1981); R. Hirschon (ed.), *Women and Property – Women as Property* (1984); D. Barker and S. Allen (eds.), *Dependence and Exploitation in Work and Marriage* (1976).

37 J. Pahl, 'The allocation of money and the structuring of inequality within marriage', *Sociological Review* 31 (1983) 237–62; L. Morris and S. Ruane, *Household Finance Management and Labour Market Behaviour* (Report to the Department of Employment

1986); L. Morris, 'Constraints on gender: the family wage, social security and the labour market; reflections on research in Hartlepool', *Work, Employment and Society* 1 (1987) 85–106.

38 D. Massey, 'Regionalism, some current issues', *Capital and Class* 6 (1978) 106–25.

39 J. Urry, *The Anatomy of Capitalist Societies: the Economy, Civil Society and the State* (1981).

40 For an account of how the term has been reworked see M. Goodwin, *The Concept of Civil Society and the Anatomy of Urban and Regional Research* (University of Sussex Urban and Regional Studies Working Paper, 66, 1988).

41 For example, see T. Marsden and J. Murdoch, *Restructuring Rurality: Key Areas for Development in Assessing Rural Change*, ESRC Countryside Change Initiative Working Paper, 4, 1990.

42 M. Bouquet, *Family, Servants and Visitors* (Norwich 1985).

43 After Bouquet's study was finished, this syndrome was abruptly altered by the introduction of milk quotas.

44 M. Bouquet, 'You cannot be a Brahmin in the English countryside' in A. P. Cohen (ed.), *Symbolising Boundaries* (Manchester 1986) 22–39.

45 M. Strathern, *Kinship at the Core* (Cambridge 1981).

46 A. P. Cohen, *The Symbolic Construction of Community* (Chichester 1985). See also *Whalsay: symbol, segment and boundary in a Shetland island community* (Manchester 1987); and his edited works, *Belonging. Identity and Social Organisation in British Rural Cultures* (Manchester 1982) and *Symbolising Boundaries. Identity and Diversity in British Cultures* (Manchester 1986).

47 Cohen, *The Symbolic Construction of Community*, 18.

48 *Ibid.*, 21.

Consolidated bibliography

A full bibliography on English rural communities would require a book in its own right. The following is acknowledged as being only partial, and is restricted to the references cited in this text.

The place of publication is London unless otherwise specified.

Ahern, G. and Davie, G., *Inner City God* (1987)

Aldridge, J. and Tregorran, J., *Ambridge – An English Village Through the Ages* (1981)

Ambrose, P. *The Quiet Revolution* (1974)

   Whatever Happened to Planning? (1986)

Amis, K., *The Green Man* (1969)

Archbishops' Commission on Rural Areas, *Faith in the Countryside* (Worthing 1990)

Arensberg, C. and Kimball, S., *Family and Community in Ireland* (Cambridge, Mass. 1940)

Austen, Jane, *Northanger Abbey* (1803)

Baker, G., 'Politics, pollution and the industrial development of a North Kent parish: Swanscombe 1840–1910', Unpublished MA Dissertation, University of Sussex 1990

Baker, M., *Folklore and Customs of Rural England* (1974)

Baldock, D. and Conder, D., *Removing Land from Agriculture: the Implications for Farming and the Environment* (Council for the Protection of Rural England 1987)

Ball, M., *Rebuilding Construction: Economic Change in the British Construction Industry* (1988)

Banks, S., '"Open" and "close" parishes in nineteenth-century England,' Unpublished PhD thesis, University of Reading 1982

   'Nineteenth-century scandal or twentieth-century model? A new look at "open" and "close" parishes', *Economic History Review* 2nd series 41 (1) (1988)

Barker, D. and Allen, S. (eds.), *Dependence and Exploitation in Work and Marriage* (1976)

Barley, M. W., 'Rural Building in England' in Joan Thirsk (ed.), *The Agrarian History of England and Wales V (ii), 1640–1750* (Cambridge 1985)

Barlow, J., 'Owner-occupier housing supply and the planning framework in the "boom" regions. Examples from Britain, France, Sweden', *Planning Practice and Research* 5 (2) (1990)

   Who Plans Berkshire? Land Supply, House Price Inflation and Housing Developers (University of Sussex Urban and Regional Studies Working Paper 72, 1990)

Barlow, J., Ambrose, P. and Duncan, S., 'Housing provision in high growth regions. A comparative study of four European sub-regions', *Scandinavian Housing and Planning Research* 5 (1) (1988)

Barnett, A., *Iron Britannia* (1982)

Barrell, J., *The Dark Side of the Landscape: the Rural Poor in English Painting 1730–1840* (Cambridge 1980)

218

'The private comedy of Thomas Rowlandson', *Art History*, 6 (4) (1983)

'The golden age of labour' in Sue Clifford, Angela King, Richard Mabey (eds.), *Second Nature* (1984)

Beard, M., *English Landed Society in the Twentieth Century* (1989)

Beier, A. L., *Masterless Men. The Vagrancy Problem in England 1560–1640* (1985)

Bell, C. and Newby, H., *Community Studies* (1971)

Bellingham, R. A., 'The use of marriage horizons to measure migration. Some conclusions from a study of Pocklington, East Yorkshire in the late eighteenth century', *Local Population Studies*, 44 (1990)

Bennett, C., 'Visions in the land of milk and honey', *The Sunday Correspondent*, 17 September 1989

Bermingham, Ann, *Landscape and Ideology: the English Rustic Tradition, 1740–1860* (1987)

Berryman, G., *The Life and Death of Doris Archer* (1981)

Betjeman, J., *Collected Poems* (1958)

Collins Guide to Parish Churches of England and Wales (1980)

Blackmore, R. D., *Lorna Doone* (1893)

Bloom, W. and Pogacnik, N., *Ley Lines and Ecology* (1985)

Blythe, Ronald, *Divine Landscapes* (1986)

Body, R., *Agriculture, the Triumph and the Shame* (1982)

Bouquet, M., *Family, Servants and Visitors* (Norwich 1985)

'You cannot be a Brahmin in the English countryside' in A. P. Cohen (ed.), *Symbolising Boundaries* (Manchester 1986)

Bourne, G., *Change in the village* (1912)

Brandon, P. and Short, B., *The South East from AD 1000* (1990)

Briers, R., *English Country Churches* (1989)

Brooke, R., *The Collected Poems* (1918)

Buchanan, C., *No Way to the Airport* (1981)

Buckatzsch, E. J., 'Place of origin of a group of immigrants into Sheffield 1624–1799' in P. Clark (ed.), *The Early Modern Town. A Reader* (1976)

Caffyn, S., 'The social structure of mid 19th-century Newick', *Sussex Archaeological Collections* 125 (1987)

Cannadine, D., *Lords and Landlords: the Aristocracy and the Towns 1774–1967* (Leicester 1980)

The Decline and Fall of the British Aristocracy (Yale 1990)

Cardinal, R., *The Landscape vision of Paul Nash* (1989)

Carpenter, S. C., *Winnington–Ingram* (1949)

Carter, Ian, *Farm Life in Northeast Scotland 1840–1914: A Poor Man's Country* (Edinburgh 1979)

Chadwick, O., *The Victorian Church*, 2 vols (1966 and 1970)

Chalker, John, *The English Georgic: A Study in the Development of a Form* (1969)

Clark, D., *Between Pulpit and Pew* (Cambridge 1982)

Clark, David, *Affordable Homes in the Countryside: a Role for Private Builders* (Action with Communities in Rural England, and the House Builders' Federation 1988)

Clark, P., 'Migration in England during the late seventeenth and early eighteenth centuries', *Past and Present* 83 (1979)

'Vagrants and vagrancy in England 1598–1644' in P. Clark and D. Souden (eds.), *Migration and Society in Early Modern England* (1987)

Clark, P. and Slack, P., *English Towns in Transition* (Oxford 1976)

Clay, Christopher, 'Landlords and estate management in England' in Joan Thirsk (ed.), *The Agrarian History of England and Wales v (ii) 1640–1750* (Cambridge 1985)

Cleere, H. and Crossley, D., *The Iron Industry of the Weald* (Leicester 1985)

Cloke, P. J., *Rural Planning: Policy into Action?* (1987)

'Rural geography and political economy' in R. Peet and N. J. Thrift (eds.), *New Models in Geography*, vol I (1989)

Cobbett, William, *Rural Rides* (various edns, e.g. 1853, 1967)

Cohen, A. P., *Belonging. Identity and Social Organisation in British Rural Cultures* (Manchester 1982)

The Symbolic Construction of Community (Chichester 1985)

Symbolising Boundaries. Identity and Diversity in British Cultures (Manchester 1986)

Whalsay: symbol, segment and boundary in a Shetland island community (Manchester 1987)

Collins, E. J. T., 'Migrant labour in British agriculture in the nineteenth century' *Economic History Review* 2nd series 18 (1976)

Colvin, C., Drew, J. and Noble, A., *Paul Nash Places* (1989)

Congleton, J. E., *Theories of Pastoral Poetry in England 1684–1798* (New York 1968)

Connell, J., 'The metropolitan village; spatial and social processes in discontinuous suburbs' in J. Johnson (ed.), *Suburban Growth: Geographical processes at the edge of the Western City* (1974)

Connell, K. H., 'Peasant marriage in Ireland: its structure and development since the Famine', *Economic History Review* 14 (1961–62)

Cornwall, J., 'Evidence of population mobility in the seventeenth century', *Bulletin of the Institute of Historical Research* 40 (1967)

Council for the Protection of Rural England, *A Place in the Country* (CPRE 1990)

Country Landowners Association, *Agreeing on Access: Landowners and the Countryside* (CLA 1983)

Cox, G., 'The farm crisis in Britain' in D. Goodman and M. L. Redclift (eds.), *The International Farm Crisis* (Basingstoke 1989)

Currie, R., Gilbert, A. and Horsley, J. H., *Churches and Churchgoers, Patterns of Church Growth in the British Isles Since 1700* (Oxford 1977)

Daniels, Stephen, 'The implications of industry: Turner and Leeds', *Turner Studies* 6 (1) (1986)

Darley, Gillian, *Villages of Vision* (1978)

Dartington Institute, *Countryside Around Towns in Scotland. A Review of Change 1976–85* (Countryside Commission for Scotland 1987)

Davey, C. 'A note on mobility in an Essex parish in the early nineteenth century', *Local Population Studies* 41 (1988)

Davies, E. and Rees, A. (eds.), *Welsh Rural Communities* (Cardiff 1960)

Devereux, P. and Thomson, I., *The Ley-Hunter's Companion* (1979)

Dodgshon, R. A., *The European Past* (1987)

Dowell, G., *Enjoying the World* (1990)

Drewett, P., Rudling, D., and Gardiner, M., *The South East to AD 1000* (1988)

Drinkwater, J. (ed.), *The Poems of Thomas Gray* (1912)

Duck, Stephen, *Poems on Several Occasions* (1736: facsimile reprint, Menston 1973)

Durand-Drouhin, J-L. and Szwengrub, L-M. (eds.), *Rural Community Studies in Europe* (Oxford 1981)

Dyer, Christopher, *Warwickshire Farming, 1349–c.1520. Preparations for Agricultural Revolution* (Dugdale Society Occasional Papers 27, 1981)

Edmondson, C., *Strategies for Rural Evangelism* (Nottingham 1989)

Edwards, Peter, *The Horse Trade of Tudor and Stuart England* (Cambridge 1988)

Eliot, T. S., 'Little Gidding', *Four Quartets* (1951)

Ellis, William D. Jnr, 'Thomas D'Urfey, the Pope-Philips Quarrel, and *The Shepherd's Week*', *Publications of the Modern Language Association* 74 (1959)

Ellman, E. B., 'Family names in Berwick from 1606 to 1812', *Sussex Archaeological Collections* 22 (1870)

Elson, M., *Green Belts, Conflict and Mediation in the Urban Fringe* (1986)

Emmett, I., *A North Wales Village: a Social Anthropological Study* (1964)

Escott, M., 'Residual mobility in a late eighteenth century parish: Binfield, Berkshire 1779–1801', *Local Population Studies* 40 (1988)

Evans, G. E., *Where Beards Wag All. The Relevance of the Oral Tradition* (1970)

Everitt, A., 'Farm labourers' in Joan Thirsk (ed.), *The Agrarian History of England and Wales IV, 1500–1640* (Cambridge 1967)

'The marketing of agricultural produce' in Joan Thirsk (ed.), *The Agrarian History of England and Wales IV, 1500–1640* (Cambridge 1967)

'Nonconformity in country parishes' in Joan Thirsk (ed.), *Land, Church and People. Essays presented to H. P. R. Finberg, Agricultural History Review* 18, 1970 supplement

'Dynasty and community since the seventeenth century' in A. Everitt (ed.), *Landscape and Community in England* (1985)

Landscape and Community in England (1985)

Continuity and Colonisation: the Evolution of Kentish Settlement (Leicester 1986)

Feingold, Richard, *Nature and Society: Later Eighteenth-Century Uses of the Pastoral and Georgic* (Hassocks, Sussex 1978)

Forsgren, Adina, *John Gay. Poet 'of a Lower Order'* (Stockholm 1964)

Francis, L. J., *Rural Anglicanism. A Future for Young Christians?* (1985)

Frankenberg, R., *Village on the Border. A Social Study of Religion, Politics and Football in a North Wales Community* (1957)

Communities in Britain (1966)

'In the production of their lives, men(?) . . . sex and gender in British community studies' in D. Barker and S. Allen (eds.), *Sexual Divisions in Society: Process and Change* (1976)

Furley, R., *A History of the Weald of Kent* 2 vols (Ashford and London, 1871)

Gardiner, M., 'The archaeology of the Weald: a survey and review', *Sussex Archaeological Collections* 128 (1990)

Gardner, J., *The Quick and the Dead* (1981)

Gibbons, S., *Cold Comfort Farm* (1932)

Gibson, Donald (ed.), *A Parson in the Vale of White Horse. George Woodward's Letters from East Hendred, 1753–1761* (Gloucester 1982)

Giddens, A., *The Constitution of Society: Outline of the Theory of Structuration* (Cambridge 1984)

Gilboy, E. W., *Wages in Eighteenth-century England* (Cambridge, Mass. 1934)

Godwin, Fay, *This Scepter'd Isle* (1989)

Goodacre, John, 'Lutterworth in the sixteenth and seventeenth centuries. A market town and its area', Unpublished PhD thesis, University of Leicester 1977

Goodchild, R. and Munton, R., *Development and the Landowner: An Analysis of the British Experience* (1985)

Goodwin, M., *The Concept of Civil Society and the Anatomy of Urban and Regional Research* (University of Sussex Urban and Regional Studies Working Paper 66, 1988)

Gosse, E., *Gray* (1889)

Gough, R., *The History of Myddle* (ed. D. Hey, 1981)

Gould, L., *Conserving the Countryside: Costing it Out* (Council for the Protection of Rural England 1989)

Grahame, K., 'The Rural Pan', *Pagan Papers* (1898)
  The Wind in the Willows (1908, 1987 edn)

Griffiths, N. J., 'Firle: selected themes from the social history of a closed Sussex village 1850–1939', Unpublished MA Dissertation, University of Sussex 1976

Grimmette, W., 'Shorne, Kent 1851–1861; age- and sex-related migration and family formation' in D. Mills (ed.), *Victorians on the Move* (Branston 1984)

Hanley, H., 'Population mobility in Buckinghamshire, 1578–83', *Local Population Studies* 15 (1975)

Hardy, Thomas, *Tess of the D'Urbervilles* (1891)
  'A Tryst at an ancient earthwork', *Stories and Poems* (1970)

Harman, R. (ed.), *Countryside Character* (1946)

Harris, John, *The Artist and the Country House: A History of Country House and Garden View Painting in Britain 1540–1870* (1979)

Harrison, Christopher (ed.), *Essays on the History of Keele* (University of Keele 1986)

Harrison, E., *The Living Landscape* (1986)

Hart, A. T., *The Country Priest in English History* (1959)

Harvey, P. D. A., 'Initiative and authority in settlement change' in M. Aston, D. Austin and C. Dyer (eds.), *The Rural Settlements of Medieval England* (1989)

Hawes, Louis, *Presences of Nature: British Landscape 1780–1830* (New Haven 1982)

Heath, Richard, *The English Peasant* (1893, reprinted Wakefield 1978)

Herbert, G., *The Country Parson* (1956 edn)

Herbert, J., *The Shrine* (1984)
  The Magic Cottage (1986)

Hewison, R., *The Heritage Industry: Britain in a Climate of Decline* (1987)

Hibbs, J., *The Country Chapel* (Newton Abbot 1988)

Hill, S., *In the Springtime of the Year* (1974)
  The Magic Apple Tree (1983)

Hillery, G. A., 'Definitions of community: areas of agreement', *Rural Sociology* 20 (1955)

Hirschon, R. (ed.) *Women and property – Women as property* (1984)

Hobsbawm, E. J., *Industry and Empire* (1969)

Hoggart, K., 'Let's do away with rurality', Unpublished paper, Rural Economy and Society Study Group, December 1989

Holderness, B., 'Personal mobility in some rural parishes in Yorkshire, 1777–1822', *Yorkshire Archaeological Journal* 42, (1967–70)
  '"Open" and "Close" parishes in England in the eighteenth and nineteenth centuries', *Agricultural History Review* 20 (1972)

Hooke, D., 'Early medieval estate and settlement patterns: the documentary evidence' in M. Aston, D. Austin and C. Dyer (eds.), *The Rural Settlements of Medieval England* (1989)

Hoskins, W. G., *Essays in Leicestershire History* (Liverpool 1950)
  The Midland Peasant. The Economic and Social History of a Leicestershire Village (1957)
  The Making of the English Landscape (ed. C. Taylor, 1988)

House Builders' Federation, *Homes, Jobs, Land: The Eternal Triangle* (HBF 1985)

Howkins, A., 'The discovery of rural England' in R. Colls and P. Dodd (eds.), *Englishness: Politics and Culture 1880–1920* (1986)

Reshaping Rural England. A Social History 1850–1925 (1991)

Hunt, E. W. and Botham, F. W., 'Wages in Britain during the industrial revolution', *Economic History Review* 2nd series 11 (1987)

Hurdis, James, *The Favourite Village, with an Additional Poem, (now first published) and a Tragedy* (1810)

Jackson, A., *Semi-detached London: Suburban Development, Life and Transport, 1900–1939* (1973)

James, M. R., *The Collected Ghost Stories* (1931)

Janowitz, A., *England's Ruins: Poetic Purpose and the National Landscape* (Cambridge 1990)

Johnson, Samuel, *The Lives of the Poets* (1776)

Jones, B. and Mattingly, D., *An Atlas of Roman Britain* (Oxford 1990)

Kipling, R., *Puck of Pook's Hill* (1906)

Rewards and Fairies (1908)

Kirk, J. C., 'Colonists of the waste: the structure and evolution of nineteenth century economy and society in the Central Forest Ridges of the High Weald', Unpublished MA Dissertation, University of Sussex 1986

Kitchen, Fred, *Brother to the Ox* (1940, 1981 edn Firle)

Kussmaul, A., *Servants in Husbandry in Early Modern England* (Cambridge 1981)

'The ambiguous mobility of farm servants', *Economic History Review* 2nd series 34 (1981)

A General Review of the Rural Economy of England 1538–1840 (Cambridge 1990)

Landry, Donna, 'The resignation of Mary Collier: some problems in feminist literary history' in Felicity Nussbaum and Laura Brown (eds.), *The New 18th Century* (New York and London 1987)

The Muses of Resistance: Laboring-Class Women's Poetry in Britain 1739–1796 (1990)

Large, Peter, 'Urban growth and agricultural change in the West Midlands during the seventeenth and eighteenth centuries' in P. Clark (ed.), *The Transformation of English Provincial Towns, 1600–1800* (1984)

Laslett, P., 'Clayworth and Cogenhoe' in P. Laslett (ed.), *Family Life and Illicit Love in Earlier Generations* (Cambridge 1977)

Levine, D., *Family Formation in an Age of Nascent Capitalism* (New York 1977)

Lewis, R. and Talbot-Ponsonby, A., *The People, the Land and the Church* (Hereford Diocesan Board of Finance 1987)

Littlejohn, J., *Westrigg. The Sociology of a Cheviot Parish* (1963)

Long, M. and Maltby, B., 'Personal mobility in three West Riding parishes, 1777–1812', *Local Population Studies* 24 (1980)

Longley, C., 'When the State takes on the mantle of Christianity', *The Times*, 8 February 1988

Lowbury, E. and Young, A., *Andrew Young: The Poetical Works* (1985)

Lowe, Norman, *The Lancashire Textile Industry in the Sixteenth Century* (Chetham Society, Manchester, 3rd series, XX, 1972)

Lowe, P., 'The rural idyll defended: from preservation to conservation' in G. Mingay (ed.), *The Rural Idyll* (1989)

Lowe, P., Cox, G., MacEwan, M., O'Riordan, T. and Winter, M., *Countryside Conflicts: the Politics of Farming, Forestry and Conservation* (Aldershot 1986)

Lowe, P. and Flynn, A., 'Environmental politics and policy in the 1980s' in J. Mohan (ed.), *The Political Geography of Contemporary Britain* (Basingstoke 1989)

Lowe, P., Marsden, T. and Munton, R., *The Social and Economic Restructuring of Rural Britain: A Position Statement* (Economic and Social Research Council 1990)

McClure, P., 'Patterns of migration in the Late Middle Ages: the evidence of English place-name surnames', *Economic History Review* 2nd series 32 (1979)

Macdonald, A., 'Gray and his critics: patterns of response in the eighteenth and nineteenth centuries' in J. Downey and B. Jones (eds.), *Fearful Joy* (Montreal 1974)

Macfarlane, A., *The Origins of English Individualism* (Oxford 1978)

McLaughlin, B., 'The rural deprivation debate: retrospect and prospect' in P. Lowe, T. Bradley and S. Wright (eds.), *Deprivation and Welfare in Rural Areas* (Norwich 1986)

Madge, C. and Harrison, T., *Mass Observation* (1937)

Malcolmson, R. W., *Life and Labour in England 1700–1780* (1981)

Marsden, T., 'The role of banking capital in the British agro-food complex' in T. Marsden and J. Little (eds.), *Political, Social and Economic Perspectives on the International Food System* (1990)

Marsden, T. and Murdoch, J., *Restructuring Rurality: Key Areas for Development in Assessing Rural Change* (Economic and Social Research Council Countryside Change Initiative Working Paper, 4, 1990)

Martin, E. W., *The Secret People* (1955)

Massey, D., 'Regionalism, some current issues', *Capital and Class* 6 (1978)

Massey, D. and Allen, J., *Uneven Redevelopment* (1988)

Massey, D. and Catalano, A., *Capital and Land: Landownership by Capital in Great Britain* (1978)

Michell, J., *Traveller's Guide to Sacred England* (1989)

Middleton, A., 'Marking boundaries: men's space and women's space in a Yorkshire village' in P. Lowe, T. Bradley and S. Wright (eds.), *Deprivation and Welfare in Rural Areas* (Norwich 1986)

Miles, A. H., *The Library of Elocution* (1882)

Mills, D., 'Has historical geography changed?', *New Trends in Geography* Unit 14, Open University 1972

  Lord and Peasant in Nineteenth Century Britain (1980)

  (ed.), *Victorians on the Move* (Branston 1984)

Mills, D. and Pearce, C., *People and Places in the Victorian Census* (Historical Geography Research series 23, 1989)

Mills, D. and Short, B., 'Social change and social conflict in nineteenth-century England: the use of the open-close village model' *Journal of Peasant Studies* 10 (4) (1983)

Mingay, G. E., 'Introduction: rural England in the industrial age' in G. E. Mingay (ed.), *The Victorian Countryside* 1, 1981

Morris, L., 'Constraints on gender: the family wage, social security and the labour market; reflections on research in Hartlepool', *Work, Employment and Society* 1 (1987)

Morris, L. and Ruane, S., *Household Finance Management and Labour Market Behaviour* (Report to the Department of Employment 1986)

Morris, William, *News from Nowhere* (1890)

Mullen, P., *Rural Rites* (1984)

Murdoch, I., *The Bell* (1958)

  The Message to the Planet (1989)

Nash, P., *Fertile Image* (1975)

Needham, S., 'The Bronze Age' in J. and D. G. Bird (eds.), *The Archaeology of Surrey to 1540* (Dorking 1987)

Newby, H., *Green and Pleasant Land?* (1979)
  'Locality and rurality: the restructuring of rural social relations', *Regional Studies* 20 (1986)
Obelkevich, J., *Religion and Rural Society, 1825–1875* (Oxford 1976)
Oldman, C., *Who Says There's No Housing Problem?* (Shelter 1990)
Opie, I. and Tatem, M., *A Dictionary of Superstitions* (Oxford 1989)
Pahl, J., 'The allocation of money and the structuring of inequality within marriage', *Sociological Review* 31 (1983)
Parker, P., 'Forever England', *The Listener* 10 December 1987
Parris, Leslie, *Landscape in Britain* (1973)
Paulson, Ronald, *Literary Landscape: Turner and Constable* (New Haven and London 1982)
Perry, M., *Deliverance* (1987)
Peyton, S., 'The village population in the Tudor Lay Subsidy Rolls', *English Historical Review* 30 (1915)
Phythian-Adams, C., *Re-thinking English Local History* (University of Leicester Occasional Paper, Fourth Series 1, 1987)
Pickles, M. F., 'Mid-Wharfedale, 1721–1812; economic and demographic change in a Pennine dale', *Local Population Studies* 16 (1976)
Piggott, S., *William Stukeley* (1950)
Potts, Alex and McWilliam, Neil, 'the landscape of reaction: Richard Wilson and his critics', *History Workshop Journal* 16 (1983)
Powys, J. C., *A Glastonbury Romance* (1933, 1953)
Powys, T. F., *Mr Weston's Good Wine* (1927)
Pred, A., *Place, Practice and Structure* (Cambridge 1986)
Rackham, O., *The History of the Countryside* (1986)
Ranger, T., 'Taking hold of the land', *Past and Present* 117 (1987)
Rawding, C. K., 'The iconography of churches: a case study of landownership and power in nineteenth-century Lincolnshire', *Journal of Historical Geography* 16 (2) (1990)
Reed, M., 'The peasantry of nineteenth-century England: a neglected class?', *History Workshop* 18 (1984)
  'Indoor farm service in 19th-century Sussex: some criticisms of a critique', *Sussex Archaeological Collections* 123, (1985)
  'Nineteenth-century rural England: a case for peasant studies?', *Journal of Peasant Studies* 14 (1) (1986)
Reeder, D. A., *Suburbanity and the Victorian City* (Leicester 1980)
Rees, A., *Life in a Welsh Countryside* (Cardiff 1950)
Rice, R. Garraway (ed.), *Sussex Apprentices and Masters 1710–1752*, Sussex Record Society, 28 (1924)
Rich, E. E., 'The population of Elizabethan England' *Economic History Review* 2nd series 2 (1950)
Richardson, J. (ed.), *Ten Rural Churches* (1988)
Roberts, B. K., *The Making of the English Village* (1987)
Rogers, H., 'The market area of Preston in the sixteenth and seventeenth centuries', *Geographical Studies* 3 (1956)
Rose, J., *The Dynamics of Urban Property Development* (1985)
Rosenthal, Michael, *British Landscape Painting* (Oxford 1982)
  Constable. The Painter and his Landscape (New Haven and London 1983)

'Approaches to Landscape Painting', *Landscape Research* 9 (3) (1984)

Rowlands, Marie B., *Masters and Men in the West Midland Metalware Trades before the Industrial Revolution* (Manchester 1975)

Rowswell, A., 'The influence of landownership on the growth/decline of rural settlements in part of East Sussex', Unpublished MPhil thesis, Brighton Polytechnic 1986

Rural Theology Association, *The Rural Church Towards 2000* (Northants 1989)

Russell, A., *The Clerical Profession* (1980)

The Country Parish (1986)

St. Croix, W. de, 'Names from the parish register books of Glynde, from 1558–1813', *Sussex Archaeological Collections* 24 (1872)

Sales, R., *English Literature in History 1780–1830: Pastoral and Politics* (1983)

Schofield, R., 'Age-specific mobility in an eighteenth-century rural English parish', *Annales de Démographie Historique*, 1970

Scotland, N. A. D., 'The role of Methodism in the origin and development of the Revolt of the Field in Lincolnshire, Norfolk and Suffolk 1872–1896', Unpublished PhD thesis, University of Aberdeen 1975

Severn, John, *Dovecotes of Nottinghamshire* (Newark 1986)

Sheail, J., 'The distribution of taxable population and wealth in England during the early sixteenth century' *Trans Institute British Geographers* 55 (1972)

Short, B., 'The turnover of tenants on the Ashburnham Estate, 1830–1850', *Sussex Archaeological Collections* 113 (1975)

(ed.), *Scarpfoot Parish: Plumpton 1830–1880* (University of Sussex Centre for Continuing Education, Occasional Paper 16, 1981)

'The art and craft of chicken cramming: poultry in the Weald of Sussex 1850–1950', *Agricultural History Review* 30 (1) (1982)

'Sussex rural communities: contemporary perspectives' in Geography Editorial Committee, *Sussex: Environment, Landscape and Society* (Gloucester 1983)

The Geography of local migration and marriage in Sussex 1500–1900, University of Sussex Research Papers in Geography 15, 1983

'The Decline of living-in servants in the transition to capitalist farming: a critique of the Sussex evidence', *Sussex Archaeological Collections* 122 (1984)

'The de-industrialisation process: a case study of the Weald, 1600–1850' in P. Hudson (ed.), *Regions and Industries: A Perspective on the Industrial Revolution in Britain* (Cambridge 1989)

Short, J., Fleming, S. and Witt, S., *Housebuilding, Planning and Community Action: the Production and Negotiation of the Built Environment* (1986)

Shorter, A., 'System, ritual and history: an examination of the work of Victor Turner' in T. Ranger and I. N. Kimambo (eds.), *The Historical Study of African religion* (1972)

Silversides, N., *Folk Religion: Friend or Foe?* (Nottingham 1986)

Simond, Louis, *An American in Regency England: the Journal of a Tour in 1810–1811* (ed. C. Hibbert, 1968)

Simpson, David, *Wordsworth's Historical Imagination* (1987)

Sinden, D., *The English Country Church* (1988)

Sisson, C. H., 'Burrington Combe', *Exactions* (Manchester 1980)

Smethurst, W., *The Archers: the First Thirty Years* (1980)

Smith, N. and Williams, P., *Gentrification of the City* (1986)

Smith, Peter, 'Rural building in Wales' in Joan Thirsk (ed.), *The Agrarian History of England and Wales V (ii) 1640–1750* (Cambridge 1985)

Snell, Keith, *Annals of the Labouring Poor: Social Change and Agrarian England 1660–1900* (Cambridge 1985)

Solkin, David, *Richard Wilson: the Landscape of Reaction* (1982)

'The battle of the books: or, the gentleman provok'd – different views on the history of British art', *The Art Bulletin* 67 (3) (1985)

Spufford, Margaret, *Contrasting Communities. English Villagers in the Sixteenth and Seventeenth centuries* (Cambridge 1974)

The Great Reclothing of Rural England. Petty Chapmen and their Wares in the Seventeenth Century (1984)

Stacey, M., 'The myth of community studies', *British Journal of Sociology* 20 (1969)

Stedman Jones, G., 'Working-class culture and working-class politics in London, 1870–1900: notes on the remaking of a working class', in B. Waites, T. Bennett and G. Martin (eds.), *Popular Culture: Past and Present* (1982)

Steele, J., 'Thomas Gray and the Season for Triumph' in J. Downey and B. Jones (eds.), *Fearful Joy* (Montreal 1974)

Stephenson, C., *Walsingham Way* (1970)

Stockwood, M., *Chanctonbury Ring* (1982)

Strathern, M., *Kinship at the Core* (Cambridge 1981)

Sumner, H., *The Ancient Earthworks of Cranborne Chase* (1913)

Sutherland, N., *A Bibliography of Thomas Gray* (New Haven 1917)

Taylor, C. C., *Village and Farmstead* (1983)

Taylor, J., 'The imaginary landscape', *Ten-8* 12 (1983)

Taylor, Kit, 'Never mind what it means', *Times Saturday Review* 2 February 1990

Tebbutt, C. F., 'A Middle-Saxon iron smelting site at Millbrook, Ashdown Forest, Sussex', *Sussex Archaeological Collections* 120 (1982)

Thirsk, Joan, *English Peasant Farming. The Agrarian History of Lincolnshire from Tudor to Recent Times* (1957, reprinted 1981)

(ed.), *The Agrarian History of England and Wales, IV, 1500–1640* (Cambridge 1967)

'Seventeenth-century agriculture and social change' in Joan Thirsk (ed.), *Land, Church and People. Essays presented to H. P. R. Finberg, Agricultural History Review* 18, 1970 Supplement

Economic Policy and Projects. The development of a Consumer society in Early Modern England (Oxford 1978)

(ed.) *The Agrarian History of England and Wales v 1640–1750* (Parts I and II, Cambridge 1984, 1985)

'Industries in the countryside' in Joan Thirsk (ed.), *The Rural Economy of England. Collected Essays* (1985)

'Projects for gentlemen, jobs for the poor: mutual aid in the Vale of Tewkesbury, 1600–1630' in Joan Thirsk (ed.), *The Rural Economy of England. Collected Essays* (1985)

England's Agricultural Regions and Agrarian History 1500–1750 (Cambridge 1987)

Tudor Enclosures (Historical Association, General Series, 41, 1987)

'The fashioning of the Tudor-Stuart gentry', *Bulletin of the John Rylands University Library of Manchester* 72 (1), Manchester 1990

'Seventeenth-Century village life in Old England' (Plimoth Plantation, Mass., U.S.A., forthcoming)

Thomas, K., *Religion and the Decline of Magic* (1971)

Thomas, R. S., *Later Poems* (1984)

The Echoes Return Slow (1988)

Thompson, D. M., 'The churches and society in nineteenth century England; a rural perspective' in G. J. Cuming and D. Baker (eds.), *Popular Belief and Practice* (1972)

Thompson, E. P. and Sugden, Mary (eds.), *Stephen Duck. 'The Thresher's Labour', and Mary Collier. 'The Woman's Labour'* (1989)

Thompson, F. M. L., 'Introduction: the rise of suburbia' in F. M. L. Thompson (ed.), *The Rise of Suburbia* (Leicester 1982)

Thomson, James, *The Seasons* (James Sambrook edn, Oxford 1981)

Thrift, N. 'Manufacturing rural geography', *Journal of Rural Studies* 3 (1) (1987)

Toulson, S., *East Anglia. Walking the Ancient Tracks* (1988)

Towler, R. and Chamberlain, A., 'Common Religion', *Sociological Yearbook of Religion in Britain* 6 (1973)

Traherne, Thomas, *Centuries* (1960)

Trollope, A., *Framley Parsonage* (1861)

Tupling, G. H., *The Economic History of Rossendale* (Chetham Society, Manchester, New Series, 86, 1927)

Underdown, D., *Revel, Riot, and Rebellion* (Oxford 1985)

Urry, J., *The Anatomy of Capitalist Societies: the Economy, Civil Society and the State* (1981) *The Tourist Gaze* (1990)

Vaisey, D. (ed.), *The Diary of Thomas Turner* (Oxford 1984)

Vaughan, Henry, 'Retirement' in L. C. Martin (ed.), *Henry Vaughan: Poetry and Selected Prose* (Oxford 1963)

Vaughan, W., 'Leisure and toil: differing views of rural life c. 1750–1850' in D. Spargo (ed.), *This Land is Our Land: Aspects of Agriculture in English Art* (1989)

Wall, R., 'The age of leaving home', *Journal of Family History* 3 (1978)

Walton, Izaak, *The Compleat Angler* (many editions)

Watkins, A., *The Old Straight Track* (1925)

Weatherill, Lorna, *The Pottery Trade and North Staffordshire, 1660–1760* (Manchester 1971)

Webb, M., *Precious Bane* (1924)

Wells, R. A. E., 'Social conflict and protest in the English countryside in the early nineteenth century: a rejoinder', *Journal of Peasant Studies* 8 (4) (1981)

West, F., *The Country Parish, Today and Tomorrow* (1964)

West Sussex County Council, *Housing Land Supply in West Sussex at 1st July 1986* (WSCC 1987)

Whitehead, A., 'Sexual antagonism in Herefordshire' in D. Barker and S. Allen (eds.), *Dependence and Exploitation in Work and Marriage* (1976)

Wiener, M. J., *English Culture and the Decline of the Industrial Spirit 1850–1980* (Cambridge 1981)

Wilcox, T. and Causey, A., *Claughton Pellew, 1890–1966* (Hove 1990)

Wilkinson, A., *The Church of England and the First World War* (1975)

Williams, R., *The Country and the City* (1975)

Williams, W. M., *The Sociology of an English Village: Gosforth* (1956) *A West Country Village: Ashworthy. Family, Kinship and Land* (1963)

Witney, K. P., *The Jutish Forest: a Study of the Weald of Kent from 450–1350 AD* (1976)

Wojciechowska, B., 'Brenchley: a study of migratory movements in a mid-nineteenth century rural parish', *Local Population Studies* 41 (1988)

Wood, William, *A Sussex Farmer* (1938)

Wright, Nigel, 'East Anglian Gentry Homes', *Centre of East Anglian Studies Newsletter* July 1988

Wright, P., *On Living in an Old Country* (1985)

Wright, S., 'Development theory and community development practice' in H. Buller and S. Wright (eds.), *Rural Development: Problems and Practices* (Aldershot 1990)

Wrigley, E. A., 'A simple model of London's importance in changing English society and economy 1650–1750', *Past and Present* 37 (1967)

'A note on the life-time mobility of married women in a parish population in the late eighteenth century', *Local Population Studies* 18 (1977)

Wrigley, E. A. and Schofield, R. S., *The Population History of England 1541–1871* (Cambridge, 2nd edn, 1989)

Young, K., Walkowitz, C. and McCullagh, R. (eds.), *Of Marriage and the Market* (1981)

Index

Buck, Samuel and Nathaniel, 4
Buckhurst Place (Sussex), 38
Buckinghamshire
    farm labourers, 87, 96
    population movement and migration,
        73, 74
    see also Olney; Stoke Poges;
        Thornborough
Burwash (Sussex), 36, 40, 76
Buxted (Sussex), 33
Byron, George Gordon, Lord, 138

Cade Street (Sussex), 33
Cambridgeshire
    farm labourers, 87, 91, 96, 99, 101
    see also Chippenham
Canon Pyon (Herefs.), 75
'Captain Swing' protest marches, 36
Cardington (Beds.), 63, 66
Castle Heaton Farm (Northumb.), 93–4,
    98
Castle Rising (Norfolk), *16*
Catholicism, *see* Roman Catholicism
Cavendish family, Dukes of Devonshire,
    32
Cerney, North (Glos.), 99
Chailey (Sussex), 35
Chanctonbury Ring (Sussex), 164
Channel Tunnel rail-link, 165
chapels, 162
    see also nonconformity
chapmen, 57, 66
Charlton, Great (Wilts.), 120
Chart, Little (Kent), 35
Chatsworth (Derbys.), 32
Cheshire, farm labourers, 87
Chevalier, Albert, 141
Chichester, Earls of, *see* Pelham
children, as farm labourers, 92–6, 99, 102,
    115
Chiltington, West (Sussex), 29
Chilvers Coton (Warwicks.), 55
Chingley Furnace (Kent), 26
Chippenham (Cambs.), 50
Christianity
    and mystical geography, 152–62, 163,
        166–7
    see also Church of England; churches;
        nonconformity
Christmas, 157, *161*
Church of England
    and mystical geography, 152–5, 156,
        157–9, 166

and 'open' and 'close' parishes, 31, 32, 33,
    39
    see also churches
churches, 9, 159–62, 214
Churchill, Sir Winston, 152
Chysauster (Cornwall), 167
Cibber, C. G., *38*
Clayworth (Notts.), 63, 73
clergymen, place in rural community, 33,
    154–5
'close' parishes, *see* 'open' and 'close'
    parishes
Cobbett, William, *Rural Rides*, 33, 58–9
Cogenhoe (Northants.), 63, 73, 74
Cohen, A. P., 214–15
Coleman, John, 86, 89, 93
Collier, Mary, 119
Colyton (Devon), 66, 72, 75, 81
Common Agricultural Policy, *see*
    European Community
community, as symbol, 211–15
community studies, images of rural
    communities in, 195–217
commuting, 175, 178, 179
conservation interests, 37
    and development of rural/urban fringe,
        179, 186–7, 188, 189, 191
Constable, John, 131
Cornwall
    farm labourers, 87, 101
    see also Chysauster; Madron
costermonger characters, in music-hall,
    141
Cotesbach (Leics.), 31
council housing, 178
Council for the Protection of Rural
    England, 182, 187
Country Landowners' Association, 187
Country Life, 4
Countryman, The, 160
Cowdray, Viscounts, *see* Pearson
Cowdray Park (Sussex), 36
Cowper, William, 130–1
Crabbe, George, 138
crafts, rural, *see* industries, rural
Cranborne Chase, 162
Cricklade (Wilts.), 58
Cumberland
    farm labourers, 87
    population movement and migration,
        81
    see also Gosforth
cycling clubs, 139